Yossele Rosenblatt

Yossele

FARRAR, STRAUS AND YOUNG • NEW YORK

Rosenblatt

THE STORY OF HIS LIFE

AS TOLD BY HIS SON

Samuel Rosenblatt

Contents

Preface

The idea of making a written record of the story of Josef Rosenblatt's rich and colorful career was born when he was still alive. About two years before his death in Jerusalem at the age of fifty-one, one of the New York tabloids published in serial form what was supposed to be an account of his life and personality, but did not do justice to either. A year later there appeared in the Yiddish daily of New York, the Day, eight autobiographical chapters, dealing for the most part with the childhood and youth of the then fifty-year-old idol of the synagogue and the concert-stage, and touching only superficially on those events that had made the beloved and admired cantor a figure of world renown. His unexpected passing in the following year, at the height of his fame, intensified the eagerness on the part of his children to compile a more adequate biography of their illustrious father, whose art had charmed and whose deeds had benefited so many of his contemporaries.

As early as the year 1936 my brother Leo, who had been my father's business manager and personal representative, commenced to collect and put in order whatever materials were to be found in the family archives, in preparation for a labor of love, which his own premature demise prevented him from executing. And so it was fated that I, my father's oldest child and the one perhaps closest to him in spirit, should take over from my brother, who had been more directly associated with him in his mundane affairs and was, consequently, in a better position than I to do the spade-work of assembling the data indispensable for this task.

Although I have tried to be as judicious as possible in the arrangement and the interpretation of the facts out of which the narrative is pieced together, and have made every effort to delineate the character of my subject without prejudice or bias, I make no pretense of complete objectivity. No son can write with absolute detachment about a father he has loved. I have, however, protected myself against the charge of excessive adulation by quoting the opinions of outsiders, by presenting the reactions to my father of persons who were able to view him more dispassionately than his own flesh and blood. Furthermore I have allowed the hero of my story, wherever it was feasible, to speak for himself.

My chief difficulty lay not in the scarcity but in the overabundance of the material at my disposal. The question I had to ask myself constantly was: "What shall I leave out in order not to pad my narrative too much and bore the reader?" Another problem was that of phraseology and styling. In all these matters I enjoyed the helpful advice and critical judgment of relatives and friends, who also supplied a number of interesting reminiscences that have been incorporated in the book. Finally I must express my indebtedness to both the Jewish Daily Forward and the Jewish Morning Journal for permitting me, through their columns, to canvass their readers for anecdotes about my father. A single notice in each of these two periodicals resulted in a response which helped considerably in enlivening the tale I was thereby able to relate.

This biography might not have seen the light of day were it not for the encouragement and moral support given me by the leaders of the Beth Tfiloh Congregation and its Brotherhood and Sisterhood, and all the friends and admirers of Yossele Rosenblatt, whose advance subscriptions made possible the manufacture of this volume. To all of them go my sincerest thanks.

Samuel Rosenblatt,
BALTIMORE, JUNE 1, 1954.

Yossele Rosenblatt

1

Earliest Memories

The earliest memories I have of my father go back to the time when I was about three years old. Our family was residing in Presburg, today better known as Bratislava, the capital of Slovakia. Four years had elapsed since my father had given up his first permanent cantorial position in Munkacs, Carpatho-Ruthenia, in order to become the chief cantor of the center of Hungarian Jewish orthodoxy.

I don't remember whether we were then still living in the Schlosstrasse, where I was born, or in the Judengasse, to which we moved subsequently. All I can recall is that I was perched on top of the table in the dining room of our second floor apartment. It was a bright, sunny spring morning. My father, beating time with his right hand, was reading music together with several members of his choir, who were recruited chiefly from among the students of the rabbinical seminary to which the city of Presburg owed its fame. His neatly-kempt black beard, by which he was destined to become so familiar in later years, was already fully grown. The complexion of his face, which it adorned, was pale and sallow; and his small frame did not yet exhibit the tendency toward corpulence which he developed under the influence of prosperity.

The scene was a typical one for that period in my father's life. Although, as his teachers, coaches and critics often observed, his was a natural talent and he had an uncanny sense of fluency in reading music, the perfection of these gifts was not achieved entirely without effort. The seriousness and diligence with which he devoted himself to his musical studies, the hours on end that he would spend reviewing his solfeggio, made my mother, who was a woman of striking beauty, utter the wish that she might be transformed into a book of musical notes ("ein Notenbuch"), so that her Yossele would occasionally deign to cast a glance at her.

At the time of which I am speaking the chief cantor ("Oberkantor") of Presburg, who was as beloved for his hospitality and piety as he was admired for his musical ability, was all of twenty-three years old. Yet, in addition to being the father of three children and having two aged parents to support, and five elder sisters to marry off, he already had behind him a lifetime of experience as precentor of the synagogue. From the tender age of eight until the time of his marriage, which took place when he was eighteen years old, he had travelled throughout the length and breadth of the Austro-Hungarian Empire. There was not a Jewish community of size or importance in this second largest concentration of Jewry in Europe where he had not officiated as cantor, in part or in toto, at a Sabbath or holiday service. The phonograph recordings of his vocal renditions, which were to spread his fame to the four corners of the earth, had not yet been made. However his published musical compositions, such as *Shirei Joseph,* had already won the approval of his colleagues and been most enthusiastically endorsed by them.

Almost every outstanding cantor of our time as well as of preceding generations served a childhood apprenticeship in the choir of some eminent interpreter of the prayers of the synagogue. By paying attention to the renditions of the master and noting his methods, he gradually acquired skill in *Chazanuth* and developed into an artist of the *Amud* in his own right. This was not the case with the phenomenon known to his contemporaries as Yossele Rosenblatt. He was not trained for but born into his calling. He sang for no one in his youth and nobody can be said to have been his teacher. It has been related that, when he was still an infant in the cradle, a friend of the family, hearing his melodious wail, predicted that he would some day become a cantor of world renown. Such prophecies are usually not taken seriously. In this instance, the forecast soon proved itself to have been fully justified. At the age of four, the delicate little dark-complexioned lad, with the large brown eyes, already exhibited signs of great musical talent. Before he had learned to read, he was able to repeat to perfection in a clear bell-like alto voice all the songs of the synagogue that he had heard chanted by his father, the reader of a small congregation in his native city. He even added flourishes of his own.

Whence did such proficiency come to a child of four? How did he acquire his ability to sing and improvise? To attempt to explain genius is as futile as to argue about tastes. Nevertheless it cannot be denied that heredity as well as environment must have played their parts in the creation of the personality of Yossele Rosenblatt, which for nearly half a century astounded the Jewish and the non-Jewish world. He was fated, as it were, to become what he did by virtue of both descent and the surroundings in which he was born and reared. Music, which remained throughout his life his dominant passion, was not only in his blood, but in the very air he breathed.

The Russian Ukraine, in which he saw the light of day,

has long been famous as a land of song and melody. Its
woods and fields seem to be instinct with music. Singing is as
natural to the Cossacks that inhabit this region as the playing
of the bagpipe to the Scot or the use of the flute to the Wal-
lachian shepherd. No wonder that the Ukraine has produced
for Jewry its foremost cantors, that Sirota and Hershman
and Kwartin, Bachmann and Minkowsky and Rozumny all
originated there. For as it has often been observed, Jews tend
to exhibit the characteristics of their gentile neighbors. At all
events the liturgical compositions of the synagogue emanating
from Southern Russia definitely betray the influence of the
Ukrainian environment.

Another important factor in the evolution of the distinctive type of *Chazanuth* which was exemplified by my father
was the East-European Jewish pietistic movement of the
eighteenth and nineteenth centuries known as *Chassidism.*
This enthusiastic brand of Jewish mysticism had brought
into Jewish life, in addition to ecstasy and fervor, a wealth of
music. Perhaps more than any other art, music may be de-
fined as what Tolstoy would call the "language of emotion."
And since the *Chassidic* mystics felt their religion intensely,
it was only natural that they should have wanted to give vent
to their feelings in song. But it was a different kind of song
from that to which Jews had been accustomed theretofore—
not the slow, subdued cadence of a people oppressed, not the
muffled cry or sob of human beings in distress, but a song of
jubilation and triumph, following the swift-moving rhythm
of the dance. It was mostly at the Sabbath table in the homes
of their rabbis, where the faithful would gather, that these
melodies would be sung. They might be made to fit the
Hebrew or Aramaic text of the Sabbath poems, or they might
be hummed as songs without words.

In such an atmosphere did young Yossele grow up. The
enthusiasm and zeal of the *Chassidim* entered into the very
marrow of his bones. Later on it expressed itself in the tempo

and the animated nature of his musical compositions and in the distinctive flavor that he injected into the traditional motifs of the prayers as he chanted them. *Chassidism* was very much at home in the part of the Ukraine in which he was born. He himself came from *Chassidic* stock and his family was very close to the Ruzyn dynasty of *Chassidic* rabbis. Among the saints of the movement his idol was that apologete extraordinary of the Jewish people Rabbi Levi Isaac of Berdychev. What attracted him to Rabbi Levi Isaac was no doubt that he saw reflected in him his own philosophy of tolerance. He adored this lover of Israel who viewed even the failings of his coreligionists in the most favorable light. As for his boundless devotion to *Chassidic* rabbis in general, his model must have been his paternal grandfather and namesake Yosie of Tilizhinitze. A fiery devotee of the rabbi of Ruzyn, this ancestor had once almost risked his life in order to procure for his master a pair of antique silver Sabbath candlesticks that were greatly coveted by the adherents of the rival Tshernobyl dynasty. He thereby created a furor in *Chassidic* circles that left its mark for a long time.

This was the background, the climate. Yet indispensable as the appropriate atmospheric and climatic conditions are to the unfolding of a flower, they cannot produce the flower itself. That is a matter of heredity. But in this respect too, nature seems to have done all it could to pave the way for the emergence of the "king of cantors." It gave him a mother who possessed a sweet, soft voice that, as he reported, "insinuated itself into the heart and permeated the entire being." And since no art can fulfill its mission without the scientific discipline called technique, nature supplied him with a father who, although but an old fashioned reader of prayers, did at least know how to read musical notations—an accomplishment rather unusual for a *Chassidic* Jew of his time and type.

Musical talent was distributed liberally among Yossele's

further of kin. One of his mother's brothers, Gedaliah Shtephaneshter, had so outstanding a voice, that the rabbi of Shtephaneshti, at whose court he functioned as cantor, remarked about him, "There is a chord of David's harp in Gedaliah's throat."

Another maternal uncle, named Todros, served as *Chazan* in the synagogue of the town of Skvira for seventy-five years. He lived to the venerable age of ninety-eight. To the very last his voice remained fresh and robust, and though he went blind towards the end, he continued to lead his congregation in prayer, which flowed naturally from his lips.

Composers, too, had a place in the family tree. The most noted was that prolific writer of liturgical music, Nissi Belzer. But Yossele's most famous kinsman in the cantorial profession, whom he resembled in physique as well as artistic endowment, was *Yerucham the Short*. "I can still picture myself," so he writes in one of his memoirs, "as a little boy sitting on my father's lap. He strokes the velvet skull-cap on my head and curls the earlocks, protruding from it, with his long and bony fingers and tells me about Yerucham, the Short. When Yerucham, the Short, stood at the reader's desk and sang, the angels of heaven seemed to sing along with him. The world has never heard nor will it ever hear the like of it. When he chanted the prayers on the high holidays, the 'days of awe,' the entire synagogue would be bathed in tears, and it appeared as though the celestial family were weeping with him and the ministering angels were pleading for the community of Israel. Such a man was Yerucham, the Short." Grandfather was apparently too modest to believe that his own offspring would one day completely eclipse this Yerucham, over whom he had waxed so rhapsodic.

The city or town of Byelaya Tzerkov, in which my father came into this world on May 9, 1882, was "a Jewish metropolis, a city of pious, God-fearing Jews, of *Chassidic*

prayer-chapels and houses of study, harboring memories of
Jewish martyrdom and self-sacrifice for the sanctification of
the name of God." Its name, which means "white church" in
Little-Russian, is derived from an ancient cloister located in
its vicinity. The Jewish inhabitants of Byelaya Tzerkov, however, always referred to it cynically as *"Schwarze Tum'oh"*
(black defilement), and not without good reason. Like many
other Jewish communities of the Ukraine, that of Byelaya
Tzerkov, which lies about fifty miles to the south of Kiev,
had seen evil days. Its soil was soaked with the blood of Jewish martyrs, hundreds of whom lost their lives during the
fateful year 1648, in which Chmielnicki's hordes swept over
Podolia and Volhynia, massacring tens, if not hundreds, of
thousands of Jews. The dilapidated, rubbed-off tombstones in
the old Jewish cemetery told the grim story. Among the
names inscribed there was that of one of my father's fore-
bears, Samson Astropolier. Together with three hundred
other Jews, he had gone clad in white shrouds to give battle
to the murderous bands of Cossacks who were storming their
city. Neither he nor any one of his companions survived.
They were cut down to the last man. Was it the cry of
anguish of these martyred ancestors of his that reechoed in
their descendant's stirring *Habet Mishomayim Ur'eh,* in
which he implored the heavenly father to have pity on his
children who were being slaughtered like sheep?

According to a tradition current in our family my father's
birth was not unheralded. Before he came upon the scene
grandmother Chayeh Sarah Rosenblatt had presented her
husband with nine children, all girls. Being women, none of
them would by the ruling of Jewish custom have been able
after the death of their parents to recite the *Kaddish* in their
memory. This made my grandfather very unhappy, and
grandmother even more so. Every time she was confined,
and the midwife announced "It's a girl," he was crestfallen,

and she felt, when she saw the downcast look in his face, as though she had failed him. But was it her fault if the Master of Fate decreed that her offspring be females?

Now there lived in the big house inhabited by the Rosenblatts a Jewish widow and her spinster daughter. The younger woman had long already reached the age of marriage; but since there was no money for the indispensable dowry and she was no ravishing beauty, no suitor presented himself to make her happy. My grandmother, good soul that she was, took the plight of the elderly maiden very much to heart, and resolved to get her married. She began by making collections for the bridal trousseau, adding kopek to kopek. Then she got after the professional marriage brokers or *shadchans,* giving them no rest, until they had found a husband for the bride-in-waiting. Thus with the help of God and the interest taken in her by Chayeh Sarah Rosenblatt, the orphan girl became a bride.

Shortly after the marriage my grandmother became pregnant again. One day her protégée, who had always felt that she owed her benefactress something in return for her kindness, came to her bursting with excitement. She related that her dead father had appeared to her in a dream and told her to go to my grandmother and inform her that she, Chayeh Sarah Rosenblatt, was going to give birth to a son. Now dreams may, as the Talmud notes, be of no significance one way or the other. This one however was believed to be true because those whom it concerned wanted it to be so. They were not disappointed. As predicted, a boy was born to my grandparents, to whom they gave the name of Josef, after grandfather Yosie Tilizhinitze.

The birth of a male child brought joy and rapture into the Rosenblatt household. Not only did the parents rejoice, but they made the entire community celebrate with them. And was there not cause for celebration when, after having brought into the world nine daughters, Chayeh Sarah Rosenblatt was at last blessed with a son? The recitations of the *Shema* and psalms of thanksgiving at the confinement and the circumcision ceremony were attended by nearly all the important people of the city. And cake was distributed by my happy grandfather to each of the five hundred little boys who had assisted in the rites marking the happy event.

A year and a half later another son made his appearance in the Rosenblatt home. He was named Levi Isaac, after the saint of Berdychev.

2

Childhood in Russia

Even if the contribution of prenatal influences to his musical development is to be completely discounted, there can be no doubt about the forces that worked on Yossele Rosenblatt once he came into the world. He was nourished on music from the moment he was born. The walls of his nursery reverberated almost without interruption to the strains of song and melody. The sounds floating in the air that impinged on the infant's ears were either those produced by his father studying the Talmud or preparing for his assignment in the synagogue, or by the members of the choir who came to the house to rehearse. And when none of the men were around, his mother would croon to him melancholy Russian folksongs, or lively *Chassidic* melodies. Only when she was alone with her child would she take this liberty, for Jewish religious law did not permit singing by women in the presence of men. "It was different, of course," so my father used to reminisce, "when only *I* was there. *I* was not yet a man. And so my mother could sing to me to her heart's content.

And until this very day her sweet singing rings in my ears. I need but close my eyes to hear her mellow, caressing voice."

Like many other children of his age, little Yossele was pretty much of a play-boy, and he never quite lost his love of fun and banter. He was always ready to join his play-mates in soldier games, school, and other such diversions. On Passover he would participate in matches of nuts. On the ninth of *Ab* he and his little friends would pelt each other with thorns. On the feast of Esther, again, they would smear their faces with makeup and run after the Purim-players.

None of these frolics were missed by young Josef. He was present at and had a hand in each of them. In order to attend them he would devise all sorts of schemes for eluding the vigilance of his mother, of his nine elder sisters, of his aunts and uncles, and of neighbors, all of whom watched him as the apple of their eye. For wasn't he, for a while at least, the only boy among so many girls, and a tiny, delicate little fellow at that, so that everybody considered it his duty to act as his caretaker and guardian? "Don't go here! Don't stand there! Don't jump! Don't run! Don't get yourself overheated! Don't let yourself get wet!" These admonitions never ceased.

All this solicitude was, however, of no avail. Much as he was watched, the restless little lad with his excess of nervous energy always found ways of giving his keepers the slip. He was like quicksilver. He couldn't stay put. In the twinkling of an eye he was off to join his comrades at play. But his favorite game was that of cantor and choir. He would invite a number of his playmates into the house. A bench covered with his mother's apron would be the prayer desk. A towel in which he wrapped himself would serve as the *Tallith*. Thus standing before the make-believe *Amud* he would act as the cantor, singing the songs that he had heard his father chant when he was rehearsing with the choir, while his little friends played the part of the choristers.

"Already in his playings is a child recognized," says the Proverbist, or, as Wordsworth puts it: "The child is father of the man." This was certainly proven by little Yossele's fondness for the game of *Chazanuth*, and a premonition thereof was felt by his parents. They must have had an inkling of things to come whenever they surprised him in his game, and beamed with inner delight. They would steal into the room unnoticed by him or his comrades, stand in a corner and look on in silence. When Yossele would lift up his eyes and see them there, he would feel abashed. On one occasion he even burst out crying. Thereupon his mother ran up to him, caught him in her arms and showered him with kisses, which made him dig his little head into her bosom and weep even harder. "Why do you cry, foolish little boy? What's there to cry about?" she said to pacify him. But the child would not stop crying. It was as though his heart told him that this child's play would one day turn into serious business, and that day was not very long in coming either.

"My first appearance in public," so my father related, "took place not in the synagogue but at home. The occasion was a family celebration the exact nature of which I can no longer recall. There was a crowd of people sitting around the table sipping wine and cracking nuts. I was running around, getting into everybody's way, going out, coming in again, turning up where I wasn't wanted. Suddenly I heard my father calling me: 'Yossele, come over here!' So I went. 'How about repeating for us the *Hashkiveinu* that you sang with the boys?' I lifted my head and noted that all eyes were riveted on me. This made the blood course more quickly through my veins. My cheeks and ears became enflamed and my heart began pounding so fast that I thought it would run out like a little mouse when the trap in which it has been caught is opened. My father turned to me again: 'Well, Yossele, why so silent? Sing! There's no need to be bashful.' And when father says: 'Sing!' one has to sing. A father must be obeyed. I always obeyed my father's orders, even when I was grown up and famous, nay, when I was a married man with children of my own. That's the kind of upbringing I received."

And so the little four-year-old lad began to sing, softly at first, with a tremulous voice, with a break due to excitement; then stronger, clearer, louder. It was as though the tones had freed themselves from the fetters by which they had been held enthralled and had come out into the open like the birds in the trees of the forests stretching round about his native city. He sang in complete forgetfulness of self and of the surroundings. For the time being he seemed alone in the big room. Only the support given him by his father, especially in the pleading passages, reminded him of the fact that he was not entirely by himself.

"When I was finished," my father concluded, "there followed several moments of complete silence. This unaccustomed quiet frightened me and I was ready to run out into the street or to hide in some corner, to creep into a closet or under the bed. But before I had a chance to make a move, I was pounced upon from all sides. Everyone began kissing and hugging me and pulling me to himself. I might have been torn to pieces if my mother had not then and there come to my rescue and checked this excessive display of enthusiasm by snapping at my admirers: 'Let go of the child! You will wear him out.' Then they released me and my mother kept me by her side."

A little while thereafter Yossele began to assist his father in the services of the synagogue as a regular member of his choir. But he was not just an ordinary chorister. The function of the average assistant to the cantor is to sing a few supporting notes, or even solos, if he happens to be particularly gifted, while the cantor himself recites the main portions of the service. In this case it was different. Even at the age of four Yossele's alto was of such honey-sweetness, his tones were so clear and the strains of his falsetto resembled so much the trills of a nightingale, that whoever heard him sing was completely entranced. His father therefore permitted him not only to assist, but to chant whole passages of the liturgy.

Reb Yechiel's *Klaus* in which the elder Rosenblatt served as *Baal Tefillah* was far from being the largest Jewish house of worship in the town of Byelaya Tzerkov with its 10,000 Jews. Also, notwithstanding his reputation as a connoisseur of music, he was, as has been noted previously, not particularly gifted. Yet once word got around about Raphael Shalom Rosenblatt's little assistant, the synagogue began to attract a wider clientele. Members of other congregations commenced to attend its services in large numbers, so that there were Sabbaths and holidays on which crowds of people, unable to get into the house of worship, would be standing in the street outside the synagogue to hear the singing through open windows.

Up to that time the elder Rosenblatt had rarely ventured beyond the confines of the city of his residence. He disliked the idea of travelling from town to town for his livelihood. He was especially reluctant to leave his home and family over the Sabbath, even if it would have brought additional income and greater comforts for his wife and children, for he was a man who was contented with his lot. True, his salary as precentor of the *Klaus*, which was supplemented by the meager pay he received for keeping the books of a local wine establishment, hardly sufficed to make ends meet. Feeding thirteen mouths never was a trifle. Yet if he was able to earn just enough to pull through he was satisfied. Neither he nor his wife entertained ambitions of getting rich. They were grateful to God for their daily bread, whatever it was, and had faith that "He who gave them life would also provide them with sustenance." This must have been the fountain that nurtured the unshakable trust and inveterate optimism which helped my father across so many crises in his oft-turbulent career.

However as the fame of little Yossele spread beyond the boundaries of Byelaya Tzerkov, grandfather Rosenblatt yielded to the pressure of those who urged him to tour the surrounding communities in order to give the Jews living there an opportunity to hear the young prodigy. Grandmother was at first opposed to the idea. She feared for the child's health. But eventually she too was won over.

"Thus," my father was wont to tell us children, "began my years of wandering. At an age when other boys would be playing leap-frog, ride on goats' backs, steal into their neighbors' orchards and pluck apples, pears, grapes or plums from the trees, I was already dragging about from town to hamlet, travelling by day or by night on coaches or in peasants' wagons in all kinds of weather, stopping at inns and taverns and enduring every type of discomfort. This was the sort of life I led up to the time of my marriage."

However so far as the peregrinations of father and son across the steppes of the Ukraine were concerned, they were not destined to continue for very long. Something happened which brought them to an abrupt halt, one of those brutal events in Jewish history that respected neither age nor station, and changed the course of life not only of the Rosenblatts, but of countless other Jews like them.

Czarist Russia had never been too friendly in its treatment of its Jewish wards. The early rulers of the Muscovite empire steadfastly refused to grant permission to Jews to tread on Russia's sacred soil. Then, when as a result of the partitioning of Poland at the end of the eighteenth century, the Russian czars found that they had automatically and despite themselves become the sovereigns of several millions of Jews, they passed laws to confine their newly won but to them undesirable subjects to the original Polish provinces. Not until the middle of the nineteenth century, during the relatively liberal regime of Alexander II, were certain categories of Jews given the right of residence in such all-Russian cities as Moscow and St. Petersburg—a right hedged about with definite restrictions.

But if for the duration of one generation the tyrannical rule of the despotic Romanoff dynasty was relieved by a brief spell of freedom and light, this period was soon succeeded by a wave of reaction that put all former cruelties completely in the shade. The accession to the throne of the reactionary Alexander III, in the spring of the year 1881, after the assassination of Alexander II, set off a series of attacks upon the hapless Jewish minority, particularly in the south of Russia, that had not had their equal in ferocity in Western Europe since the Middle Ages. The assaults by the Russian peasantry and lower middle class upon the lives and property of the Jews dwelling in their midst were followed by legal pogroms carried out by the governmental agencies themselves. These latter were even more effective than the popular outbursts in convincing Russian Jewry that, if it was to survive at all, it would have to look for homes elsewhere. The result was the beginning of a mass migration, the largest portion of which was headed in the direction of the New World.

Among those who left the inhospitable terrain of Russia during the eighteen eighties was the family of Raphael and Chayeh Sarah Rosenblatt. They were in no immediate danger since Byelaya Tzerkov was by-passed by the wave of violence that swept over other Jewish communities of the Ukraine. Nor was economic pressure the cause of their sudden departure from their Russian home. A mere technicality sent the reader of Reb Yechiel's *Klaus* across the border one day during the fall of the year 1889. The technicality was that he, Raphael Rosenblatt, was legally a subject of Austria. It was the avowed policy of the imperial Russian government to find excuses in order to rid itself of its unwanted dependents; and suspicion alone sufficed to accomplish the end

where more positive grounds were wanting. Although an un-
announced raid on the Rosenblatt apartment one night failed
to produce clear evidence of contraband harbored, that did
not prevent an ukase from being issued the next morning
giving the helpless aliens twenty-four hours to leave the country.

The day on which this happened was, as my father recalled, dark and dreary, as dismal and gloomy as the spirits of
the children of the wandering race, who found themselves
homeless again after a brief respite. A pall of despondency
hung over the house which was crammed full of bundles and
luggage packed for the journey. Dejection was written on the
faces of grandfather and grandmother Rosenblatt and of my
father's elder sisters, as friends and neighbors, who called to
say good-bye, came and went. Every now and then a sigh or a
moan would be heard and Chayeh Sarah's handkerchief
would be lifted, wiping the tears from her eyes.

The only ones who seemed to be unconcerned were the
children, that is, seven-year-old Yossele and his little brother
Levi. To them the very idea of emigrating to a foreign country appealed as a lark. It signified adventure, a leap into the
unknown; and adventure to youth is always fun. Where they
were bound for they did not know, and if they knew, they did
not realize what it meant. They heard it said that they were
going to a place called "Galicia," and that Galicians were
people who spoke with a broad drawl and with a sing-song in
their voice. They were ruled by an emperor named Francis
Joseph—a man with big side-whiskers and a smooth-shaven
chin. Every time they thought of what he must have looked
like—this Francis Joseph with the whiskers and the shaven
chin—they chuckled. But as for the location of Galicia—they
did not have the faintest idea of it, nor did it bother them.
For all they cared it could lie on the other side of the legendary river Sambatyon. As for the Galicians, they might be the
little red Jews that are said to live beyond the further bank of

this stream that rests on every Sabbath. With such pleasant fancies did the youngsters amuse themselves, as their seniors were pulling long faces and painting the future that lay ahead of them in the gloomiest colors.

3

At the Rabbi's Table

The first objective of the involuntary exiles was the town of Sadagora, Bukowina, which was but a stone's throw from Czernowitz, the capital of the province. The crossing of the border into Austrian territory was made on foot, as the little cash the family had for transportation had quickly given out. Carrying the few bundles that constituted their worldly possessions in their hands or on their backs, the travellers were, like many others before them, escorted out of Russia by grim soldiers, sent to make certain that they would never return. The brutality of these instruments of Russian tyranny was responsible for an injury sustained by one of my father's sisters which left her crippled for life.

The reason for the choice of Sadagora was that it was the headquarters of the scion of the Ruzyn dynasty of *Chassidic* rabbis, Rabbi Friedman, whose father had united Raphael and Chayeh Sarah Rosenblatt in wedlock. Being somewhat related to the rabbi my grandfather hoped that with his assistance he might find the means of maintaining his family.

The rabbinical mansion of Sadagora, as it stood out in my father's memory many years later and as the photograph of it in our home indicated, was an edifice of regal splendor. It consisted of a network of buildings, with turrets in each corner, surrounding a central courtyard. Included among these was the synagogue or rather the *Beth Hamidrash* as it was called, in which the congregation was wont to assemble for prayer. According to the impression it made upon the childish mind of the young Yossele the auditorium was as large as a forest.

Particularly vivid in his recollection was the Friday night after the family's arrival, on which he and his father and his younger brother went to worship there for the first time. The place was crowded with *Chassidim* wearing *shtreimels* on their heads and clad in long kaftans. These *shtreimels*, with their velvet caps and their borders of sable skins, were a complete novelty to the little Russian emigre. He had never seen anything like them before, because in Byelaya Tzerkov it was not the custom to wear them. As for the rabbi himself, he was not present among the worshippers. According to a practice that had been established by the founder of his dynasty and was continued by him, he said his prayers in the privacy of his own room.

It did not take long for the newcomers to attract public attention. Nobody could help noticing the two little boys, who, standing beside their father, were praying with so much fervor. All eyes converged on the children as they shook and gesticulated like grown-ups, curling their earlocks and responding *viva voce* after each benediction: "*Boruch hu uvoruch sh'mo*" and "Amen." By the time the services were over everybody knew who the strangers were. Grandfather Rosenblatt was accorded a broad welcome by the people that crowded around him and his sons. The two lads were, for their part, given, as a mark of affection, pinches in their cheeks. These expressions of love caused the flesh to smart so much that my father's brother was ready to burst into tears because of the pain.

After the conclusion of the prayers father and sons joined the rest of the devotees at the rabbi's table. There the elder Rosenblatt was invited to render a melody. The two children assisted him and made a deep impression. Later on an opportunity presented itself for Yossele to do a piece alone and the audience went wild with enthusiasm.

The cantor attached to the rabbi's prayer-chapel was a certain Reb Israel. He was an excellent musician. Many of the tunes sung at the rabbinical court of Sadagora and chanted by the adherents of the dynasty until this day emanate from him. This Reb Israel was so deeply impressed with Yossele that he decided to take him under his wing. It came to pass after grandfather had officiated in the communal synagogue of Sadagora one Saturday, and his Yossele had sung several solos with great success. Reb Israel, who happened to be present, instead of showing his approval by means of a pinch, kissed him on the forehead. From then on Reb Israel saw to it that Yossele participated not only in every Sabbath and holiday service, but also at every function held at the rabbi's table. Thus was my father introduced into the world of Galician *Chassidism* in which he was destined to live during the most formative and impressionable years of his childhood.

However the honor and privilege of performing at the rabbi's board and affording pleasure to the man of God and to his followers were in and by themselves not sufficient to fill the hungry mouths of a family consisting of a father and a mother and ten children that still lived at home. The question of "What shall we eat?" still had to be answered. For even little Yossele, small and delicate though he was and consequently not much of an eater, even *he* demanded food when his stomach was empty. Grandfather Rosenblatt had entertained the hope of being able to follow his calling of precentor in Sadagora, but there was no vacancy. The position of communal cantor was already filled and even the rabbi's *Klaus* had a competent man for the performance of that function. The offer to Yossele by the chief cantor, Reb Shlomo, of a place in his choir was proudly declined by the spirited eight-year-old, who was all too conscious of his powers.

"What will be my duties as a chorister?" was the first question he shot at his would-be-patron. And when the latter informed him that in addition to singing he would be required to perform such menial tasks as carrying out the garbage and shining the cantor's shoes every morning, the little fellow stopped him short by saying: "As far as shining shoes is concerned, other cantors will do that for me."

Faced with the problem of earning a livelihood, grandfather decided to consult the rabbi, and the holy man counselled him to repair to Czernowitz. "Czernowitz," he said, "is a large city, and with a treasure like your Yossele you should have no difficulty in establishing yourself." Raphael Rosenblatt took the rabbi's advice. He went to Czernowitz to try his luck and thus started his son Josef on his career of itinerant cantor.

"Czernowitz," wrote my father in his memoirs, "was the first urban center of any size with which it had been my fortune to become acquainted during the eight and a half years of my life. The towns and hamlets to which I used to accompany my father theretofore in order to officiate at Sabbath services were all small and unsightly. They were of the type concerning which it is said that if you drive into them in a carriage, the heads of the horses would be at one end and the rear of the wagon at the other. Their streets were invariably muddy and dusty, and the houses small and poorly built. Now, however, I found myself in a large city, with broad well-paved streets, with big stores and tall buildings. At night the shops were illumined by gas-lamps that emitted a sort of greenish light. And the people! They were so well-dressed and looked so different from those I had met previously. I was told they were Jews. But who ever heard of clean-shaven, beardless Jews, with turned-up mustaches, and hats and short jackets? Of course there were also real, genuine Jews in Czernowitz, Jews with beards and kaftans. On Saturdays they would don their *shtreimels* and wear their long gaberdines. All this was very confusing to me at the beginning. I was frightened by the immensity of the metropolis. I was afraid of getting lost in the maze of its houses and so I held on tight to my father's coat and wouldn't let go of it."

It was in this capital of the province of Bukowina, which harbored side by side the modern and the traditional in Jewish life, that the boy-wonder from Byelaya Tzerkov made his debut as an artist of the *Amud* in the Austro-Hungarian empire. His first performance proved to be so phenomenal a success that at his second appearance, which occurred on the Sabbath following, 16 policemen, 8 firemen, and 2 inspectors were required to maintain order among the crowd and to keep out the throng that could not get in for lack of room. Nominally, it was his father who conducted the service. For, since the young virtuoso still had more than four years to go before reaching his majority, which according to Jewish law he was to attain upon his thirteenth birthday, he could not yet officially serve as cantor. Actually, however, it was the son who was the principal performer, while the father and the younger brother acted as his assistants.

Altogether grandfather Rosenblatt and his two sons spent eight weeks in Czernowitz. For every Sabbath that they officiated they received as compensation ten gulden, or the equivalent of four dollars in American currency. This amount was far from being a fortune. Yet it represented to the family, under the circumstances in which it was situated then, a tidy sum of money, enough to keep the wolf of starvation from the door.

Besides material emoluments their appearances in Czernowitz also brought publicity, which was so vital for assuring a steady flow of engagements. Connoisseurs of liturgical music came to listen to them in the synagogues in which they officiated. Articles were published about their performance in the local German language newspaper. Among those who manifested interest in my father was the cantor of the local "Reform" temple and the director of his choir. One day he was taken by grandfather to the choir director's home to have his voice tested and to obtain advice on how best to develop it.

It was also in Czernowitz that my father met for the first time the later celebrated Viennese cantor Don Fuchs. The latter was then still in his twenties, a tall and handsome man with an established reputation as an opera singer. He tried to talk grandfather into letting his gifted son study for the opera in Vienna. The only response he elicited from him was: "The gentile world has enough renegade Jews already. There is no need of my supplying it with another."

4

The Wandering Years

The extraordinary success of the Czernowitz venture, toward which my father, the then eight-year-old Yossele, had contributed the lion's share, definitely marked out for him the course that he was thenceforth to follow. It seemed to be decreed by heaven, with the help of my grandfather, that he was to become the interpreter of prayer for the Jewish masses living in the motley collection of countries ruled over by the easy-going, cavalier-like emperor Francis Joseph. His mission was to soothe and to stir, to rouse to ecstasy or fill with hope, through the medium of the sacred music of the synagogue, his fellow-Jews in the countless communities that dotted the Austro-Hungarian empire.

There was a ready market for the cantorial art in that part

of the world. It was a type of merchandise that was very much in demand. For the overwhelming majority of the Jews of Eastern Europe were at the end of the nineteenth century still relatively untouched by the sophistications of modern Western society. They lived completely in accordance with the traditions of their fathers. The synagogue was not only their religious home, but also their social club, their theatre, their place of amusement and communal center. They knew of the opera only from hearsay. The symphony was to them a mystery. Musical instruments were used only at weddings. The sole form of musical art patronized by them and, consequently, cultivated by their gifted sons, was that of cantor. They would give a great deal to hear a person, who had ability and a pleasing voice, chant the traditional prayers of the synagogue, which expressed so well every emotion that filled the heart of the Jew, his joy and his sorrow, his triumphs in spite of oppression, his abiding faith in the midst of suffering. To listen to a talented *chazan* perform on a Sabbath or a holiday was one of the few pleasures that the East-European Jew of the old order allowed himself, one of the rare types of recreation he indulged in. It satisfied the hunger of his soul. It fulfilled his natural craving for the aesthetic, the harmonious, the beautiful.

Yossele had the capacity for satisfying this hunger and for fulfilling this craving. Even as a child of eight he possessed a remarkable power of improvisation; I mean the faculty, without previous preparation, of suiting the music to the words he was reciting in free song, depending entirely upon the inspiration of the moment. He was then already exhibiting signs of that mastery of *"sogachz"* which he developed later on. He could pass with the greatest dexterity and case from mode to mode and genre to genre. He was particularly adept in deftly weaving into the traditional motifs, which were for the most part in the minor key, the lively tunes that he had heard the *Chassidim* sing at the table of the Rabbi of Sadagora. He thereby introduced thitherto unknown variations into the liturgical stereotypes that relieved their monotony and produced the most pleasing effects upon the ears of the listeners. It was these musically unorthodox methods that made such of his compositions as *Mekimi* (Psalm 113), *Minachal* and *Elokai, Neshomoh* so popular.

My grandfather was fully aware of his son's genius. He did not have to wait for the celebrated surgeon, Professor Trzubicki, to inform him, when he once examined Yossele's vocal cords, that his Yossele had a fortune of a million (gulden) in his throat.

Yet although as the head of a large family, grandfather always was pressed for money and compelled by the force of circumstances to exploit his child's talents, he was not so mercenary as to sacrifice the youth's spiritual development for material gain. Also he was too conscientious a Jewish father not to recognize his obligation of "Thou shalt teach them diligently to thy children," that is, of imparting to his son a knowledge of Israel's religious heritage.

However to send the boy to *Cheder,* the regular one-room elementary school which used to be attended by most Jewish children in Eastern Europe, was out of the question. He was too much on the road. Grandfather, therefore, engaged a private teacher who accompanied his children on their journeys. The luggage they took along included among other things copies of the classics of Jewish sacred literature. Every spare moment he had, every hour when he was free from the performance of his professional duties, Yossele had to devote to his studies. He would receive instruction while travelling from town to town, which often took whole days, as well as upon reaching his destination.

The coaches or uncovered wagons, which were generally used as conveyances instead of the railroad trains in order to save expense, traversed fields and forests. They passed by peasants at work, merchants going to market, or tailors, shoemakers and furriers making the rounds of the villages in quest of a livelihood. Yossele paid but little attention to them, for he durst not lose time. He had barely arrived at the inn where he was to put up for the night when he was made to sit down at the table, open up a volume of the Bible or the *Talmud* and read his assignment under the direction of his tutor. His father acted as supervisor, and a stern task-master was he. He saw to it that the youth did not fritter his precious time away in frivolity. In addition he took charge of his musical education. He taught him to read musical scores, acquainted him with the compositions of the outstanding cantors of the time, such as Nissi Belzer, of whose family relationship he was very proud, and others. The musical curriculum included furthermore the popular choral selections of Seidel Rovner, who later emigrated to America where he lived to a great age.

While grandfather Rosenblatt looked out for my father's spiritual progress and well-being, grandmother worried about his material comfort and his physical health. She tried, whenever it was at all possible, to join him on his journeys so that she could cook for him and supervise his diet. If she was unable to go herself—there were still quite a number of children at home and a household to be maintained—she sent my father's eldest unmarried sister along to watch over her darling and his younger brother. Evidently she did not trust grandfather in these things. "After all he is a man. And what does a man know about such matters as a child's food or need of rest? What certainty is there, if left to their father's mercies, that my Yossele and Levele will eat on time and go to bed at a reasonable hour?"

This parental care and solicitude was not without telling effects. The acquaintance made by my father, as soon as he was old enough to read, with the elements of the Hebrew language and its script and his introduction in early childhood into the classics of Jewish lore showed their results in his remarkable interpretation of the prayers of the synagogue, in his ability to translate their contents into music and to transmit their innermost meaning to his audiences by the medium of sound. Such renditions of quotations from rabbinic literature as his *Omar Rabbi Elozor, Bameh Madlikin,* and *Akavyoh ben Mahallalel omer* would have been impossible for anyone to whom the *Mishnah* and the Talmud were sealed books.

On the other hand, the pains taken by grandmother in fulfilling her child's physical requirements showed their beneficial results in his developing, notwithstanding his diminutive size and initial frailty, a fairly robust constitution, which gave him the stamina to bear up with hardly any illness under the strain of a wandering life. The only surgical operation that I can recall my father ever undergoing was one of a minor nature.

Yet all the watchfulness and care of a devoted and loving mother could not overcome the exhaustion and fatigue which were the unavoidable consequences of the living conditions with which an itinerant boy-cantor was forced to put up in those days. When the weather was mild and the sun was shining, travelling in open, roofless coaches or peasant carts from city to city or from one town to another was fairly tolerable notwithstanding the inconvenience and the roughness of the roads. But in the long winter months, when the ground was covered with snow and the temperature was below zero, or when the rain came down in torrents or in slow penetrating drizzles and the dirt underneath the wheels turned into mud, such trips were no joy-rides. Add to this the other discomforts that the roving virtuoso often had to put up with, such as stopping overnight in cold, unheated inns, and sleeping on the floor without adequate bedding, and you will agree that the wandering years of Yossele Rosenblatt were far from pleasant. No wonder that grandmother had fainting spells whenever her Yossele, who was the apple of her eye, had to go off on one of his trips without her. Nor is it surprising that my father's younger brother Levi had to be kept from dozing off during services or to be awakened by means of pinpricks, when he had fallen asleep right in front of the praying-desk.

The second large city to be visited by the wandering boy-cantor, who was then just turning nine, was Lemberg (Lwow in Polish), which lay but sixty miles from the Russian border. The Jewish community of this capital of Galicia, which numbered at that time close to 40,000 souls out of a total population of about 130,000, was able to look upon a distinguished history that went back to the thirteenth century. Jews had always played an important role in its commerce and industry. Since the sixteenth century its rabbis had stood in the forefront of Jewish religious and intellectual life. From it came some of the leaders of the *Haskalah* movement in Austria at the beginning of the nineteenth century as well as the staunchest sponsors of Zionism in Galicia at the end of the century.

It was a well-organized community, equipped with all necessary public institutions. It boasted in the eighteen nineties three large synagogues and nine smaller ones, two *batte-midrashim*, a choir-synagogue, a large Jewish hospital, an orphan asylum, a Jewish technical school, free Jewish elementary schools for the children of the poor, and several *Yeshibot*. One of the tombstones in its old Jewish cemetery is dated as early as 1348.

It wasn't a simple matter to secure permission from the president of the community, the *Rosh Hakahal*, for the right to officiate in one of the synagogues on a Sabbath. Once, however, this obstacle had been hurdled, the road was clear. The first service attracted an audience of a size unprecedented in the annals of Lemberg. Several hours before the scheduled time of prayer the crowd had already begun to assemble. By the time the principals arrived, it was impossible for them to get into the synagogue, and they had to be hoisted above the heads of the worshippers to gain entry. Inside of the house of prayer people were packed like sardines. There was such jostling and crowding that the doors were battered down and the railing of the *Almemar* was broken. It was a miracle that no one was trampled to death. There were, however, some casualties. Several of the patrons were injured and a good many lost their *shtreimels* and the buttons of their coats.

After services that Saturday morning the boy-cantor was carried to the home of the president of the community for *Kiddush*. The entire congregation turned out for the occasion, so that the president's house resembled a fortress besieged. A total of seven weeks did little Yossele tarry in Lemberg, officiating in some of the largest synagogues. The elite of the citizenry of the metropolis, Christians as well as Jews, came to hear him, and both German and Polish periodicals took note of his performance. The fee father and son received in Lemberg amounted to one hundred gulden per Sabbath, which was considered very good pay in those days. It was the beginning of prosperity for a family that had up to that time lived in penury, if not in actual want.

My father was befriended during his stay in Lemberg by the community's chief cantor, Halpern. Grandfather was asked to bring him to the cantor's home every day, and each time my father had to sing for him. One day, when he met grandfather Rosenblatt on the street, the cantor said to him: "I wonder, Reb Raphael, whether it is the best thing for me to have you bring your Yossele to my house." "But what's wrong with it?" asked my grandfather taken aback. "Well you see, every time I hear Yossele sing, I become more closely attached to him, so that I dread the very thought of our eventual separation, which I realize is inevitable."

Cantor Halpern was childless. All his unspent parental affection was, therefore, poured out upon the talented youth whom he had taken to his bosom. The friendship shown by the older man to the promising youngster was not misplaced or wasted. My father always thought of Cantor Halpern with the deepest veneration and esteem. He was fond of speaking about the latter's generosity, his kindness, his broad Jewish learning as well as his musicianship. And in later years, when the protege had attained world-wide fame as a singer and he found his then aged friend and former patron in distress, he came to his rescue, in grateful remembrance of those childhood days in Lemberg.

5

In the Congregation of the Pious

During the next three years of his life, my father moved in an atmosphere of scrupulous Jewish piety and intense religious enthusiasm. In his itinerary as wandering boy-cantor there figured such places as Komarno, Sambor and Munkacs in Carpatho-Ruthenia and Rymanov, Sandec, Gorlice and Radomishl in Galicia. The world to which these towns belonged was a universe apart, with its own peculiar sets of standards, fashions and values that had very little in common with those current in the fashionable society of the West.

In this world the fear of heaven was rated higher than the possession of wealth; and helping a brother in need, because it was a divine commandment, afforded greater joy to those that performed it than the best entertainment. No one went to sleep in this world without reciting the *Shema* and putting a bowl and a glass of water beneath his bed so he could upon awaking in the morning wash the tips of his fingers before walking more than four cubits. The men wore long kaftans that reached down to their toes, and tucked the bottoms of their trousers into their shoes. They allowed their earlocks to grow long and never shaved their beards.

Time counted for little among the hundreds of thousands, aye millions, of Jewish pietists, who followed the doctrine of Rabbi Israel Baal Shem Tob in the service of God. They would spend hours every morning in preparation for prayer, which included an ablution in a ritual bath or immersion in a natural body of water like a river or pond, the icy surface of which sometimes had to be cracked open in the winter. The morning service, since it was begun late, might last into midday; for in his ecstasy and fervor the *Chassid* would repeat his prayers many times. It was his wife, who was absolved from the duty of public worship—women did not count in the quorum of ten necessary for public services of the synagogue—that took charge of the little shop from which the family derived its livelihood. Who else could be counted upon to support the household while her husband was basking in the sunshine of his *rebbe*, the man of God, whose ways he longed to study and imitate and whose teachings he absorbed as eagerly as a thirsty person drinks water?

One never went empty-handed to these saintly men of *Chassidism*. Some of them, the *Tzaddikim* of Sadagora, Tshortkov, Belz and Ger, for example, were able, thanks to the gifts of thousands of devotees, to maintain establishments that resembled courts of royalty. In return for the *pidyonim* they received from their followers, the *Chassidic* rabbis would mete out blessings, offer advice in business undertakings or marriage matches, or distribute amulets for protection against disease and other hazards or dangers. My father in the days of his youth wore several such talismans. They had been presented to him for good luck in his calling as a singer in Israel by such *rebbes* as the Sandecer, the Gorlicer and the Rymanover, at whose tables he had sung. It was considered an honor to sing at the table of a *Chassidic* rabbi, whether on Friday nights at dinner or on Saturday afternoons at the third meal or at a *Melavah Malkah*, the banquet tendered to Queen Sabbath after the conclusion of the sacred day. Even to be able to partake of the left-overs of the fish or other food eaten by the holy men was regarded as a rare privilege.

In *Chassidic* circles of the better type the practice of having boys, who had not yet become *Bar-Mitzvah*, act as precentors, was frowned upon. How could children worthily represent congregations consisting of men of learning and merit? Even if they did not recite the more important prayers, it did not seem right, however gifted they might be musically, to allow such youngsters to stand before the Holy Ark and offer supplication for their elders and betters. Altogether the abuse of the *Amud* by many so-called child-marvels, often motivated by purely venal considerations, was looked upon as a desecration of the holy, a form of sacrilege.

Reb Raphael Rosenblatt's son, however, was different. He, Yossele, was looked upon as being in a class by himself. That was settled once and for all by the rabbi of Komarno. The spiritual head of this stronghold of *Chassidism* was a man renowned for his piety. His followers, knowing how unbending their master was in his adherence to the letter of the law, felt certain, therefore, that he would never approve of having a youth who had not yet attained his majority officiate in the synagogue. As it turned out they had been completely mistaken in their prognosis. When Yossele and his father went to pay their respects to the rabbi on Friday night after services, they wondered, like everybody else, just what the holy man would have to say, and how they would be received by him. Would he show them a mark of his favor or reveal his displeasure over the offense given to the rules of the etiquette of the house of prayer? They found the rabbi seated at the head of the table, sunken in thought, his eyes closed, humming a tune to himself. The *Chassidim*, their faces turned in the direction of their master, listened, with bated breath to his subdued, muffled droning that floated from the chair up above. Suddenly the rabbi opened his eyes, fixed them on Yossele and said to him:

"Sing something, Yossele!"

"Thereupon," said my father, "it seemed to me as though a tune had rolled spontaneously out of my throat. I sang like a person hypnotized, seeing nothing around me except the rabbi's eyes peering through the thick eye-brows. I don't remember how long that lasted. All I can recall is that it appeared to me as though my song would never end, that it would continue to eternity. When I finished, everybody at the table was silent. No one uttered a sound. The first to break the spell was the rabbi himself. In a tone of voice, such as a person uses when speaking to himself, he exclaimed:

"He has a pure mouth, and his prayers will be heard!"

With lightning rapidity the verdict of the rabbi of Komarno spread throughout Galicia. Wherever *Chassidim* met and Yossele Rosenblatt's name came up for discussion, the holy man's statement was repeated. "He has a pure mouth."

Rabbis were not the only doubters whose skepticism young Yossele had to overcome. There were cantors, too, that needed to be convinced that it was possible for a little boy not yet in his teens to be a genuine artist. One of these was Cantor Alter Bauman of Stanislav, Galicia. Herman Wohl, who was later on to become my father's favorite choir director, was then serving as a member of that celebrated cantor's choir. One day, he relates, it was reported that a certain *Chassid* was touring the country with a nine-year-old son of his who possessed a voice like that of a canary. When the little fellow would recite a prayer at the *Amud,* he would draw tears from everyone's eyes. Well, the boy came to Stanislav and the town went agog. When his father brought him to Cantor Bauman's for an audition, people literally hung from the windows of the cantor's house.

Reb Alter received Yossele Rosenblatt with grave misgiv-

ings. There were then, just as there still are today, many so-
called boy-wonders on the loose, and very few of them ever
amounted to anything. But when Yossele, standing in the
middle of the room, opened his mouth to sing, he just commanded attention. Reb Alter screwed up his eyes in deep
concentration and listened. When the lad had finished, his
auditor remained motionless for awhile, his eyes still closed
and his face beaming. Suddenly the elderly gentleman tore
himself loose from the chair, ran up to the little singer, threw
his arms about him and showered him with kisses.

"God bless you," he mumbled. "You are growing up to be
a genius in the realm of music. I, a veteran cantor, who have
served at the prayer-desk for many years, confer upon you
my ordination."

This recognition by so competent an authority in the realm
of *Chazanuth* flattered the youth enormously. He felt that he
was already an accomplished *chazan*, and he began to pur-
sue in all earnestness the calling to which he had been ap-
pointed by the Master of Fate.

Life, on the whole, was serious in this *Chassidic* world of
which my father was so integral a part during this period of
his young life. Even though *Chassidism* preached the gospel
of joyousness, there wasn't much time for tomfoolery or play.
Once in Radomishl, when the boy-cantor joined some of his
playmates in a game of nuts, he drew from one of the elders
a sharp reprimand. "How shameful for a young man who
leads the congregation in prayer to while his time away with
such nonsense."

But although the day by day existence of a *Chassidic* lad
like Yossele Rosenblatt, especially one on whose narrow
shoulders rested the burden of maintaining an entire
family, was one of deep earnest, it was not on that account
filled with gloom for one who possessed the faculty of
detecting the humorous and comical in human life. Yossele
was blessed with such a gift and, thanks to it, able to extract

the honey out of many an otherwise bitter fruit, thus making a virtue of necessity.

Once, for example, he was engaged to conduct the Sabbath services in the town of Drohobycz. The crowd that had collected in front of the synagogue was so large that the little cantor was unable to squeeze through. "If you don't let me in," he said to the human wall that was impeding his entrance, "you may as well all go home."

On another occasion—he was then about ten years old but looked like a child of seven—the would-be audience that sought admittance into the house of worship in which he was to officiate had become so unwieldy that police reserves had to be called to maintain order. The chief performer, who was responsible for the collection of the throng, made several attempts to break through the mass of humanity, but in vain. Yet young as he was, he did not lose his composure. He neither fretted nor raged, but waited patiently outside, laughing to himself. A man seeing a child so amused, asked him: "Little boy, why are you laughing? What seems to be so funny?" "What am I laughing for?" repeated my father. "If it weren't for me, those fellows over there"—and he pointed to the policemen—"would be out of a job."

Again there was that Friday evening in Sambor, when the wax candles that illumined the synagogue melted down to the bottom. Even the naphtha lamps went out for lack of kerosene, so that the congregation was wrapt in pitch darkness. Yossele and his father were not a bit disturbed. They went on with the services to the very end as though nothing had happened.

One Sabbath eve in Komarno after services, the worshippers waited at the front entrance of the synagogue for a glimpse of the nine-year-old prodigy whose rendition of the prayers had thrilled them so much. Yossele, however, was in no mood for being pulled to pieces by his enthusiastic admirers. So he sneaked out through a back door and left the crowd standing.

Among the most memorable episodes of his boyhood days recalled by my father, was one going back to the time of his first visit to Cracow. He suddenly felt an urge for gloves. Knowing that his pious father would not give his consent to the gratification of such a fancy, which was befitting only a dandy, he went into a haberdashery by himself and asked to be shown some handgear. The attendant at the counter, a woman, took measure of her customer—a bekaftaned oaf with curly earlocks and so puny that it would seem that he had just been let loose from his mother's apron strings—and looked at him with dubious eyes. "Did you say you wanted gloves?" she asked. "Yes, gloves," answered the determined lad who was not to be put off by her refusal to serve him. Very reluctantly she showed him some gloves, but quoted so high a price that, eager as the little man was to feel them on his hands, he just could not agree to such robbery. He began to bargain, but the sales-woman would not reduce the amount she had asked. Finally, in a desperate effort to get rid of him, she exclaimed angrily: "Geh gesunterheit (Go in good health). I won't run after you." Whereunto the proud youngster retorted: "You *will* run after me."

As he was leaving the store, a throng of people who had seen him enter and recognized him, were awaiting him and followed him as he hurried back to the pension where he was staying. Among those who pursued him was the saleslady of the haberdashery. It had suddenly dawned upon her who her would-be customer was and she regretted her treatment of him. The next morning the proprietress of his pension handed my father a little package. It contained the gloves that he had selected. They were offered with the compliments of the haberdasher woman and her husband.

6

A Letter to America

It was in the middle of November 1893 that my father, his brother Levi and his parents arrived in Cracow. More than four years had elapsed since they had come from Byelaya Tzerkov and since the eldest daughter, my father's sister Chaveh, had moved to America. How the boy-cantor and his family fared in this most ancient seat of Polish-Jewish culture is revealed in the following letter by my grandfather, dated December 28th and addressed to his daughter Chaveh in New York.

"First of all," he declares in this epistle of his, written in a very picturesque Yiddish, spiced with Hebrew quotations from the Bible and rabbinic literature, "I beg to inform you that we are all well, thank God. May the Lord thus grant me to see you in joy. Secondly, I wish to let you know that I received the dear letter you wrote me on the eve of the festival of *Chanukah* announcing the birth of your second daughter. May she bring you much good fortune and may both your children grow up in health and happiness.

"I beg you not to be angry with me for writing you so rarely. We are seldom at home because the necessity of making a livelihood compels us to travel. However I am very grateful to the Almighty even for this, and pray that He may help us so that our luck may not fail. I have reason to be hopeful that things will continue to improve as we go along, because God has blessed me with a gift the fame of which has spread over the whole of Austria. I have reference to my two sons who are written up in all newspapers. When, for instance, my son Joseph, your brother, conducts services in the large synagogue of any city, it is necessary to call out the police. Otherwise it would be impossible to pray there on account of the crowd, since everybody is eager to hear him. For that reason also tickets of admission are charged for our performance.

"This is the sixth Saturday that we are spending in Cracow. The first two Sabbaths' services netted us 175 Gulden while the synagogue also profited to the extent of 200 Gulden . . . Without tickets of admission it would have been impossible to have services. My entire revenue for the past five weeks has been 450 Gulden. May the Almighty help to keep my children well and may no evil eye have dominion over them.

"I trust to God that I may soon be able in joy to marry off my daughter Gittel. My only care is that God provide her a suitable mate. I am also in a position to inform you that I have already had an opportunity to pay off the debts incurred in Sadagora and buy some clothes. I have had fur-coats made for myself and my son Joseph at a cost of 75 Gulden, and also one for my son Levi Isaac at a cost of 15 Gulden. I now have in my possession 300 Gulden in cash . . . Please let me know what sort of a living you are making.

"I shall also send you the posters that are pasted on the billboards whenever we officiate or sing. I would have sent you pictures of us. But first of all it is not fitting for me to be photographed. Secondly you are liable to forget about us, for I still hope to God that you may come to visit us . . ."

As is evident from this first-hand account the experience of Lemberg was repeated in Cracow. The cantors of the city all came to hear the young prodigy. In the audiences there were among others a goodly number of high government officials, attracted by curiosity about the boy-wonder who had caused such a stir among the Jews. One Saturday, just as previously in Lemberg, the railing of the *Almemar* was broken by the record throng.

To have been permitted to perform at all in Cracow was itself already a great achievement. It would have been a feather in the cap of even a cantor of maturity and standing in his profession, let alone a young boy who was not yet Bar-Mitzvah. For the Jewish community of Cracow was the most venerable in Poland, and one of the largest and most influential in the entire Jewish world. It had the reputation —and deservedly so—of being a Mustergemeinde, a model congregation. Hence it was but natural that it should have lured the outstanding artists of the *Amud*. Its chief precentor, Leizer Kremenitzer, was known far and wide as a leader in his profession.

To meet the standards that would satisfy so critical an audience as the Cracow public was difficult. "In our city," Cracow Jews told my father, "when a visiting cantor comes for a guest performance, no matter how high a position he may occupy in his calling, he officiates for several Sabbaths and then he has to pack up and leave." Nevertheless my father sang in Cracow for seventeen weeks, and on every Saturday that he performed he drew the same record audience. The total revenue for the family from these seventeen weeks of service was seventeen hundred gulden. It represented real prosperity. Grandfather's eyes brightened and the wrinkles of worry disappeared from his usually earnest face. It was in this city that he met the renowned Professor Trzubicki whose name was mentioned before.

Not far from Cracow lay a little hamlet or village known as Brzesko in Polish but called Brigel by the Jews. The regular maps did not give any indication of its existence. Its size was, to use my father's own description, no greater than that of the yawn of a flea. Nevertheless he would not have traded Brzesko, whose sole claim to fame lay in the beer it brewed, for Paris or Vienna or London or even New York. And the reason was that Brzesko was the scene of his only romance, the birthplace of the one lady-love he had ever had or known and with whom he spent thirty-three blissful years from the day of their marriage until the moment of his death.

He visited Brzesko for the first time when he was about twelve years old at the request of one of my mother's two musical brothers. The elder one had heard my father in Cracow and was so impressed that he prevailed upon my grandfather to spend a Sabbath in Brzesko in order to afford the two hundred Jewish families living there some real Sabbath joy. That Sabbath morning there came up to the women's gallery of the local house of worship, among others, twelve-year-old Taubele Kaufman. Together with her girl-friends she stood bent over the railing of the women's gallery devouring with her eyes the small figure of a boy standing upon a specially constructed raised platform in front of the prayer-desk, wrapped in a huge prayer-shawl, while her ears were entranced by the divine music that issued from his mouth.

"As I left the synagogue," my father related, "the worshippers, as they usually did, followed me, and she, who later became my wife, among them. However Taubele ran faster than everybody else. She wanted to be sure of a good look at me. I paid no attention to all this because I was already accustomed to such pursuits.

"For *Kiddush* I and my father were invited to Taubele's home. I still recall, just as though it were today, how I sat at the table and felt fixed upon me all the time the brilliant brown eyes of the little girl with the pretty black tresses and the beautiful rosy face. She looked at me and I was too abashed to lift my eyes. But our eyes did meet, and when they did, I felt the blood rushing into my face. She, too, reddened and quickly lowered her eyes. This happened sev-

eral times. I sang, but my thoughts were elsewhere. I had
that far-away look, so that my father, noticing it, asked me
whether I was feeling well.

"After that Taubele left the room and I did not see her
any more until we met again five years later. In the meantime I began to sense a certain restlessness. It seemed to me
as though the world had become empty with her departure,
as though I were left all alone. The little girl would not go
out of my mind. Wherever I went I saw Taubele standing
before me."

My father learned a great deal of what had transpired in
the synagogue that morning from the mouth of my mother
herself after they were married. She told him how, as she ran
after him when he was leaving the synagogue, her girl friends
teased her, saying: "Taubele is in love with the little cantor
(*mit dem kleinen chazendel*) . . . Taubele wants Yossele
for a bridegroom . . ." and my mother stamped her foot
and said: "It isn't true . . . I will never marry anybody who
is such a midget that he has to stand on a platform in order to
reach the prayer-desk."

The truth of the matter was that my father, who never
grew beyond five feet in height, was at that time no taller
than an eight-year-old child. And it happened more than
once, when he sang in some town or hamlet, that the children who were taken along by their parents to hear him and
who were as yet unable to differentiate in their pronunciation between *chazendel* (the diminutive of *chazan*, "cantor") and *chazerel* (the diminutive of *chazer*, "pig"), would
ask to be hoisted up so they could see the "little chazerel"
(*das kleine chazerel*).

Exactly how *Chassidic* society, which was carried away by
Yossele's singing, explained his genius to itself is illustrated
by the following incident after one of his successful performances. He was then about twelve years old and officiating in
a town which had the venerable Moses Lutzker for its can-

tor. When the services were over, the old gentleman walked over to where the little virtuoso was standing and picked up his long gaberdine as though he were looking for something that might be concealed underneath.

"What are you looking for, Reb Moshe?" asked the somewhat puzzled youth.

"I am looking for the *dybbuk* that is hidden in your bosom. Only Yerucham the Short could sing as you did. The only way I can figure it out is that a *dybbuk* of his has entered into you."

There were times when the enthusiasm of the admiring public created embarrassing situations, especially when proper precautions were not taken. Once, for instance, my father arrived in the town of Gorlice on Friday morning in preparation for the Sabbath services that were to be held the same evening. Between three and five in the afternoon the tickets were sold out. Nevertheless the management decided to dispense with police protection. The result was that the synagogue gates were battered down. Many people who had purchased tickets could not get in, whereas a large proportion of those who had gained admittance had not paid for the privilege.

7

Francis Joseph's Loss

Thus far the boy-cantor from Byelaya Tzerkov had remained strictly within the boundaries of the empire of *Chassidism*. Communities like those of Czernowitz, Lemberg and Cracow, despite the veneer of modernism that a certain portion of their upper stratum had acquired and notwithstanding the inroads of Zionism and the presence in them of choral synagogues—the equivalent relatively speaking of American Reform temples—were still, on the whole, part of the *Chassidic* world. Now, however, what was really the *Kulturwelt,* the cultured society of the West in the best sense of the word, was to learn of his existence. This occurred when in the fall of the year 1894 the Rosenblatts, father and sons, visited Vienna, the glamorous, gay capital of the Austro-Hungarian empire.

At the end of the nineteenth century Vienna was at the height of its glory. It did not have the forlorn, bedraggled look that it acquired after World War I when it was cut off from its large provincial hinterland, the chief source of its industry and its wealth. Nor had it become the ghost town which it is today under Russian and Allied occupation. It was a city of music and literature and art, of parks and gardens, of tastefully furnished and well-stocked shops and magnificent public edifices. Its opera house, royal museum, palaces and parliament buildings were among the showplaces of the world. Its Prater was a synonym for amusement, its cafes the rendezvous of writers and thinkers, statesmen and journalists, whose views attracted international attention. People from everywhere gravitated to Vienna, and not without good cause. For was it not the home of Arthur Schnitzler who set the tone for the novel and the drama? Was it not there that Johann Strauss, to whose waltz music the entire world was dancing, wielded the baton? Did not the most renowned physicians conduct their clinics in its hospitals and expound their theories in the lecture halls of its university?

In all this pulsating life, in all these activities of the Austrian capital its Jews played a most prominent part. Indeed without them, as the tragically murdered Hugo Bettauer, the author of "The City Without Jews," demonstrated so convincingly, Vienna would not have been Vienna. It was entirely natural that the Viennese Jews, to measure up to the general standards prevailing in the metropolis, which they themselves had helped to establish, should have built for the service of God the most sumptuous houses of worship. Nor is it surprising that a man who was considered the foremost composer of synagogue music of all time, Salomon Sulzer, should have been their chief cantor for more than half a century until his death in the year 1890.

This sophisticated, cultured, artistic Vienna with its refined tastes and high aesthetic ideals, took the self-made, musically almost untutored *Chassidic* youth, who possessed none of the refinements of the West, but sang completely à la naturelle, to its heart. It gave the young prodigy a reception such as was not accorded anyone before or since. Weeks before his first appearance tickets were sold out. As to whether the expectations were justified by the performance, we have the testimony of an article penned by Dr. Josef Bloch, in the December 28, 1894 issue of his Oesterreichische Wochenschrift. Though belonging by vocation and training to the West, this outstanding journalist and champion of Jewish rights in the Austrian parliament was by birth a Galician Jew. He was close enough to the source to appreciate fully the traditional Jewish art of the *chazan*. And so, after hearing Josef Rosenblatt, he wrote:

"Vienna (the World's Youngest Cantor)"

"Prodigy!—much abused designation for every type of halfbaked precocity brought forth by parental vanity or greed. We hear nowadays of so many prodigies, that a child that would not be recognized as such might be the true prodigy. All this has nothing to do with the eleven-year-old lad about whom we wish to speak now. We had the opportunity to listen to him in private surroundings and must bear witness to the great and amazing musical talent that is manifested in him. Josef is the little son of *Chazan* Rafael Rosenblatt of Sadagora, and himself already a fullfledged *Chazan*. But not an ordinary, but an unusual, a fascinating *Chazan*. His memory is stupendous, his musical sureness astounding.

He has already mastered today whatever can be learned in his calling, and in addition thereto much that cannot be acquired by training and study but must be congenital, native, inborn.

"Without ever wandering off the beaten track he is able to find his way through the mazes of Oriental melody with its ramified coloratura. His presentation exhibits not the slightest trace of the mechanical, the studied or parroted. The little fellow sings with taste, with profoundest understanding of the words of the sacred text, with depth of feeling.

"We can well picture him moving a large congregation to tears in solemn moments of the High Holidays. His voice has power and good resonance. He uses his mezza voce in the Polish manner. Similarly does he employ head and palate tones. He is deftly assisted by his younger brother and his father. We have no doubt of the boy's future, if only he could be kept from having to continue to work for a livelihood so that he might be able to devote himself to further study."

During the three months that my father tarried in Vienna he officiated in the largest synagogues of the city. Not only his fellow-countrymen, the Galician and Polish Jews who lived in the second Bezirk came to hear him, but also the aristocratic Temple-Jews in their high hats and their trained Kaiser Wilhelm mustaches or side-whiskers à la Francis Joseph. His auditors included such distinguished personalities as Vienna Jewry's celebrated preacher, Professor Guedemann, who became very fond of him, Dr. Josef Bloch and a host of prominent Viennese cantors.

One of the staunchest friends he made in Vienna was the merchant Jacob Maerz. Himself a singer and musician of no mean attainments, Maerz used to officiate on the High Holidays and turn over all the proceeds to charity. A man of great wealth, his house was always open to the poor and needy. He was a patron of rabbis and scholars, and developed a special fondness for the boy-cantor from Sadagora. My father was in the habit then of beating time by stamping the floor with one foot. This was very annoying to the tenants in the apart ment beneath that of Mr. Maerz in which he was staying for a while, and they complained about the disturbance in no uncertain terms. In order to save my father embarrassment Jacob Maerz sat his young protege on his lap and let him step on his feet instead.

One day the aforementioned Dr. Bloch came to the hotel in which my father and his brother and father were stopping and approached the latter with the following proposition. "Mr. Rosenblatt, do you know what I am minded to do? I would like to take your little Josef to the imperial court and present him to the emperor."

"You would like to do what?" inquired my grandfather, his face becoming pale. Dr. Bloch repeated his statement. "But why, for what purpose?" asked Raphael Rosenblatt visibly frightened.

"It would do us Jews great honor," replied Dr. Bloch. "I am certain the emperor will be pleased with his singing and very probably recommend him to the imperial conservatory of music."

"Never! Never!" exclaimed my terrified grandfather. "Under no circumstances will I permit my child to be sent to the conservatory. He was born for the *Amud* and at the *Amud* he will remain."

Such having been the feeling of my grandfather in regard to even the smallest deviation from the strict line of tradition, one can well surmise what his reaction could be where more was at stake. Among the invitations extended to my father to officiate was one issued by a certain Reform temple. This was quite a departure from the accepted rules, for it was not customary for Reform congregations to permit boy-cantors or anyone but their official readers to conduct services in their temples. My grandfather was under the impression that the house of worship in which my father had been asked to perform was a synagogue like other synagogues. Had he known it to be otherwise, he would most certainly never have accepted the invitation. In his eyes the changes introduced by Reform Judaism were equivalent to apostasy.

As per agreement, then, grandfather, accompanied by my father, went to the temple, and the two of them were about to enter the auditorium, when he noticed through the open door men and women seated on the same floor while an organ pealed forth music. That was all he needed. He yanked his son's arm with such force, that the boy almost lost his balance, and ran with him as one runs from a fire. To this day, what happened that Friday night in the temple, when the expected performers failed to make an appearance, remains a secret.

After Vienna the next important étape in my father's tour of the communities of the Austro-Hungarian empire was Budapest, the beautiful capital of Hungary on the Danube River. More provincial and smaller than Vienna, Budapest was, nevertheless, from the Jewish standpoint, more important. For one thing its Jewish population was numerically larger than that of the first city of the realm. Secondly, Hungarian Jewry, which drew its chief inspiration from Budapest, represented more than that of Vienna, with its German Kultur, a blending of the East and the West. Hungary at that time included, in addition to purely Hungarian territory, also Slovakia, Carpatho-Ruthenia, Transylvania and a portion of what is today Yugoslavia. Although the Reform movement emanating from Germany had made considerable inroads into certain parts of Hungary, whose Jews were almost without exception ardent Hungarian patriots speaking the Hungarian language, the majority followed the traditions of their fathers. Most of the Hungarian Jews spoke in addition to their native Hungarian also German. Many of them were well versed in German literature. And since the fledglings of their *Yeshibot* combined the Jewish learning and piety of the East with the culture of the West, they were very much in demand as rabbis of Orthodox congregations in Germany, where fluency in the German language and the ability to deliver sermons in that tongue were desiderata.

To a greater extent even than the Jewish community of Vienna did Budapest Jewry contribute to Jewish scholarship and the development of the Jewish Volksgeist. It is noteworthy that both Theodor Herzl and Max Nordau, the two founders and leading spirits of political Zionism, were born and reared in Budapest, and that two such savants as the philosopher David Kaufmann and the philologist and historian of the Talmud Wilhelm Bacher served on the faculty of its rabbinical seminary.

If Vienna had among its celebrities in the field of *Chazanuth* so eminent a composer of synagogue music as Sulzer, Budapest's Rombach temple could pride itself on having as its cantor a man with the most phenomenal heroic tenor voice that has ever been heard, Jacob Bachmann. This Jacob Bachmann, whose praises my father never tired of rehearsing, was also among his ardent admirers. His verdict about Yossele's voice agreed fully with that of Professor Trzubicki of Cracow. However for a more detailed appraisal of what Budapest Jewry thought of the youthful virtuoso, who officiated in its midst for several weeks, we must refer the reader to a critique written in one of the German-language Jewish weeklies of Budapest on January 7, 1896 by a certain Dr. Ignatz Friedlieber. It was entitled: "The Oldest Jewish Synagogue and the Youngest Cantor in Budapest."

"This unusual contrast," said the writer, "quite spontaneously impresses itself upon the mind of a person who enters the threshold of the house of worship of the Polish Jews, that is located in the socalled Simonyi House, on a Friday evening. For the past several weeks a beardless, only fourteen-year-old youth has been functioning there. He has been assisted by his still younger brother with a piping voice and his father, a short, long-bearded Jew from Kiev, who in consequence of the expulsion of Jews from Russia has settled in Sadagora, Bukowina. For weeks people from all strata of society have been making pilgrimages—upon payment of an admission charge—to this temple, of the very existence of which they had theretofore been completely unaware, and not one left dissatisfied. Even the uninitiated cannot help being impressed by the precision with which the little precentor reads the text to the worshippers—I mean *recites the prayers,* because his entire presentation consists of free and unfettered improvisation. Everyone is full of admiration for the lad's magnificent coloratura, which comes to the fore in many passages of the prayers in inimitable fashion.—As for the initiated, who are conversant with the mysteries of the Hebrew language and whose ears have been attuned since their youth to these peculiar minor motifs, they are just transported to ecstasy when they hear so magnificent an interpretation of the old and well known chants. . . ."

The writer, like Dr. Bloch before him, voices the hope at the conclusion of his review that his subject might be given the opportunity of developing his talent and be relieved of the responsibility of working for a livelihood lest his further progress be impeded by the exertion. He suggested also that his father "be compensated for the surrender of his orthodox scruples with regard to the secular training of his son, who is for him a heavenly as well as earthly treasure in the literal sense of the word, if he can at all be persuaded to agree thereto."

It is needless to say that these well-meant suggestions and best-intentioned advice fell on deaf ears. My grandfather would never have consented to give up his orthodox scruples and he could not afford to renounce his family's sole certain means of support.

8

Adolescence

During the interval between his sojourn in Vienna and his appearance in Budapest the boy Josef Rosenblatt grew to man's estate as a Jew. In reality he was at thirteen still far from being a man. He was very much below average in physical development and almost as completely under his strict father's thumb as theretofore. However Jewish law decreed that, having reached his thirteenth birthday, he be regarded as an adult. That gave him the privilege of acting from then on as a cantor in his own right, qualified to lead any congregation in Israel in prayer and chant the main portions of the synagogue liturgy. No ado was made about his coming of age. No party was tendered him, as is customary nowadays among Occidental Jews, to mark his confirmation. Grandfather merely showed him one morning how to wind the leather thongs of his phylacteries around his left arm and how to place the box, designated as a frontlet, above his forehead. Thereupon he told him that he was a *Bar-Mitzvah*, a person charged with all the obligations of Judaism.

Actual maturity was first attained when the lad was about fifteen years old. It was then that the boyish alto passed almost imperceptibly into a manly tenor, a tenor of the same power and sweetness that had characterized the child's voice out of which it had evolved and the place of which it had taken. By all the rules of musical science and according to the theories of professors of voice culture since time immemorial, the young singer should have given his vocal cords a complete rest of at least a year or two during the period of transition, in order not to do injury to his voice but give it a chance to become strong and flexible. These rules were apparently not observed by my father, for the record of his performances makes no allowance for any interruption in his professional career. After his appearance in Budapest at the beginning of the year 1896 we find him successively in Sopron Keresztur (Tzelem), Presburg, Duna Szerdahely, Nyitra and Miskolcz. The next year he officiated in such places as Gyongyos, Gyarmat, Papa, Ujhely and Nagyvarad (Grosswardein); then in the year 1898 in Dees, Beregsas, Mihalewicz and Nagy-Kapos, and in 1899 in Zenta. That all these towns, the names of which have been preserved in testimonial letters written in German, Hungarian and Hebrew, were located in what was then the kingdom of Hungary, was no accident. Hungarian Jewry was at that time the most prosperous section of the Jewish population of the Austro-Hungarian empire, and in a better position than the rest to remunerate the talents of a gifted *chazan,* the appreciation of whose art they shared with all of East-European Jewry. It was my father's fate, for the greater portion of his career as a precentor of the synagogue, to serve congregations of Hungarian Jews.

Wherever the boy Yossele performed he met with the same universal acclaim for his musical ability, voice, coloratura and power of improvisation as well as for his piety. The pattern of recommendations was set by Rabbi Saul Broch of Magendorf. In a letter written in the summer of 1892 about the then ten-year-old boy-cantor he stated that Yossele stood out among the rank and file of the prodigies of the time by his unswerving loyalty to Jewish tradition, which was so often abandoned by others.

Also in another respect was he differentiated from the common run of Wunderkinder. Whereas these others ceased, upon reaching manhood, to be preeminent, and consequently no longer attracted attention, in the case of Yossele

Rosenblatt the situation was almost the reverse. The older and maturer he became, the more did the wonder of him grow and his popularity increase.

Blessed with the musical gifts that he possessed and a very attractive personality, young Yossele was sought out by well-to-do lovers of music, and every citizen of importance in the Jewish communities in which he sang sued for the privilege of entertaining him as a house-guest. Those who were fortunate enough to have their invitations accepted became the envy of all their fellowtownsmen.

"When my uncle Hirsh Godol, the richest man in our community and a connoisseur of music besides," reports an eye-witness, "heard Yossele officiate at the Sabbath morning service, he insisted on his having the Sabbath meal with him —despite the fact that he resided at some distance from the town . . . Once he had him in his home, however, and especially after the beautiful *Zemiros* sung by the boy at the table, the host would not let his guest go anymore.

"Immediately upon the termination of the Sabbath he sent his coachman to fetch Yossele's and his father's luggage from the hotel in which they had their quarters and put at their disposal two rooms of his ten room mansion. And of course, as far as food was concerned, they lacked for nothing.

"My uncle's children were all fairly competent pianists, and therefore in a position to play the accompaniment while Yossele sang. All this was so enjoyable to me that I stayed at my uncle's for as long as Yossele was there. I was then past my Bar-Mitzvah and had already accumulated a considerable stock of learning. So I spent a good bit of time with Yossele in learned discussions and became rather chummy with him.

"However as the week wore on and the townspeople noted that my uncle was still retaining for himself the little *Chazan* and his father, they began to grumble. To pacify them my uncle negotiated for Yossele and his father to remain for another Sabbath service, offering to pay out of his own pocket as much as the community had paid for the previous Sabbath's performance. Thus the anger of the public was appeased. Everybody was satisfied. What pleasures the rich can indulge themselves in!"

My father was always generous with his talents toward his hosts. He never begrudged the use of his voice for the pleasure of those who had extended to him courtesies or attentions. That was one reason for his popularity. Another was his quickness at repartee. Thus, for instance, when, as a fourteen-year-old lad, he was the guest of the president of the community of Dukla in Galicia, his host said to him in the course of the meal: "Yossele, let me hear an *Av Horachamim* of yours, but let it be a good one." Whereunto the youth, without losing a moment, shot back: "I never knew that there was such a thing as a *bad Av Horachamim* ('Father of Mercy')."

It was at this juncture in his career that the creative urge first formally manifested itself in my father. Originality had, as has been noted previously, from the very beginning characterized his performance. In earliest infancy he had exhibited the faculty of improvisation. However to take pencil and paper and jot down an idea for a song, a hymn or an oratorio, was something that he first began to do when he was about fifteen years old. It happened, as a boyhood friend of his reported, in Beregsas. They were both bathing in a pool and splashing about in the water, when my father suddenly stopped and began very quietly to hum a tune. Immediately thereafter he jumped out of the water, found himself a stub of a pencil and a piece of paper, and scribbled down a melody. When he finished, he announced that he had written a new *Lecha Dodi* for the inauguration of the Sabbath. "This," concluded our informant, "transpired just one hour before services began. He sang the new composition with such skill and with fugues of such beauty that a Johann Sebastian Bach would have approved." The inspiration of his catchy *V'chol*

Maaminim, composed sixteen years later, came to my father amidst similar circumstances.

Thus there commenced for him an era of composition that produced nearly five-hundred musical works for cantor and choir, many of which have become favorites among *Chazanim.* By using head-tones instead of the full voice while composing or rehearsing, he developed that extraordinary falsetto that gave his performance as *chazan* the distinctive Rosenblatt touch. The amazing feats of coloratura and the trills that this falsetto enabled him to execute astounded all critics in later years when he appeared on the concert stage.

For several years since the family's arrival from Russia, Sadagora was mentioned as the permanent residence of the wandering Rosenblatts. In the letter dispatched by my paternal grandfather to his daughter in America at the end of December 1893 from Cracow, the home of Madame Feige Schapira in Drohobycz, Galicia is given as the forwarding address. It was written by my father himself. The actual wording of the note, penned in Latin characters, and faulty German spelling, was: "Dize Adresse Schreib Ich Zelbst Dein Bruder Jozef Rosenblüth Aus Biale Cerkow" (This address I am writing myself your brother Josef Rosenblüth from Biale Cerkow). Some time during the year 1898 my grandparents must have established headquarters in the West-Galician village of Novy Targ (Neumarkt). There was no special reason for their settling there except that their daughter Gittel had married a native of that place. The names that figure in the letters of recommendation preserved in the family archives from this period are those of towns of the vicinity, such as Rymanov, Zuczawa and Brzesko. Novy Targ was destined to be the last station in my grandparents' peregrinations on earth.

The boy-prodigy from Byelaya Tzerkov was now maturing into manhood. In certain respects one might say he never quite grew up. For notwithstanding the veneer of worldliness that he acquired as a result of his many and varied contacts throughout his rich and colorful career, he always retained his childish playfulness and buoyancy. Throughout his life he kept that youthful optimism and naive trust in human beings, which was at once a most important factor in his phenomenal success as well as the chief cause contributing to his undoing. Thus did nature, which showered its gifts upon him so lavishly in some respects, compensate for its prodigality by impoverishing him in others. Grown-up or not, however, as he reached the age of seventeen, with ten years of wandering behind him, the former child-marvel became tired of the hectic existence of an itinerant cantor. He began to long for security and rest, for a place in which he might settle down permanently and no longer have to move about from city to city and from town to hamlet to eke out a livelihood.

One day his path crossed that of Rabbi David Moshe Friedman, the head of the *Chassidic* dynasty of Tshortkov. He officiated in the rabbi's prayer-chapel and made an unforgettable impression. In the presence and within the hearing of the large assemblage of devotees the patriarch bestowed upon the still beardless youth his fatherly blessing and voiced the hope that he would become "a great man in Israel." Under the spell of the moment, my father expressed a desire to become the official precentor at his patron's private synagogue. What could be more satisfying than a life in the entourage of such a saint? Besides it would put an end to his interminable wanderings. However the venerable sage, who was a wise and practical person, dissuaded him from this plan of his.

"You are the possessor of a precious instrument," he said, "by means of which you will be able to make a name for yourself and rouse Jews to greater piety. Here there is no future for you. Continue travelling. With the renown you will achieve for yourself you will rise to great heights." So he continued travelling, and at the age of eighteen he obtained his first regular position, being elected cantor of the community of Munkacs in Carpatho-Ruthenia. The recommendation of the rabbi of Tshortkov went a long way in helping him secure it.

Yet before he could enter upon his post, he had to fulfill one proviso without which no orthodox Jewish congregation in Europe would have engaged him as cantor. He had to get himself a wife. Whether he was ready for marriage or not—and psychologically he was then certainly still far from being fit for the assumption of the responsibilities of family life—did not come into consideration. So long as he was unmarried he would not be permitted, on a permanent basis, to lead a congregation of the faithful in prayer. My father, therefore, had no choice but to comply.

9

Settling Down

Various matches had been proposed to him. Officially it was to my grandfather that the offers were made. Marriages in those days among the Jews of Eastern Europe were usually arranged by the parents. The principals themselves rarely met before the performance of the rites that united them in wedlock, let alone that they should have exchanged words. Some of the brides proposed had attached to them considerable dowries, for my father was looked upon as quite a catch. Others had the qualification of pedigree. But my father would have no part of them; and although it was not considered seemly for a young man and woman to participate personally in the negotiations leading to their betrothal, they could not be forced to marry against their will. The marriage troth, according to Jewish law, requires the consent of both parties.

Among the brides-to-be whose virtues were sung by the marriage-brokers was the daughter of the rabbi of Neumarkt, known as "Freckles" among her girl friends. A large *Nadan* was promised my father if he would marry her. The prospective bridegroom proposed a mask as a return wedding gift. So the matter was dropped and the subject never mentioned again. Another time a match was suggested that seemed very desirable to my grandfather, and he was ready to give his approval. However when he saw the unhappiness in my father's eyes, he discontinued the conversation concerning it.

The real reason why none of these offers appealed to my father was that in his mind's eye he was still carrying around with him the image of rosy-cheeked, dark-eyed Taubele Kaufman, with the long black tresses, whom at the age of twelve he had met in Brzesko. It was to her that his heart belonged. When therefore, five years later, chance brought him to Brzesko again and, as was to be expected, he came in contact once more with one of Taubele's brothers, he unburdened himself to the latter and Taubele's brother did the rest. He was, as a matter of fact, quite thrilled over the prospect and confided to my father the secret that to his sister *he* was very pleasing also.

This made my father very happy. He felt as though he were in heaven, and well might he feel that way. My mother, who is still today considered very attractive, was at the age of seventeen, as a photo from that time indicates, a beautiful young woman. "Greek goddess" is what people called her because of her classic, delicate features, her slender figure, erect carriage and head of curly hair. Endowed with much native intelligence, worldly wise and an excellent student in the Polish school in which she had enrolled without the knowledge of her parents, she had at one time been all set to go to Worms on the Rhine to study nursing or medicine, when she was compelled by parental intervention to give up her plan.

My maternal grandfather, Judah (Idel) Kaufman, the community *Shochet* and a native of Sandec, had been raised in Bartfeld (Bardiov), Czechoslovakia (at that time Hungary). A descendant of Rabbi Alexander Sender of Zolkiev, the author of *Tebuot Shor*, a supercommentary on certain phases of Jewish law, grandfather Kaufman was the acknowledged lay leader of the town, beloved and respected and trusted by everybody, Jew as well as gentile. Whenever a collection had to be made for some charitable purpose, whether it was that of marrying off an orphan bride, or helping a family whose house had burned down, it was Reb Idel Kaufman who was charged with the task of canvassing the community. If people had some extra cash on hand—savings banks were non-existent in small towns like Brzesko—they would entrust it to Reb Idel to take care of for them. He was a soft-spoken, even-tempered person, who seldom raised his voice except in the enthusiasm of prayer. Scrupulously observant himself in matters of religion, he was tolerant toward others. But what was most remarkable about him was the tidiness of the man. To keep clean in a place like Brzesko, the wooden one-story structures of which had no sewage or sanitary plumbing whatever and the floors of which consisted of hard dirt, was an achievement. Of course there was the public bath-house which was frequented every Friday in preparation for the Sabbath. Nevertheless such rules of hygiene as are current in the modern Western world were either unknown or not practiced in the villages of Galicia at the turn of the twentieth century.

Financially grandfather Kaufman, though he performed many religious functions outside of his calling gratis, was fairly comfortable. He was in a position, therefore, to give his daughter a respectable dowry. And so the arrangements for the nuptials were quickly concluded, the marital agreements were set down in writing and the engagement of "the talented and God-fearing young *Chazan* and singer Josef, the son of the reader, Raphael Rosenblatt of Neumarkt, and the beautiful and accomplished maiden Taube, daughter of the *Shochet* Judah Idel Kaufman of Brigel," was celebrated at a banquet which was attended by nearly all the townspeople.

The date of the marriage itself was set for a year later, when my father was to reach the age of eighteen, which, according to tradition, was the appropriate time for entering the nuptial canopy. Actually, the full twelve months needed for the preparation of the trousseau and the acquisition of household furnishings were not observed, because my father was anxious to take advantage of the offer of the position with the Munkacs community. And so the wedding took place in Brzesko under the open sky in the courtyard of the synagogue on Wednesday evening, the 21st of *Ab* of the year 5660 (August 15, 1900).

It was a festive wedding, marked by all the joyousness and fervor of *Chassidic* tradition. There was much of singing as well as of the display of Jewish learning at the table by both principals and guests. My father, grandfather Rosenblatt, my uncle Levi and my mother's brothers supplied the musical program, while the rabbis present contributed the menu of Torah. The meal was interrupted by dancing, but not dancing as we know it, for there was no mingling of the sexes. When men and women danced together at all, the means of contact was a handkerchief, the man holding one end, the woman holding the other.

The dominant mood among all the wedding guests was one of extreme happiness. It was generally agreed that there could not be a more perfect match. If there was anyone among the celebrants whose joy was tempered by a note of sadness, it was the little bride. Just before the wedding

ceremony took place, she was made to part with the beautiful, long, chestnut-brown hair, which was her pride and
glory, and which was at least one reason why her Yossele had
fallen in love with her. It was the price she had to pay to the
custom prevalent among the pious Jews of Eastern Europe,
a custom which both families insisted upon upholding.

The festivities were concluded with the traditional
"seven days of feasting" that followed the wedding. And so
on the ninth of Elul of the year 5660 (September 3, 1900)
Rabbi Tobias Lipschuetz, the president of the rabbinical
court of Brzesko and its environs, was able to inform the congregation of Munkacs that "the sweet singer in Israel Reb
Joseph, nee Rosenblatt, whose fame was spread far and wide,
and whose noble qualities he had had a chance to observe
during his sojourn of several weeks in Brzesko, had taken
to wife the daughter of the local *Shochet* Reb Idel Kaufman.
He was, therefore, qualified to represent in prayer any community that saw fit to appoint him to such a position."

The contract signed by the Munkacsers on Saturday night,
August 18, 1900, or three days after the marriage, engaging
Yossele Rosenblatt as their permanent cantor, was the fulfillment of a vow taken eight years previously. It was at that
time that the Jews of Munkacs had travelled en masse across
the wooden bridge that separated their city from the neigh-
boring town to hear the then ten-year-old boy-cantor. So
impressed were they with the performance that they promised themselves that they would accept the young man as
their chief precentor as soon as he would reach the age of
eighteen and have taken unto himself a wife. That condition had now been carried out and so the execution of the
pledge fell due automatically.

The city of Munkacs, high in the Carpathian Mountains,
in the portion of Ruthenia which was in 1900 a part of Hungary, had a very unusual Jewish community. Constituting
nearly one half of the total population of 15,000, it differed

from those of cities of comparable size and importance by its utter unworldliness, by its thorough aversion for anything that smacked of modernism, whether in matters of dress or speech or methods of education. Completely under the domination of the *Tzaddikim* of the Spira dynasty, who ruled them with an iron hand, the Jews of Munkacs regarded even the Orthodox Agudat Israel as an organization of apostates. All Jewish men in this town donned *shtreimels* during the week as well as on Saturdays and holidays. The four-cornered garments with the fringes, worn in full view of everybody, reached down to the knees, and earlocks were a foot long. They were known as zealots, these Jews of Munkacs, zealots intolerant of ways other than their own, and ready to resort to any measures necessary to make their views prevail.

My father gave his Munkacs parishioners and their spiritual leaders no cause for complaint. Yet even for him, who remained throughout his life a symbol and champion of loyalty to Jewish tradition, their extremism was more than he could bear. At the beginning he felt quite contented with his lot. He had a wife and a position that paid him a fairly respectable salary. His travels were at an end, and the twenty-five gulden a week that he earned were sufficient to live on according to the prevailing standards. The fact that he had to stint himself because his parents, his brother, and a sister made their home with him, and that the money brought him by my mother as a wedding dower had been used to marry off another sister, was certainly not the fault of the good people of Munkacs. They fulfilled scrupulously their part of the agreement. When his first week was up, and no other funds were available, they turned over to their cantor as his wages the entire revenue from the ritual bath—a sackful of groschen (pennies) weighing a total of thirty pounds.

The young cantor had been in Munkacs only a few months, when he found the atmosphere in the town too confining for the further development of his talents. Although

he had until then had but little contact with the modern
world of music, he recognized instinctively that there were
many things he could learn from it. But in order to take advantage of what it offered, he would have to leave Munkacs.
At best the retarded community with its provincialism and
its religious conservatism would not have held him for more
than a year. That the break came sooner than that was due
to a dispute between cantor and congregation over the matter of a choir. Since accompaniment by instrumental music
at divine services was proscribed in the Orthodox synagogue,
the support of a choir of vocalists was an absolute necessity to
any cantor worthy of the name. Now competent singers always commanded a good price, but all that the Munkacsers
were willing to spend for a choir for an entire year was the
hopelessly inadequate sum of 600 gulden.

My father felt completely frustrated. This was the last
straw, the end of his connection with Munkacs. He looked
longingly toward the progressive city of Presburg, whose
Cultusgemeinde was then listening to applicants for the position of cantor. But what excuse could he offer his parishioners, who were watching him most jealously, for absenting
himself from his pulpit for a Sabbath, so as to be able to
demonstrate his qualifications to the Presburgers? He
thought for a while. Then he asked the board to release him
for a weekend so that he might look over the field in Presburg for voices for his choir. The request was granted.

Instead of coming back with new choristers, however, he
returned with a contract in his pocket from the Presburg
congregation, which had selected him from among 56 rival
candidates to serve for an initial term of two years. It was
an extraordinary triumph for an eighteen-year-old. Presburg, the crown of Hungarian Jewry, had chosen him. But
would Munkacs let him go? True, there was no stipulation
of time in his agreement with the community of Munkacs.
But it was usually taken for granted that when a cantor was

engaged without such a limit, he would serve for life. To set
his mind at ease my father again turned to his patron and
spiritual advisor, the old rabbi of Tshortkov, for counsel.
What should he do? He had the opportunity, if he accepted
the Presburg offer, to improve his financial status as well as
serve a larger congregation, whereas in Munkacs there were
no prospects of professional advancement or artistic growth.

The patriarch listened attentively to what his protege had
to say, looked him over and understood . . . Forthwith he
dispatched a letter to the leaders of the Munkacs congregation in which he wrote among other things: "Do not stand in
the way of this young man's progress. He may one day become a source of pride to Jewry."

When the news became known to the Jews of Munkacs
that their beloved Yossele, whose chanting of the Sabbath
prayers had afforded them so much spiritual pleasure, had
accepted a position in Presburg, consternation reigned in
the community. Where would they find a *chazan* to replace
him? Who was there who could chant *Mizmor Shir Leyom
Hashabbos* as beautifully as he did? Their spiritual leader,
austere, uncompromising Rabbi Hirsh Spira, wrung his
hands in desperation and rent his garments as a sign of
mourning, but for another reason. The step my father had
taken was in his eyes equivalent to apostasy. "Yossele is
kalie geworen" (strayed from the path), he exclaimed. His
Yossele, who had sanctified the name of God by his staunch
adherence to orthodoxy in spite of his great gifts, refusing
steadfastly thitherto to barter away his religious principles
for material gain, had at last yielded to pressure. He had
sold his birthright for a mess of pottage. But what had he
done that was wrong? Hear, oh ye heavens, and shudder!
He had exchanged the holy community of Munkacs, whose
Jews wore *shtreimels* every day of the week, for the unholy
city of Presburg in which they are donned only on the Sabbath.

The letter of the *Tzaddik* of Tshortkov notwithstanding, every effort was made by the Munkacsers to retain their cantor. Luckily for him he had given the president of the Presburg community a solemn pledge confirmed by a hand-clasp (*"Tekias Kaf"*). Such a promise, which was equivalent to the signature of a contract, could not be lightly brushed aside, especially since there was a penalty of 400 kronen attached to any failure to live up to the agreement. Thus it came to pass that after having served for eleven months as *chazan* in Munkacs, the citadel of *Chassidic* intransigency, my father assumed his post as Oberkantor of the Orthodoxische Israelitische Cultusgemeinde of Presburg. He arrived in time to comply with the condition that he enter his new position at the latest four weeks before the New Year's Day of the year 5662 (1901).

10

Presburg

My father was no stranger to the Jewish community of Presburg (pronounced "Preshbórg" or "Pshbórg" by the native Jews), which he served for five years, acquiring thereby the nickname of Yossele Presburger. He had officiated in its synagogue as well as in the prayer hall of its *Yeshibah* as a boy of fourteen and, according to the testimony of Rabbi Simchah Bunim Schreiber, left an indelible impression. These memories contributed in no small measure to his winning the award of a contract.

Presburg was far from being the largest, yet it was certainly the most influential as well as the oldest Jewish community in the kingdom of Hungary. It was the second but not the last Hungarian Jewish congregation my father was to serve as cantor.

His incumbency of the cantorate in Presburg marked a definite step forward in my father's artistic development. Munkacs, where he had had his first post, was ideologically a part of Galician *Chassidism* and it was to the recommendation of a *Chassidic* rabbi that he owed his position there. The precentorship of Presburg he had obtained on his own merits. For all its piety Presburg belonged more to the German sphere of culture. More German was spoken and written by the 8,000 Jewish inhabitants of this Hungarian city of 70,000 than either Hungarian or Slovakian. Unlike the Jews of Germany, however, who used German exclusively in their correspondence, the Presburgers occasionally employed the Yiddish vernacular in their official documents. The *Yeshibah* students, who hailed not only from every part of Hungary but from other countries as well, were as punctilious in their compliance with Jewish ritual as those attending other such institutions. They were modern in their appearance, however, and very few wore beards.

The new cantor's connections with the *Yeshibah* of Presburg soon became very close. His choir, as has been noted already, was to a large extent constituted from among its students. These students were always welcome guests in his abode. A goodly number of them were even boarded by him. He loved young men who were dedicating their lives to the study of the Jew's most treasured possession—the *Torah*. Those who were endowed with musical talent and good voices became, under his inspiration and tutelage, eminent cantors in their own right. All of them, however, felt at home with him and would often exchange pleasantries and match wits with him.

Among the members of the faculty to whom my father was particularly attracted, was Rabbi Leib Gross. Rabbi Gross was a scholar blessed with a sense of humor. His wit manifested itself in the dressing-down he would administer to the arrogant and the foppish, especially those whose conceit was coupled with ignorance. There was among the frequenters of the prayer-chapel of the *Yeshibah* a middle-aged gentleman of rather slender intellectual attainments. To show off his zealousness for his religion, he would cover his head with his prayer-shawl during services in the manner of the erudite. Reb Leib could not bear such a display of virtue by a boor. So he said to him one day as he saw him swaddled in the prayer-shawl: "Reb Israel, as a man with claims to learning, you ought to be acquainted with the rule that it is not befitting for an ignoramus to pray with his *Tallis* over his head."

My father always related this story with a chuckle, for he enjoyed nothing more thoroughly than to see those who deserved a lesson put in their place.

The quiet and peace of Presburg, the appreciation and understanding with which his gifts as a singer and as an interpreter of the prayers of the synagogue met, encouraged the young cantor to devote himself in all earnestness to the theoretical study of music and the cultivation of his voice. He received instruction in voice culture from Professor Van der Staats of Vienna, which was only an hour's ride by trolley from Presburg. The teacher predicted a brilliant future for his pupil. He lived to see his prophecy fulfilled when in the year 1923 Josef Rosenblatt returned to Presburg a world renowned figure.

The Presburg period was also one of the most productive for him from the standpoint of the composition of Jewish liturgical music. Pencil and paper were always on the night table at his bed-side, so that if an idea for a song occurred to him in the middle of the night he could write it down before forgetting it. It was during this time that he published his *Shirei Joseph,* a compilation of 150 recitatives and choral pieces which he was able to try out on his own very adequate

choir. It met with the enthusiastic approval of such outstanding authorities on synagogue music as Bela Guttmann
of Vienna and Jacob Bachmann and Adolf Lazarus of Budapest. It was also in Presburg, in the summer of 1905, his
last year there, when the phonograph was still a very recent
invention, that he made his first recordings. The manufac-
turers were the Edison Company of Vienna.

So far as my father was concerned, the five years spent in
Presburg were the most tranquil and serene of his entire career. He found himself in an almost ideal environment,
ideal for productivity, for professional growth and spiritual
satisfaction. Quite the reverse was the situation of his pretty
young wife. For her, life in Presburg was anything but a
sinecure. Right from the very start she was saddled with an
even larger household than in Munkacs. For my father's sister Gittel, together with her husband, who was never much
of a bread-winner, and her children now came to live with
the family. Of the companionship of her husband mother
enjoyed very little. Her Yossele was always occupied either
with his musical studies or professional duties.

In addition she was very much handicapped by her young
spouse's immaturity. Preeminent as my father was already
then in his chosen field of Jewish music, he was in worldly
matters still a child. It was not at all unusual for the Oberkantor of Presburg, whose hirsute chin testified to his being
chronologically a man, to be surprised playing a game of
marbles with the boys. And more than once did it happen,
when he already had several children of his own, that he
was chastised for some reason or other by his stern and oft
intolerant father. He bore such rebukes meekly, for he was
still as submissive to his parents as he had been in the days
of his bachelorhood, so much so that he was afraid, even
where he was fully justified, to assert his independence as an
adult and a pater familias.

Resentful though she may have been at times of this domination of her husband by her parents-in-law, my mother was willing to put up with it out of a sense of filial respect. But what irritated her exceedingly and caused her infinite unhappiness was the fact that my father was also completely under the thumbs of his sisters. Even after he was married, they continued to treat him as one would a little brother, ordering him around and trying to plan his life for him, despite the fact that he was the sole means of their support. As his wife, my mother had to perform all the menial chores. The help of a maid was out of the question. The family's budget at that time could not afford it. Scrubbing the rough wooden floors of the apartment was therefore her assignment. It was an almost daily task because the Hungarian fleas stubbornly defied all attempts at extermination.

Out of her husband's meagre earnings my mother had to provide food not only for him and his parents and brother and sisters, but also for the guests that came in an almost unending stream. Her Yossele loved to entertain; he was the very soul of hospitality. Then, when grandfather Rosenblatt was stricken with a fatal paralysis and lay helpless on his couch, it was not his daughters but his young daughter-in-law who took care of him as one would of a babe in arms.

In part the hostile behavior of my father's sisters towards my mother may have sprung from jealousy. My mother was blessed with something of which they had but little—external attractiveness. Also it must have been difficult for them to become reconciled to the thought that a total stranger, an intruder as my mother was in their eyes, should reap the benefits of their brother's talents which but for her would have accrued entirely to them. So they lost no opportunity of conveying their feelings towards her. It was particularly Gittel who was lavish with her darts of disparagement. When after the lapse of the first year of her married life my mother had failed to produce a child, aunt Gittel taunted her with being unable to bear offspring. And in the sight of the East-European Jews of the era there were but few divine visitations more dreaded than that of barrenness.

Fortunately aunt Gittel was unable to make use of this weapon of humiliation for long because the next year, on May 5, 1902, I was born. On October 3rd of the year follow- ing my brother Leo arrived and twelve months later my oldest sister Nettie.

My father might have been content to remain in Presburg for the rest of his life. However with the birth of children, his household expenses increased and the community of Pres- burg was in no position to raise his salary sufficiently to cope with his needs. It was necessary for him to look elsewhere for opportunities to augment his earnings. Just then he heard that there was a vacancy in the position of chief cantor in the city of Hamburg, the second metropolis of the pro- gressive and enlightened German Empire of William II. With the blessing of his good friend Rabbi Simchah Bunim Schreiber, who had always been extremely fond of him, he boarded the train one day early in 1906 to go to Hamburg for a trial service in the Kohlhoefen synagogue of the Deutsch-Israelitischer Synagogenverband. The Sabbath on which he officiated happened to be the one denominated in the Jewish calendar "the Sabbath of Song." His success was instantaneous. On the Saturday following his appearance the Hamburger Fremdenblatt reported:

"The position of chief cantor of the local Synagogue-Union is about to be filled. Various candidates have applied, among others the precentor of a large congregation in Presburg, Mr. Josef Rosenblatt, who presented himself on Friday and Sat- urday of last week in the great synagogue of the congregation located at Kohlhoefen. There prevails, as we hear, a una- nimity of admiration regarding the singing of Mr. Rosen- blatt. He possesses a phenomenal tenor voice and an excep- tional manner of presentation that puts him in the category of the great artists. The overwhelming majority of the members of the congregation would gladly welcome the election of Mr. Rosenblatt as chief cantor."

It did not take very long for this wish to be realized. A week later the same periodical announced that Josef Rosenblatt of Presburg had been chosen at a "joint session of the presidium and the college of delegates as chief cantor of the Synagogenverband." An official letter, dated February 27th and signed by the president J. H. Levy, confirmed this fact to the applicant. The only matters that had to be settled before he could enter upon his new position were those of securing a passport from the Austrian government and obtaining from the German authorities in Hamburg the permission to settle there. This was taken care of in time for him to assume his duties which, according to the contract, were to commence on July 1st.

The negotiations back and forth must have consumed several weeks. It also required some time to liquidate our family's affairs in Presburg and set up house again in Hamburg.

Exactly how long my father lingered in Hamburg before he came to fetch my mother, brother, sister and me, I do not remember. According to my mother it was three months. In my childish eyes, however, it seemed like an eternity. I was, as always, greatly attached to my father, and as his absence from home was prolonged, I became very lonesome for him. One incident, which is indicative of the effect of our separation upon me as well as upon my brother Leo, still lingers in my memory. We were visiting our maternal grandparents in Brzesko in the company of our mother prior to our departure from Austria-Hungary. Our sister Nettie, then an infant a little over one year old, had just been put to bed. Suddenly it was noticed that Leo and I were missing. After several hours of frantic search we were discovered by mother's brother Samuel, wandering through the woods on the outskirts of the town and humming a mournful tune. Overjoyed to have found us, mother asked me, without scolding: "Shmilekel, why did you go away from home? What were you doing in the woods?" "I went with Leo to look for daddy," was my reply. Several days later my mother surprised me sucking my thumb and crying in the same singsong as when I was discovered walking in the woods: "Oi mein taierer Tateshu farwus bistu fin uns aveck? Wielang noch westu sein in Hamburg?" (Oh, dear daddy, why did you leave us? How long yet will you be in Hamburg?).

11
Hamburg

Hamburg marked another etape in my father's career. It constituted his graduation to the world of the West. Presburg was still East-European. Hamburg was completely Occidental. The transition did not present too much difficulty to our family. One reason was the absence of any language barrier.

Secondly Hamburg represented a step upward economically for my father. The salary of 7000 marks a year that he was being paid was more than he could ever have dreamt of receiving in Presburg. It is true that one third of it was sent away conscientiously to his parents, who had returned to their home in Neumarkt, and that the allowance, granted him by the congregation for furnishing our apartment on Bornstrasse number 34, was turned over to his sister Feige for her dowry, with the result that our furniture had to be bought on the installment plan. Nevertheless the position in Hamburg permitted us greater latitude and made possi-

ble conveniences and comforts that we had not known theretofore.

In the third place, Hamburg was a big, beautiful and clean
city. The edifices along the Alster River, headed by the massive Renaissance style City Hall (Rathaus)—in fact the entire central business section—were truly imposing. And then
there were parks like the one adjoining the synagogue,
and wide streets like the Grindel Allee and Rotherbaum
Chaussee shaded by trees.

Finally what could not help impressing the newcomer was
the orderliness and regularity of Jewish life in Hamburg. It
was a reflection of that punctiliousness which is one of the
outstanding traits of the German character. Nothing was left
to hazard. Everything down to the smallest detail had its
rules and especially assigned place, even the prayers of the
synagogue. The contract delivered to my father contained
definite instructions in regard to the selections of the liturgy
which he, the Oberkantor, was expected to recite and how he
was to chant them, whether aloud or in an undertone, and
the parts that were to be pronounced by the Unterkantor.
The community had a chief rabbi or Oberrabbiner, with his
specific duties, and an assistant rabbi, who had his particular
field of activities marked out, in order to head off any possibility of conflict of authority or jurisdiction.

Hamburg was the real cradle of the Jewish Reform movement in Germany. It was there that the first house of worship marking this new departure in religious Judaism was
established in 1818. Yet it still harbored, when we arrived
there in the summer of 1906, a considerable Orthodox community, which was numerically larger than that of the
friends of reform. By and large, the members of the Deutsch-
Israelitischer Synagogenverband were very strict in their religious observance. One of the distinctions of German Jewry
was its logical consistency, its freedom from compromise.
German Jews were either believers, followers of the right

teaching, adhering to every iota of the law, or they did not believe and, therefore, went to the other extreme of complete liberalism. There was no middle ground between these two poles.

The mania for law and order, which was a characteristic of all Germans, Jew as well as non-Jew, was undoubtedly a most admirable trait. It contributed greatly to whatever eminence was attained by the German people in such fields as science and industry. However when carried to extremes it could lead to absurdities. This my parents were destined to find out not long after they had settled in Hamburg.

One morning, shortly after the birth of my sister Gertrude, the door-bell rang and an officious-looking woman, attired in a stiff mannish suit, entered. My father greeted her with his usual politeness, bade her be seated and then asked: "What do you wish gracious lady? How can I serve you?"

The woman, whose roving eyes had taken in every detail of the house, without bothering to return my father's courtesies, went straight to the point. Speaking in a curt, gruff voice, she said, "I am district directress of the Federal Social Welfare Commission of the municipality of Hamburg. I have come to persuade you to move out of the city at once. You have now had your fourth child with Miss Kaufman, without being legally married to her. Our government cannot close its eyes to this irregularity any longer. The best advice I can give you is to leave immediately."

My father was aghast. He looked at his visitor as at a person out of her mind. "I, not legally married? Then what is the meaning of this Jewish marriage contract"—and he produced the Hebrew document drawn up by the rabbi of Brzesko who had married him—"and the names of the witnesses, testifying to my union with my wife?"

"This piece of paper," said the woman, who happened to be a Jewess besides, "is worthless so long as you have no official marriage license authorizing your wedding." All the attempts of my father's elder colleague, the second cantor Dreiblatt, to enlighten the lady about the legality of the marriage proved unconvincing. It was a most embarrassing situation, which only a very much belated civil ceremony could remedy. To avoid publicity my parents decided to go away to England. So they booked passage on the first boat leaving for London and there went through the necessary formalities.

The cause of the predicament in which my parents found themselves was the fact that they had been reared in the empire of the easy-going Francis Joseph, which has often been described as "a despotism tempered by inefficiency." In Austria-Hungary, especially the part of it that was known as Galicia, Jewish couples never bothered to apply for official permits to marry. It was sufficient for them that their union was solemnized by their rabbi in accordance with the laws of "Moses and Israel"; and very few of them ever violated their marriage troth. The marriage of my parents was of such a nature. However in the eyes of the municipality of Hamburg their tie was illegal until His Britannic Majesty had put his seal of approval upon it after the birth of their fourth child.

The congregation to which my father became attached when he was twenty-four years old, was, like the Cultusgemeinde of Presburg, orthodox. But it was a different type of orthodoxy, this orthodoxy that was practiced by the German Jews of the great free port on the Elbe, from that of the Jewish spiritual capital of Hungary. The latter still had the inner warmth of East-European Jewry. This quality was completely absent in Hamburg.

That there was something aesthetic about the manner in which the ceremonial laws of Judaism were observed in Hamburg is not to be denied. The decorum at divine services, the high hats and walking suits worn by the men in the synagogue on festive occasions, the neatly decorated booths

erected on the lawns or balconies of Jewish homes for the
Feast of Tabernacles—all these things lent to Jewish religious life in this German city a dignity and beauty which
it did not have anywhere else in the Jewish Diaspora.

To be sure the coupling of rigid adherence to the traditions of the past with the polish and culture of the present
day world resulted in inconsistencies which escaped the attention of those that were accustomed to them. They were,
however, detected at once by East-Europeans like my father.

He had been in Hamburg only one month when he attended one of those elegant weddings that were quite common in this community. There he noticed that the dresses
of some of the women were cut unusually low. It struck him
as a violation of the Jewish code of modesty, and he called it
to the attention of the rabbi. Dr. Marcus Hirsch was a sincerely pious man. At the same time he was a member of western society in which decolleté evening gowns were accepted
as the proper attire at marriage celebrations. He had grown
so used to seeing them that he never gave the matter a moment's thought. When, therefore, my father pointed out to
him the exposed bosoms, he exclaimed: "Amazing! I have
been rabbi in Hamburg for twenty-five years and I never noticed that our women were improperly dressed, and here
comes Yossele, a complete stranger, and sees at the first
glance what has escaped my eyes all this time."

On one occasion—he was then still fresh in his new environment—my father's ignorance of the rules of modern
etiquette led to an embarrassment which bordered on scan-
dal and almost became a cause célèbre. He had been invited to a social function which was attended by the elite
of Hamburg's Jewish society. His singing had been one of
the highlights of the evening's entertainment. After the formal part of the program was concluded, the bearded little
cantor, whose performance had thrilled the audience, was

introduced to one of the aristocratic ladies present in the gathering. In a natural gesture she extended her hand to the artist. To her great amazement, however, he allowed it to remain suspended in mid-air. Such rudeness was unheard of. "Eine Ungezogenheit!" "Unerhoert!" were the angry exclamations of the bystanders who had seen what had happened. "What's the matter with this man? Where are his manners?"

There was no use explaining that it was not customary among the pious Jews of Eastern Europe to shake hands with women. In polite society in Germany, even among the orthodox, such customs were not heeded. They were superseded by the usages of the land. It took some time for the storm to subside and for tempers to be allayed. The incident was not without effect on the perpetrator. There was no recurrence of the faux pas. Little by little the unworldly East-European *chazan* learned the amenities of the West. He became a patron of the opera and the theatre. It was at the operatic performances given at the Hamburg Stadttheater that he heard Caruso. He at once adopted the great singer as his model, studied his technique and tried to copy his methods of tone production. The admiration, by the way, was mutual. In his personal memoirs Caruso makes mention of a most unusual cantor by the name of Josef Rosenblatt whom he had had occasion to hear in a Hamburg synagogue. Later on when both men had settled in America and become more intimately acquainted with each other, the Italian master of song presented his Jewish counterpart and admirer, who rarely missed a performance of Caruso's, with a book of his caricatures as a token of his esteem.

His visits to such places of frivolity as the theater turned my father into a mortal sinner in the eyes of his younger brother Levi, who never overlooked an opportunity to throw the matter up to him. Once when he was asked by my father to accept his share of a certain family obligation, Levi re-

plied indignantly: "Who empowered you to give orders? Am
I not just as pious as you are? Did anybody have to look for
me in a theater in order to inform me of our father's death?"

Of course the Oberkantor of the Synagogenverband of
Hamburg did not take the reprimand too much to heart.
From the standpoint of the Hamburg conception of orthodoxy, which he had made his own, he had not violated
any code of Jewish law by entering the Stadttheater in order
to hear a great singer. If there was anything that he disliked
about the ways of the Jews of Hamburg and that he could
never get used to, it was not this, but their stolid Prussian
rigidity, their insistence that everybody conform to their Pro-
crustean standards. A Lithuanian Jewish punster once remarked, "German Judaism is 'ein Uhrjudentum' "—that is
"a Judaism of the clock" rather than "original" or "traditional" Judaism. It certainly appeared as such in the eyes of
Josef Rosenblatt.

At six o'clock in the morning every day, in every kind of
weather, he had to present himself in the weekday synagogue
for morning services. And he was invariably late, for as an
artist, who is accustomed to staying up far into the night, it
was absolutely impossible for him to keep regular hours.
Getting up early in the morning, especially on the cold, bleak
days of winter—and it could get very cold in Hamburg—was
torture.

Then, again, he was expected to observe every fast-day
listed. The orthodox Jews of Hamburg kept not only the
ancient days of mourning, such as the fasts of Gedaliah and
Esther, the tenth of Tebet and seventeenth of Tamuz. They
abstained from food also on the *"Mondays, Thursdays* and
Mondays" after Passover and the Feast of Tabernacles. Once
when the president of the congregation was informed that
the cantor had been found eating on one of these minor days
of austerity, he threatened the offender with restraint from
performing wedding ceremonies if he continued in his per-

versity. Whereunto the culprit replied: "In that case, I suppose you, Mr. Von Son, will solemnize the marriage rites."

12

German Jewry

Even less, however, than their rigid discipline was my father able to endure the German Jews' lack of fervor and emotion. "A strange breed of Jews, these Germans," he used to remark. "They never lift their voices at *Shema Koleinu*. They never gesticulate when they say: 'All my bones exclaim: O Lord, who is like unto Thee?' They stand erect and motionless even when they are supposed to be making the most impassioned plea to the Heavenly Father. And when one of their closest and dearest relatives passes away, they say with perfect resignation 'Tsk, what can one do? It was the will of God.' They are like the ice-cream certified by the chief rabbi of Frankfurt am Main—'Gefrohrenes unter Aufsicht des Oberrabbiners Dr. Breuer' (Frozen under the supervision of Chief Rabbi Dr. Breuer)." One Saturday when in the course of the prayer for the new moon he lapsed into a lachrymose mood as he came to the supplication for "sustenance," one of the pillars of the congregation inquired whether anybody was sick in his family. Even so devoted a friend as Herr Bachrach, who loved him dearly, could not restrain himself from remarking on one occasion, "Mr. Rosenblatt, you sing so divinely. Why, then should it be necessary for you to sigh and wail?"

My father's ire was greatly provoked by this type of criticism. "How do you like that! I serve the most delectable dish, the Jewish sob, which is the sauce of *Chazanuth,* and along comes my good friend and tells me that I wail."

But what irritated him most of all was when, after he had given an excellent account of himself, his voice ringing like a bell, and his falsetto sounding like a flute, the chairman of the board would come up to him, and, complimenting him upon a fine service, say: "Herr Rosenblatt, Sie haben wunderbar geort. (Mr. Rosenblatt, you prayed marvellously.) Aber warum haben Sie so oft wiederholt? (But why did you repeat the words so often?) Es steht ja nicht in der *Tefilloh* (It isn't written that way in the prayerbook)."

Eventually this strait-jacketing was one of the contributing causes of his leaving Hamburg for America. At the beginning, however, he did not mind these restrictions because there were many compensations that life in the German Jewish community had to offer.

One of these was the classical finish that his six-year tenure of office there gave to his art as a *chazan.* The congregation that he had been engaged to lead in prayer included in its midst men of great wealth and distinction in commerce and industry, like the banker Max Warburg and the shipping wizard Albert Ballin. In addition it was composed also of a large number of intellectuals and professionals, holders of degrees from German universities. Frequenters of the opera and patrons of the symphony, it was but natural that their musical standards should have been rigorous and that they should have been exacting in their demands from their cantor. They not only expected him to be vocally in trim but also insisted that his repertoire be of a high order. They enjoyed hearing him render a Yiddish folk-song and often went into rapture when he sang a *Chassidic* melody at a wedding meal or a banquet. In the synagogue, however, they allowed the chanting by cantor or choir only of compositions that emanated from such recognized creators of Jewish liturgical music as Sulzer and Lewandowski.

To meet these demands my father was compelled to write recitatives and choral selections that conformed to these patterns and measured up to the requirements. He complied fully. It was particularly in his original rendition of the *Kiddush* on Sabbath eves and the chanting of the additional service of the New Year that he excelled. What was remarkable about his compositions that date from the Hamburg period is that, though they reveal the most interesting variations of the traditional motifs, not a single word of the text is repeated. These factors, plus the qualities of his voice, caused the Hamburg Jews to refer to him as their "Jewish Caruso."

Of course the artist in him felt cramped and circumscribed. It was not the practice of the cantors of the orthodox Jewish communities of Germany to go on concert tours. Even to officiate at religious functions in synagogues other than their own was considered out of order. But if Josef Rosenblatt was unable thus to exploit his talents, he was, on the other hand, left free to devote himself to musical studies, to composition and to the commencement of those recordings on the gramophone which caused his fame to spread across the Atlantic and to earn him world renown. He celebrated his twenty-fifth birthday in Hamburg by publishing twenty-five recitatives and other types of liturgical selections, which he entitled *Tfilos Josef.* This collection was to be followed later on by *Zemiros Josef* and *Shiv'oh Ofanei Hakiddush.*

While my father, an individualist at heart, found the atmosphere of Hamburg too confining, my mother, on the contrary, loved it. She admired German orderliness, German culture and the German language. A student of Goethe and Schiller, she was fond of quoting from these German classics and of thus displaying her proficiency in German.

Secondly she was intrigued with the spaciousness and the cleanliness and comfort of the living quarters she could now afford. True, central heating was still very rare in Hamburg—

tile stoves were almost universally used—and illumination
was by gas-light. But the rooms were large, bright and airy,
and the furniture she was able to acquire was fine and elegant. Furthermore she felt affluent enough before very long
to engage a maid to assist her in her household duties.

But what mother relished most of all was the opportunity that her separation from my father's family gave her
to be her own mistress, not to be dictated to or criticized or
bossed anymore by this or that relative, but to have the right
to make her own decisions. Attempts were, of course, still
being made, by remote control, to guide my father's destinies
and run his household. But it wasn't the same as the daily
and hourly nagging and importuning by those whose immediate physical presence was a constant challenge to her
peace of mind.

We lived graciously in Hamburg, enjoying most of the
comforts of modern civilization, and yet frugally. Mother
quickly learned how to prepare the savory dishes which were
the specialty of the German Hausfrau. Our every-day clothes
as well as the table linens were often patched. Yet whenever we Rosenblatt juniors went out on a Saturday or holiday
or some other such occasion, we looked as though our parents were people of wealth.

Summer vacations for the entire family were beyond our
means. The only one who was allowed an occasional rest-
cure was mother. After the birth of each of the first three
children she had in Hamburg, she went to recuperate for
two weeks in Salzschlirf in the Hessian mountains. As
for father, he contented himself with the annual excursions,
in June or July, of the upper classes of our school and the
congregational choir to Cuxhaven, on the North Sea, or
Blankenese on the Elbe or a trip into the Harz woods. After we had reached school age, brother Leo and I would accompany him.

Of course, father was never at a loss as to where to go or

how to spend his leisure hours. Still as restless as he had been in his childhood, he had to be up and doing all the time. If a new bridge was completed, he had to be present at the dedication. When a celebrity came to town, he had to go to see him. If a parade was arranged for the emperor, he had to be there to watch it. And when Hagenbeck's famous zoo opened up, he couldn't think of missing the occasion. He loved to take motor-boat rides along the Alster to the Uhlenhorst Ferry House and feed the pigeons, to promenade along the Rathaus and meander through the Esplanades. Since he enjoyed doing it in company, his children, to whom he was deeply attached, often went with him.

As soon as we were old enough, we were sent to the private kindergarten conducted by a Fräulein Lanzkron, where we played games and learned German nursery rhymes and soldiers' songs. Upon reaching school age, Leo and I were enrolled in the Talmud Tora Realschule. My sister Nettie entered the Israelitische Toechterschule. Both of these fine institutions were maintained by the Jewish community.

It was a proud day for me, that brisk and sunny day in April of the year 1909, when with a fur-lined green knapsack on my back I trudged off for the first time to school, accompanied by my father. How my younger brothers and sisters envied me for being so grown up! But even prouder than I was my father, when old Mr. Isaak, nicknamed "Kindermädchen" (nurse-maid), because he taught the beginners' class, remarked to him, as he enrolled me: "Ihr Samuel hat so ein treues Gesicht. Er wird einmal Rabbiner werden." (Your Samuel has such a spiritual look. Mark my words, he will one day be a rabbi.)

As a result of our exposure to the influences wielded by this school the younger set of Rosenblatts were speedily molded into German superpatriots and in a short time we acquired a distinctly Hamburgese accent which made us sound like natives. However, deeper even than the impression exercised by the formal instruction received at the Talmud Tora Realschule was that produced by the general atmosphere pervading the synagogue and the homes we frequented. Every festival was marked by its distinctive symbol. Every occasion of joy or sorrow had its peculiar charm that left its imprint on the childish mind. There were the low stools in front of every prayer-desk on the Ninth of *Ab,* and the white caps and robes worn by all the men in the synagogue on the High Holidays. *Simchat Torah* meant for us youngsters not only the gorgeous spectacle of the entire board of the congregation lining the steps leading up to the Holy Ark holding aloft the Scrolls of the Law, but—more important than this—the haul of sweets brought home that day, enough to last us for weeks. *Purim* was identified with eclairs and whipped cream tarts; the Fifteenth of *Shebat,* with Johnny bread and the Feast of Weeks with cheesecake; while *Sukkot* meant making the rounds of the booths of friends to partake of refreshments. *Chanukah* was the time for dominoes and Passover the season of the year when the grocer would turn his shop inside out to make sure that there would not be the slightest admixture of aught that was leavened in the merchandise he offered for sale for the holiday week. As for the weekly Sabbath, Cantor Rosenblatt's rendition of the divine services on this day of repose and rest invariably brought to those who were within hearing of his voice what the Hamburgers called an *"Auneg Shabbos."*

The Jews of Hamburg were conscious—all too conscious perhaps—of the superiority which their wealth and culture gave them over their less fortunate brethren from Eastern Europe, hundreds of thousands of whom had since the turn of the century been passing through their city on the way to America. Germany, the Germany of William II, was at this time a first-rate power, competing successfully with the British Empire in the conquest of the markets of the world. In the growth of its commerce and industry German Jewry played a very important part. It was the Jew Albert Ballin whose organizing genius created the Hamburg-America Line, the most successful rival of the great English passenger steamship companies. Hamburg, now a city with a population of nearly a million, and the most important seaport in continental Europe, owed much of its prosperity to the activities of this line, and its 18,000 Jewish inhabitants shared in the material riches that accrued to it. It was the latitude which their economic advancement afforded them that enabled them to build such fine communal institutions as the Bornplatz Synagogue in which my father officiated, our school—the Talmud Tora Realschule, and the Jewish Hospital.

They had reason to feel proud of their achievements, these Jews of Hamburg. And though one may not be able ethically to condone their attitude, one can at least understand why they should have looked patronizingly upon their poor relations, those *Nebichs* from the East, the *Ostjuden* with their rags, their uncouth appearance and their atrocious jargon, which was, in the eyes of their German brethren, a travesty upon the noble idiom of the fatherland. To the average Jewish native of Germany, every Jew hailing from Eastern Europe, whatever the land of his origin may have been, whether it was Russia or Galicia or Roumania or Hungary, was a "Pollak"; and the word "Pollak" was a synonym for untidiness, for lack of culture and want of manners. He might remember his Talmud better than his German coreligionist. He might even be possessed of a certain amount of native shrewdness which would enable him eventually to succeed in extricating himself from his degrading misery. But then he was at best only a "Drehkopf," a sort of manipulator, not a person of breeding and refinement and scientific knowledge like the successful German Jewish man of business.

Thus the few East-European Jews, who had contrived to

settle in Hamburg on a permanent basis, found themselves virtually ostracized by their German brethren, and they looked for a haven of refuge where they could feel more at home. Where else could they discover in Hamburg an atmosphere that was more congenial to their spirits than in the abode of Reb Yossele Rosenblatt? For, although on account of his talents he was accepted among the Germans—genius, it must be remembered, is international—he still looked, in his beard, skull-cap and frock-coat, neat though they were, like an East-European Jew. He spoke the latter's language and understood his needs. With Yossele, the plain, simple, warm Jew of the old school, they did not have to stand on ceremony. They could pour out their hearts before him and he would listen to their stories sympathetically and endeavor to help them. No one in need ever left his dwelling empty-handed.

Thus our home became a rendezvous for the entire East-European colony in Hamburg, an oasis in a desert of German social snobbery. One would meet there cantors, *shochetim* and other religious functionaries, most of whom were of East-European provenance. Nearly all the professional *servi synagogae* had to be imported by the Jewish congregations of Germany from the East, and, like my father, very few of them ever attained the privilege of citizenship in the Reich. It was as a subject of "his imperial and royal apostolical majesty, Francis Joseph I, emperor of Austria and king of Hungary" that my father was permitted to reside in Hamburg. It was on an Austrian passport that he travelled to America and under Austrian jurisdiction that he remained until he became a citizen of the United States.

In his capacity of chief cantor of the largest congregation in the city my father was, of course, invited to many an aristocratic home and came in contact with the greatest. Yet his intimates were his professional associates, including gentle Chief Rabbi Marcus Hirsch, after whom he named one of his children. Our closest friends were the second cantor Drei-blatt, the reader of the Torah Wigderowitsch, the former chief cantor Suesskind, and his successor Emil Gross, members of the choir and other such folk. Among the laity his staunchest standby and warmest admirer, in whose villa he gave many an informal concert, was Bernhard Lewandovski. In his, the nephew of Lewis Lewandovski of Berlin, the celebrated German-Jewish composer of synagogue music, the little East-European *chazan* found sympathy and understanding. But then Hermann Lewandovski belonged, by descent and breeding, to the musical fraternity, which is a species apart.

My father was never content with merely entertaining those of his brethren who came to his home and with making them feel welcome in it. Like the patriarch Abraham, whose hospitality to strangers he strove to emulate, he went out of his way to look for subjects upon whom to practice this virtue. Often he would visit the lodging houses, near the harbor, in which the East-European would-be-immigrants to America were staying while waiting for their ships to leave, and sing for them to make the time pass more quickly. Occasionally he would bring some of these involuntary exiles, whose future was then still so uncertain, to our apartment to cheer them up.

After having lived in Hamburg for five years, our family—that is all of us with the exception of my father—seemed very well integrated with the German milieu. Although not yet citizens, we regarded Germany as our home. It was more than just rhetoric when, a year later, as the ship that was to bring us to America was moving away from the German mainland, we children sang as a farewell song the ballad, "Nun, adee du mein lieb Heimatland" (Now adieu my dear homeland). We might have stayed on until the coming of

Hitler, were it not for two compelling factors that forced my father to seek his fortune elsewhere—his family's mounting needs and the Hamburg congregation's parsimony.

Father was always in need of money. He never had sufficient funds to pay off all the debts that kept accumulating—a thing that his parishioners were simply unable to understand. "Why should a cantor," they would ask, "who doesn't gamble and makes no investments in speculative business ventures and is not a high liver, have so much expense?" There was no use telling them that his salary had been mortgaged far ahead into the future to marry off single sisters and maintain old parents who had no other means of support.

Ordinarily my father would make light of it, if his perpetual requests for advances on his salary were turned down or his applications for private loans were refused. It was a custom in the Hamburg synagogue, at the kneeling ritual on the Day of Atonement, for a prominent member of the board to help the cantor, who was not permitted to change his position throughout the service, up on his feet. Once it was a wealthy banker who was given the honor. On the day after the solemn festival, when my father met the gentleman on the street, he remarked "What tough luck I have! The one time a rich man gives me a lift, he doesn't carry any money with him."

However the time came when this impecuniousness was no longer a laughing matter. Our family kept increasing. In the spring of 1912 my mother was expecting her seventh child. Our parishioners never got over the marvel that a woman with a girlish figure, such as my mother had managed to retain until that time, could have born so many children. "Sieh mal," they would say to their companions, if they chanced to see her walking in the street, "diese Frau hat sieben Kinder." (Believe it or not, this woman has seven children.) Large families were unusual among the well-to-do

German Jews of Hamburg. On account of the high standards that had to be met by husbands, Jewish men rarely married before they were thirty years old.

On top of my father's other cares his sister Gittel became
widowed. Since the plan of having her live with us permanently didn't work out—my mother took a firm stand
against that—the expense of maintaining her in an establishment of her own imposed additional burdens upon
an already greatly overstrained budget. The attachment to
our household in the year 1911 of aunt Gittel's oldest daughter Caroline aggravated the situation. My father had no alternative but to apply again to the *Vorstand* (board) for an
increase in his rather modest salary. When the request
was turned down there was only one choice left, namely to
look elsewhere for a solution of his problems.

There was one person in Hamburg who might have prevented what was about to happen. That person was the new
chief rabbi Dr. Samuel Spitzer, who had been chosen to succeed Rabbi Hirsch after the latter's death in 1909. Not
nearly as eloquent a preacher as the assistant rabbi Anton
Nobel, Dr. Spitzer, on account of his learning, carried great
weight with the congregation's leaders, and a word from him
would have gone far. For some reason best known to himself, this man, who owed his election as rabbi of Hamburg
chiefly to my father's recommendation, refused to exert
himself in his behalf. And so matters took their inevitable
course. As it turned out this indifference worked out to my
father's best interest. "Dr. Spitzer," he used to say in later
years, "did me a real service by not putting himself out on
my account or I might still be vegetating in Hamburg today."

However it be, my father's financial embarrassment, coupled with the congregation's parsimony, the chief rabbi's
apathy and the sense of repression that the artist had always

felt in the regimented society of German Jewry, all these factors contributed to his seeking a means of escape. The opportunity was not long in presenting itself.

13

America Calling

In December, 1909 a world Zionist Congress was held in Hamburg. Among the delegates to this assemblage were representatives of the rapidly growing and already populous Jewish community of the United States of America. A number of them attended the services at the Bornplatz Synagogue, where my father was officiating, and were deeply impressed. Returning home they brought back with them glowing reports of the young cantor with the mellow tenor voice and the genuine Jewish "sob" that they had heard in Hamburg.

These reports, supported by such phonograph recordings as that of the prayer for the new-moon, reached the ears of the board of directors of the First Hungarian Congregation Ohab Zedek of New York. The resignation in the fall of 1911 of their chief cantor Isaiah Meisels, a man as tall as his voice was high-pitched, had created a vacancy in the position. That this vacancy might be filled by the twenty-nine-year-old cantor of Hamburg, came as a suggestion on the part of a friend of our family, Mr. Strobel.

Mr. Strobel was at that time serving in the capacity of dietary supervisor on the passenger ships of the Hamburg-America Line. As such he was in close contact with the Jewish communities of both Hamburg and New York. Hungarian by birth, it was his custom, whenever he was in New

York on a Sabbath, to worship in the synagogues of the First Hungarian Congregation. Though he had never formally discussed with my father the question of his availability for a position outside of Hamburg, he knew of his eagerness for a change. When, therefore, he heard of Cantor Meisels' resignation, he suggested to the leaders of Ohab Zedek that they write my father and invite him to come to New York to conduct a Sabbath service. "I am sure," he declared, "that once you have heard Mr. Rosenblatt, you will not let him go."

The leaders took Mr. Strobel's advice and on January 9th the secretary of the congregation, delicate, silvery-haired Mr. David Berliner, opened correspondence with my father in German, inviting him to officiate on two Sabbaths in one of the congregation's houses of worship. Ohab Zedek, he stated, was among the largest orthodox congregations in America, and had always enjoyed the services of the best cantors, "such as A. Karniol, Baer, Judah Leib Abrahams and S. Meisels." It was then served by two rabbis as well as two cantors. Nevertheless it was looking for "a good *Chazan*," especially "one who was acquainted with the Hungarian, typically Jewish method of the presentation of prayers." That was why among other reasons it turned to him.

In a letter following this one, after asking my father to let him know whether he would be able to come to New York immediately after Passover, before the more substantial members of the congregation would be leaving for their summer vacation, Mr. Berliner wrote: "It is quite possible that our president, who will be on his way to Karlsbad right after Pesach, will visit you. *It is true that he is not a Hungarian. Yet he is an extraordinarily fine and decent person* (Er ist zwar kein Ungar, aber doch ein selten feiner ordentlicher Mann), with whom you will be able to discuss matters further orally."

The arrogance implicit in this casual remark did not escape my father. It gave him a momentary qualm. But there was nothing he could do about it. For he was at the time a man seeking to improve his situation. As such he could not afford to be too fastidious. So he decided not to permit this sample of Hungarian conceit to stand in his way, but proceeded with the negotiations.

The Ohab Zedek Congregation at first offered him fifty percent of the receipts from the proceeds of two Sabbath services besides paying for his passage, second class, to and from America. That was too uncertain, and he held out for something more definite. Finally two days after Passover a cable arrived from New York. It guaranteed the sum of four hundred dollars as remuneration in addition to travelling expenses. That settled the matter. And so he betook himself immediately to Bremen to await the departure of his ship.

He had not yet left Bremen when a special messenger arrived from Hamburg. It was my mother's brother Samuel who was then visiting us. "What brings you here, Schmiel?" asked the astonished fugitive. "Brace yourself, Yossel, I have bad news for you," said uncle Samuel. "What happened? You don't mean . . ." "No, word has come to us from Neumarkt that your mother died, and Taube wants you to return at once." "My mother, my poor darling mother," my father broke down. "Of course I will come. How can I go on a trip during the *Shiv'oh?*" However there were also other even more potent reasons why my mother wanted him home. It had just been reported during that same weekend that the White Star liner Titanic, the largest ship afloat, had been sunk, after having struck an iceberg, with a loss of more that 1500 out of about 2200 persons aboard. This made my mother anxious to have my father cancel his trip to America for the moment.

He was just about to return, when the ubiquitous Reverend Dreiblatt, together with another emissary of the congregation, appeared on the scene. They had been sent specially to bring my father back; and it did not now, of course, require much persuasion to render him amenable to their request. When the trio returned to Hamburg arm in arm with my father, there was joy and jubilation in the synagogue. Herr Dreiblatt considered it a personal triumph that he had been able to entice the would-be-fugitive back to his prison. A special poem, entitled "The Singer's Flight" (des Sänger's Flucht) was composed in celebration of this victory. All was now well again. Even the hard-hearted *Vorstand* had softened. It did not insist anymore on its rights, but mercifully granted its runaway cantor the requested increase in salary.

However the elation of the members of the Synagogenverband was destined to be short-lived. The lure of America was too strong for the singer. Four hundred dollars, the equivalent of about 1900 German marks, was a substantial sum of money. It was more than one fourth of his total annual salary. Besides America held out other opportunities which Germany did not offer. Barely four weeks after his first venture, therefore, my father made a second attempt to get away. And this time the persuasive Herr Dreiblatt did not catch up with him. The singer landed in New York on May 26th and there he remained.

For this drastic step he had the wholehearted approval and blessing of my mother. In a letter addressed to him at Bremerhaven, full of expressions of tenderness and love, such as one might expect from a newlywed bride, she bade him godspeed on his journey.

"Dear Josef, beloved of my heart," so it began. "Received your telegram and postcard from Bremen and rejoiced greatly over them. May the Almighty continue to lead you on the right way . . . That I am lonesome for you, you can well understand." Then it goes on to inform the correspondent that his friend Herr Bachrach thought that it would be proper for him to return within four weeks, even if it were only for the purpose of calling for his family and making his adieus. That would give the lie to the malicious charge of the president Von Son that their cantor's request, prior to his first departure, for a mere brief leave of absence had been a trick (Schwindel), that his real intention had been to get away. At all events, whatever he might decide to do, she, his wife, was ready to go along. Echoing the protestations of loyalty of the biblical Ruth, she said: "Wherever you will go, my dearest one in the world, there will I go . . . The main thing is that with the help of God you make good. Then all will be well." Both Wigderowitsch, she added, and the new sexton Rosenmann, with whom my father had been on intimate terms, agreed that there was no future for him in Hamburg. A distant relative of hers, who lived in New York, assured her that his predecessor at the Ohab Zedek, Cantor Meisels, did not in the least measure up to her Yossele. He had every reason, therefore, to feel confident of doing well in America. Her only concern was that the time might pass quickly so that they might all soon be together again.

As happened on several occasions before, my father's trial performances, this time at the Harlem synagogue of the Ohab Zedek Congregation, proved to be an instantaneous success. The crowds that had come to hear the new cantor were entranced by the beauty of his voice, the phenomenal nature of his falsetto, the agility of his coloratura and the sincerity and soulful fervor of his praying. He represented to them the true *Sheliach Tzibbur,* a person worthy of representing his congregation before their Father in Heaven.

My father never knew what it meant to coddle himself the way many other cantors do. So on the first Saturday, because he had failed to heed his wife's warning to keep out of drafts and not to overexert himself, he suffered from a cold. Consequently he did not function at his best. By the next Saturday, however, he had overcome this affliction. His voice was rich and clear and the worshippers were thrilled by what they saw and heard.

That same Saturday night at a special meeting of the board of directors of the congregation, which then counted some four-hundred dues-paying members, my father was unanimously elected as *chazan*. The salary of $2400 a year that he was to receive was the highest ever paid by an orthodox congregation in America to a cantor. His side income, he was assured, would at least equal his salary, for it was the custom in the synagogue at the reading of the Torah to make offerings for the cantor. Together with his income from weddings and funerals, this would bring the total of his earnings up to $5000 annually.

After the vote had been taken and the recommendation of the committee to engage my father had been adopted, the chairman, Mr. Aaron Garfunkel, vice-president of the congregation, a tall dignified gentleman, the scion of an old American Jewish family of Savannah, Georgia, arose and said to all assembled: "Gentlemen, today I feel genuinely proud to be a member of the Ohab Zedek Congregation. I am proud because you have shown how highly you rate the character of Cantor Rosenblatt by the price you are willing to pay him for his truly Jewish rendition of the services of the synagogue, which cannot help having a salutary influence upon all sectors of our community. By your action you have immeasurably raised the prestige of *Chazanuth* in America. You have given encouragement to synagogue attendance, particularly on the part of the younger and growing generation of American Jews, who will be attracted by Mr. Rosenblatt's art."

My father immediately cabled my mother to dispose of our furniture, pack the rest of our belongings and come with the children to join him in New York.

While we children, who were about to leave the scenes of

our childhood, and our mother, who had so quickly become accustomed to the orderly existence of Germany, were light of heart and looking forward to the change of habitat with pleasant and even eager anticipation, it was quite the reverse with everybody else we knew in Hamburg. Consternation bordering on mourning reigned in the Jewish community when it was learned that the treasure that they had harbored in their midst for six brief years had vanished, that their Yossele, who had been their pride and glory and, in spite of his high demands, the cause of the congregation's prosperity, was gone never to return. Some of them, the leaders whose niggardliness had driven my father to America, were angry. Yossele had become money-mad, they claimed. He had allowed the almighty dollar to seduce him. He had sold his Jewish birthright for a pot of American gold. The overwhelming majority, however, were grief-stricken. They could not forgive those who had deprived them, on account of a few paltry marks, of the many thrills and pleasures the great little cantor had given them. They knew very well that they would never get anyone to take his place. There were many *chazanim* in the world, but artists of the *Amud* like Yossele Rosenblatt were rare. Vainly did they strive to induce him to return by means of such pleas published in the press as: "Yossele, come back! All is not yet lost" (Jossele, kehre zurueck! Noch ist nicht alles vergeben). Of no effect either was the poem "American Hallel," which, while lauding the fugitive singer and justifying his desire to make his fortune in America, attempted to win him back with the argument that after all worldly prosperity was illusory, deceiving. "All men are," as the Psalmist put it, "liars." It was to no avail. Yossele would not return.

Among those who were deeply distressed over my father's decision to remain in America was his widowed sister Gittel. She dreaded the thought of perhaps permanent separation from her beloved brother, who had been so long her mainstay, aye her very staff of life. Another relative who greatly disapproved of the step was my uncle Stauber of Verbo, the husband of my father's sister Feige. Looking upon himself as a man of the world, he warned my mother against being led astray by the American mirage. If America were really so wonderful, why did Caruso, after the phenomenal success he had made there, after having been idolized in that country, return to Europe? Why did cantors of renown like Sirota refuse to settle there? Why did Pinie Minkowsky, after a three-year sojourn in the United States, come back to the Old World? Did she think, he asked, that her Yossele, a beginner compared to all these celebrities, could go further than they did in the land of Columbus? Furthermore, although the American dollar looked very big when sent to Europe and exchanged for German marks, in America its purchasing power was relatively small. Twenty-four hundred dollars was not the equivalent there of 10,000 marks in Germany. Besides, the position with the New York congregation was not even permanent. The contract was made for only five years, not for a life-time. There were no prospects of tenure. There was no security of any kind. Finally what would Yossele's father, who had sacrificed so much to raise his son as a devout and pious Jew, have said, had he been alive, about his beloved child's going away to a country where the Torah of Moses was honored only in the breach?

None of these pleas made the slightest impression on my mother. Like my father she felt irresistibly drawn to the new world of the West. She was as fed up as her husband with all the dickering and haggling and smallness of the Hamburgers. Only later on, after she had settled in the "golden land," did she appreciate fully those qualities in which German Jewry, at that time, excelled.

It was on a pleasant and sunny June day in 1912 that our family boarded the middle-aged, medium-sized steamer Amerika, of the Hamburg-America Line, to make the pas-

sage from Hamburg to New York. Our party included besides my mother and her seven children, ranging in age from
three months to ten years, also my mother's unmarried
brother Samuel, who made the trip with us so that he might
help his sister with her brood. My cousin Caroline, who had
been with us for a year, had returned to her mother.

The crossing itself, which took ten days, was uneventful.
We travelled second-class, had our share of sea-sickness on
the days when the ocean was rough, and consumed enough
ice cream to last us for several years and make us want not to
look at the stuff for a life-time. Of course we quickly changed
our minds once we were ashore. The hero of our voyage, who
attracted most attention, was my brother Marcus. He had
just turned three and with his dark eyes, jet black hair and
rosy-cheeked olive-complexioned face he looked like a cupid-
doll that had stepped out of a show-window.

We were still aboard ship on the 4th of July, America's
Independence Day, and the fireworks and other forms of celebration gave us a foretaste of the spirit of the vast new country in which we were to make our home. On the morning of
July 6th the outlines of the American shore became visible
in the distance. A few hours later our boat steamed slowly
into New York harbor where the Statue of Liberty, holding
aloft the torch of freedom, was bidding us welcome.

14

The Land of the Free

As second-class passengers, and therefore preferred immigrants, we were not detained by quarantine like our less fortunate fellow-travellers of the third class and steerage. After

a cursory examination of our eyes we were hurried through the customs and permitted to go ashore where father was anxiously and eagerly awaiting us. He looked and seemed to be very happy. America was a country after his own heart. No more chains! No more fetters! No more cramping rules and stifling restrictions! No more getting up at unearthly hours in the morning to attend services! No more walking on a tight rope of synagogue regulations! He felt like a bird released from the cage in which it had been imprisoned for six wearisome years.

The First Hungarian Congregation Ohab Zedek that had engaged his services as cantor did not impose any unreasonable burdens upon him. Aside from requiring him to officiate every Friday evening and Saturday morning and the festivals, it made few demands. He could sleep as late as he wanted, he was free to repeat the words of the prayers to his heart's content, and he was at liberty, during the week, to accept any outside engagements that might come his way. In short, he was no longer a helpless employee at the mercy of a ruthless and exacting *Vorstand,* but an artist in his own right whose talents were available to those who wished to engage him. Such was my father's immediate reaction to this young and still growing America that had taken him to its heart and acclaimed him almost instantly as the greatest *chazan* of his generation, nay of the era.

Quite different was the impression that the American environment made upon my mother. She viewed her new surroundings not with the eyes of an artist surveying his audience, but of a woman, the maker of the home and the person chiefly concerned with the raising of her children as people of refinement and culture. Judging by these criteria it seemed to her that she had gotten the worst of the bargain by coming to America. The Germany she had left behind was *the* land of Kultur, in which life ran in well-regulated and orderly grooves.

And what had she been offered in exchange for what she had given up? To be sure Harlem was at that time the aristocratic Jewish neighborhood of New York, where most of the well-to-do Jews resided. But that was true only of the blocks between Lenox and Seventh Avenues, where the better private homes were located, not of the tenements between Fifth and Lenox Avenues into one of which we moved when we arrived. The flat that had been rented for us on the fourth floor of the oldish building on 2 West 119th Street consisted of six dingy, stuffy rooms, three of which were always dark because their windows faced the wall of the houses behind ours in the courtyard, thus effectively shutting off the sunlight.

It was our luck to strike one of the hottest summers within the memory of New Yorkers. We were unaccustomed to such heat in the parts of Europe from which we had come. The result was that for the first few nights of our stay in New York we were unable to sleep—a situation which did not buoy up mother's spirits. To add to her woes the place wasn't even clean. There was a musty odor in the rooms, and on the morning after we had taken possession of our home something unusual transpired, something that could never have happened in Hamburg where every apartment was regularly fumigated. As we children opened the bottom drawer of one of the cupboards to put our clothes in, something screeched and we beheld a tiny blue-skinned rodent, the like of which we had read about in books but never seen. "Mamma, sieh mal, ein Tier," ("Mother, look, an animal!") we exclaimed in glee.

But mother did not seem to share our happiness. She was mortified, shocked and disgusted. "Where did you take me?" she upbraided my father, forgetting all her noble professions of several weeks before. "What did I need it for? Weren't we well off enough in Hamburg? Why, Hamburg was paradise compared to this. And the people! *There* our parishioners were persons of breeding, of education, of etiquette. Youth looked up with deference to old age. Children respected their parents. Who ever heard a child talk back to his father or mother? And what have we here? Rabble, riffraff collected from the four corners of the earth (ein zusammengelaufenes Volk), people without manners or refinement or knowledge, loud-mouthed youngsters and elderly men and women without dignity."

Unfortunately most of mother's complaints were quite justified. America was at that time still like a diamond in the rough that needed a lot of refining and polishing. The standards, material or intellectual, were not what they are today. Although the United States was the land of invention, in technological progress it lagged far behind Germany and the percentage of the youth going to college was much smaller than it is now. The first two English expressions that struck our foreign ears and that we set down in our American vocabulary were "Sharrap" ("shut up!") and "Gerrarehere" ("Get out of here"). Neither of them were calculated to give us superior aliens a high conception of American culture. It took us a little while to learn that the English tongue was not restricted to these two terms, that in reality it was a language of great richness and beauty capable of formulating the loftiest thoughts and giving utterance to the noblest human sentiments.

Mother soon discovered that not only in these respects but also in others her brother-in-law Stauber had been right. Economically she was not as well off as she had been in Hamburg, because the $2400 a year that my father was earning did not have the purchasing power of its equivalent in German marks. True, the cost of living was then much lower than it is today. A dollar was a dollar. Good cuts of meat could be gotten at 15 cents a pound and eggs cost a penny apiece. Yet with nine mouths to feed and money to be sent abroad, $200 a month was not quite enough. Her expectations of wealth and splendor in Columbus's golden land turned out to be an illusion.

And so my mother kept on wringing her hands, and wailing and mourning about her "paradise lost" for two years, until the World War broke out. Then at last she stopped. She became reconciled to America with all its shortcomings and deficiencies, and made peace with her lot.

As for my father, he had had no problems to begin with. America was his country and of American cities New York was his favorite. He loved its bustle, its activity and movement, its subways and elevated railroads and its friendly, unconventional people. The fact that it was not as clean and orderly as Hamburg bothered him not at all. He wasn't interested in externals, but in what was beneath the surface. And it seemed to him that notwithstanding its lackadaisical, happy-go-lucky exterior America was far more wholesome than Germany with its sophisticated politeness and its correct manners.

American informality suited him perfectly. When he was invited for the first time to a wedding-dinner at the fashionable Astor Hotel on a hot summer night—air-conditioning had not yet been invented—he was shocked to see men take off their jackets and sit down in their shirt-sleeves to eat. In Hamburg that would have been *verboten* as the height of impropriety. Yet, once he had gotten over the initial surprise he was inordinately pleased, because the heat would have been unbearable.

And so my father could not wait to take out his first papers and apply at the earliest opportunity for his American citizenship. He was sworn in as a citizen by the Supreme Court of the State of New York on November 9, 1917, after having been a resident of America for a little over five years.

The story that I am now about to relate was told on the occasion of a celebration in honor of the completion of several decades of devoted service by a distinguished orthodox rabbi of New York to his congregation. The narrator was no less prominent a figure in the lay leadership of the congregation than the president himself, and the purpose of the story was to illustrate the high veneration and esteem in which the said president held the said rabbi.

"One Saturday afternoon," recounted the speaker, dipping into his past, "I was walking along Lenox Avenue with a cigar in my mouth, when, lo and behold! who should be coming in my direction but our spiritual father, Rabbi Cohen. What was I to do? To smoke in the presence of the holy man in violation of the Sabbath code would be offending his religious sensibilities. To throw the lighted cigar away would make what I had been doing too obvious. Therefore, in order to remove the cause of offense from sight as quickly and imperceptibly as possible, I hurriedly stuck the smoldering butt into my pocket until there was a safe distance between me and the rabbi. When I took it out again, I found that it had burnt a hole through the garment."

Nowhere except in America could such a story have been related, because nowhere except in America would a man who could have allowed himself to make such a boast at a public gathering have been chosen to head an orthodox congregation. In certain parts of Eastern Europe he might have been run out of town as a heretic if he as much as carried a handkerchief on the day of rest. In this free new world it was not held against him even that he smoked on the holy day. It did not disqualify him from the highest office in an orthodox congregation. Such was the complexion of orthodoxy in the United States at that time.

But how did my father fit into this scheme of things? How did he, a sincerely pious man, without hypocrisy or pretense, explain to himself these glaring inconsistencies between theory and practice? True, he was endowed with a sense of humor which enabled him to laugh off many an unpleasant experience that would have annoyed one not blessed with such a disposition. Once, for example, shortly after his arrival in the United States he remarked to one of his companions: "What a wonderful country, this America! Even its street-cars observe the Sabbath. I saw with my own eyes a sign in one of them, which said: No Smoking!" But certainly in his more serious moments he could not have been blind to the shortcomings of the overwhelming majority of his coreli-gionists in America in matters pertaining to Jewish law. What made him, who was so strict with himself, so tolerant towards others?

One explanation of his attitude is perhaps his unbounded love for his fellow-mortals, a love that made him seek out the best that was in them and overlook their faults.

I remember the day when he took me for the first time to visit his eldest sister, whom he had not seen since he had left Russia at the age of seven while she and her husband had gone on to America. One would imagine that people, who had had their home in the land of opportunity for twenty-three years and who entertained no scruples about the length of their working week, should have accumulated some capital during all that time and attained a measure of economic in-dependence. What a disappointment, therefore, was it for me to be led into a modest, three-room flat on East 106th Street, furnished with the utmost simplicity, and to be in-formed that that was where my father's sister lived. Even greater was my shock when I was introduced to a wrinkled, prematurely old lady who, though she had been in America for more than two decades, could hardly speak a word of English, and was told "Meet your aunt Chaveh, son."

My father, however, was not the least bit embarrassed by the poverty of the surroundings. He greeted his sister as though she were a queen and sat down at her table and par-took of her humble fare as if they were royal delicacies. To her children, who were simple working-people, he was plain

Uncle Yossele, without any flourishes or airs, while he in turn admired in them their innate qualities of decency and home-spun respectability.

The same cordiality characterized his demeanor toward all his relatives and kinsmen that he found in America. It was manifest in his relationship to his cousin Sarah Perl, the daughter of his uncle Gedaliah Shtefaneshter, who was a plutocrat compared to aunt Chaveh. It showed itself in his behavior toward the more affluent Pilatskys and to his two elderly uncles Vetter Ephraim and Vetter Moshe Wolf.

Another reason why he was able to get along with people whose views were the direct opposite of his own was that he looked upon piety as a private affair between the individual and his Maker. Therefore, although stringent with himself, he never attempted to force his beliefs on others, and, when he tried to exercise suasion, it was done in the most inoffensive manner. This trait in him made him beloved among all sections of the Jewish population of New York, from the most radical to the most conservative.

Joseph Rumshinsky, the well known composer of music for the Yiddish theater, which was then in the heyday of its glory in America, relates as an example of my father's personal piety coupled with tolerance toward others the following incident. He was walking down Second Avenue with him late one weekday afternoon. With the oncoming of dusk, recalls Rumshinsky, Yossele became restive. He had not yet said his afternoon prayers and the time for the discharge of this obligation was running out. Rumshinsky noticed Yossele's restlessness, but the reason for it never dawned on him.

At length they came to a corner drugstore, and Yossele, mumbling an excuse to his companion, darted into the place. Five minutes passed. Ten minutes rolled by, and as Yossele still did not emerge, Rumshinsky, growing impatient, decided to investigate. Entering the drugstore, he espied Yossele standing in a telephone booth, the receiver at his ear, an arm rest-ing on the receiver support and his lips moving as though he were talking to somebody. Rumshinsky understood at once what had happened. Amused by the ingenuity of the scheme, he remarked teasingly: "What a long conversation you had over the telephone with the receiver down, Reb Yossele!" Without the least bit of embarrassment, as though it were something self-evident, Reb Yossele replied: "But where else in this bustling city could I find the privacy to *daven Minchah?*"

Once he was rehearsing his program for the coming Sabbath at the home of a choir director. When he was finished, he said goodbye to his host and looked, as was his custom, for the *Mezuzah* on the right doorpost of the entrance, but could not find it. He left without saying a word. The next morning the choir director heard a peculiar hammering at the door. Curious as to what might be the cause of the noise he opened the door and, to his amazement, saw Yossele Rosenblatt, with hammer in hand, nailing the little oblong box to the right doorpost. The choir director became red in the face and stammered out an apology. "I confess, Reb Yossele, that the *Mezuzah* should have been put up when I moved into the apartment several months ago and I had in mind to attend to it immediately. But you know how it is. I became involved with other things and so it escaped my attention." "Well that's taken care of now," was all that Yossele had to say to that.

Anxious as my father was to see his coreligionists in America more punctilious in the observance of the tenets of their faith, he realized that adherence to the letter of the law at times entailed a sacrifice that not all were ready or able to make. He, therefore, welcomed any opportunity to remove the obstacles that economics posed to religion. On several Friday evenings, for example, he had seen a wizened old Jewish woman selling candies right outside the synagogue. The spectacle of the violation of the Sabbath by a person of her age affected him very painfully. "Tell me, Mamenyu," he asked the old lady, "how much do you take in on an average on a night like this?" When she divulged to him the extent of her modest profit, he said to her: "Listen to me. I will make a bargain with you. If you will promise me to keep the Sabbath, I will pay you whatever an evening's work like this may net you." From that time on, for a number of years, she received on every Friday afternoon with clocklike regularity the sum of $3.00.

15

Getting Adjusted

It has already been noted that my father very quickly felt at home in America. One factor that facilitated his acclimatization was the presence in the country of a large community of East-European Jews. Many of them still remembered him from the days when, as a child prodigy, he had travelled through the towns and hamlets of the Ukraine and, later on, of the Austro-Hungarian empire. Reared in the same surroundings and coming from the same cultural background as he, and still making extensive use of his Yiddish mother-tongue, they were able to understand him, admire him for his piety and appreciate his art. And there was hardly a group among them that did not claim kinship with him. The Hungarians called him their own because he had lived in Hungary and cut his cantorial teeth, so to speak, in Hungarian congregations. The Galicians felt close to him because he had grown up in Galicia and married a native of their home-country. The Lithuanians, despite the wide variation of pronunciation that differentiated their Yiddish from his, looked upon him as a fellow-countryman, for was not their Lithuania just as much a part of the Russian empire as his Ukraine? With the Jews hailing from Little Russia he shared in common the place of birth, while the Roumanians regarded themselves as related to him because his maternal uncle had his home in Shtephaneshti.

It was different with his children. Products as we were of the German school, we looked down with disdain upon the vernacular of the millions of East European Jews which we were accustomed to refer to in Germany as "Jargon"—a medley of grammatically incorrect and phonetically mispronounced German with an admixture of Polish, Hebrew and other dialects to fill in the lacunae. English was as yet unknown to us. We, therefore, had a language barrier to overcome before we could become completely integrated with our new environment. Fortunately for us the process was neither difficult nor long-protracted. After three months in the neighborhood public schools, to which the four oldest of us were sent in the fall when the school season began, we were transformed into full-fledged Americans with not a trace of a foreign accent. For the purposes of our Americanization the American public school was an excellent medium. It brought us into direct contact with our fellow Americans, black and white, Christian and Jewish, Latin and Anglo-Saxon. The Sabbath presented no problem, because the schools were closed on Saturdays as well as Sundays.

The question of our Jewish education was not so easy to solve and gave my father considerable concern. The *Yeshivah* of Harlem, which corresponded roughly speaking to the schools we had attended in Hamburg, was not particularly appealing to us. The facilities as well as the discipline were poor, and the language of instruction for the Jewish studies was Yiddish, which definitely ruled it out for us. It was also on this account that, after having taken in several sessions of the Salanter Talmud Torah, an afternoon Hebrew School operating five days a week and three hours a day, my brother and I stopped going there. We could not endure the distortion of the German language, nor did we take kindly to the method of instruction. Since in such matters as Jewish education, money was with him no object, my father decided to engage a private tutor for us. His choice was a Warsaw intellectual who spoke both English and German, and a happy choice it was. A competent Hebrew grammarian, a connoisseur of the Bible, who was also well versed in the literature of the nineteenth century Hebrew revival movement, Mr. Weisbart was an excellent pedagogue. I remember him to this day with affection and gratitude, for it was he who started me on my career of Jewish scholarship.

Before very long we were well rooted in America. Although the transition from the old world to the new brought about some changes in our daily routine, most of our personal life continued more or less in the same grooves as before. The form of services at the Ohab Zedek synagogue was essentially identical with the ritual followed by the Synagogenverband in Hamburg. The difference consisted of such externals as decorum, attire and architecture. To bolster a financial structure, which was still rather insecure, the custom prevailed at the Ohab Zedek, as it did in other Orthodox synagogues at that time in America, to announce the offerings made whenever a worshipper was called up to the reading of the Torah. This did not contribute to the orderliness of this part of the service. Furthermore there was missed by us newcomers in the Ohab Zedek the formality to which we had been accustomed in Hamburg. In the American synagogue only the officers and officials wore frock coats and high hats on Sabbaths and the festivals. Finally the unpretentious exterior of the Ohab Zedek synagogue building, wedged in as it was between other edifices, and its rather simple inte-

rior, contrasted sharply with the spaciousness on the outside
and the decorous inside of the structure in which we had
worshipped in Hamburg.

Notwithstanding these deficiencies Ohab Zedek was by far
the most aristocratic and best patronized synagogue of New
York in that generation. It made up in enthusiasm what it
may have lacked in polish and decor. Whenever it was
known that its chief cantor, Yossele Rosenblatt, would officiate, its main auditorium was sure to be filled to capacity.
On Sabbaths preceding the beginning of Jewish months,
when the prayer for the new moon was recited, or on the major festivals, it was impossible for anyone, who arrived after
the *Kedushah* of the morning devotion, to secure a seat.

There were occasions when an admission charge, limiting
the size of the crowd seeking entrance into the synagogue, was
absolutely imperative. One such occasion was the service inaugurating the annual penitential season on the Sunday
morning before the Jewish New Year. As early as 2 A.M. the
entire block of 116th Street between Fifth and Lenox Avenues would be black with men and women, some of whom
had travelled great distances to hear Yossele Rosenblatt say
Selichos. They would remonstrate with the chief usher, Mr.
Schwarz, who, as a former policeman, was accustomed to
handling crowds, and implore him to allow them to enter.
"I came all the way from St. Louis for the privilege of hearing
Reb Yossele," one pleaded. Another was on a visit from San
Francisco. He had had no time to provide himself with a
ticket, and he might never be in New York again. Could not,
therefore, he asked, an exception be made in his case. The
visitors from afar often offered to pay several times the regular price of admission. But Mr. Schwarz was ruthless. He
knew only one rule: No ticket, no admittance.

Even Yossele had a hard time pushing through the throng
that blocked the entrance on the outside, while within the
building every bit of empty space was taken up by worship-

pers eager to hear the *chazan*. It was lucky that the floor of
the synagogue did not give way under the load it had to
carry, and that no fire ever broke out, since no precautions
were taken against such hazards.

If seats were at a premium on the first day of *Selichos,* despite the fact that the service began at the unearthly hour of
4 A.M., all the more difficult were they to obtain for the
High Holidays, when most American Jews, then as today,
made provision for divine worship. The rental of pews at
the Ohab Zedek Synagogue, during the years that my father
was officiating, yielded up to $50 per person and the total
revenue to the congregation from that source alone ran as
high as $33,000 a season, a staggering sum for those days.

One factor that made Ohab Zedek outstanding among
American Jewish congregations was undoubtedly the calibre
of its membership. It included, in addition to persons of
wealth, such distinguished public servants as Judges Otto
Rosalsky and Gustav Hartman. Its learned rabbis were leaders in their respective fields. But it was not these fine men
that were connected with the congregation or stood at its
helm that were the real cause of its popularity during more
than two decades. In spite of his dignified patriarchal appearance and his flawless literary High German—that was
way over the heads of most of his audience—Dr. Klein's forte
did not lie in the field of oratory. As for American-born Dr.
Bernard Drachman, despite his Shakespearean diction, he
was not the most effective speaker.

What attracted the multitude to the Ohab Zedek synagogue and brought wealth to its coffers was, by the admission
of all, its cantor. Illustrative of the fascination he exercised
was the case of the man who later became my father-in-law.
A native of Bukowina, who had been living in Paris, Isser
Woloch had settled in the Bronx when he first came to America. As soon as he learned that the boy-prodigy he had known
in his youth was serving as *chazan* in Harlem, he decided at

once to move into that neighborhood. He wished to make certain that his children would grow up in a synagogue which represented all that was beautiful in Judaism.

Why were lovers of music like Isser Woloch drawn so powerfully to Reb Yossele? Because every performance of his was a sacred concert, a most elevating religious experience, as soul-filling and satisfying as the finest symphony. He sang with such ease that it was hard to tell where the notes came from and whence the tones derived their power. When those who substituted for him chanted the service, it was usually all effort and no art ("A Melocheh und kein Chochmeh"). "But when Yossele *davened,*" so it was said, "it was all art and no effort" ("a Chochmeh und nisht kein Melocheh"). He would stand almost motionless before the prayer-desk and melody would issue from his mouth like music from the strings of a violin. He was invariably at his best at *Neilah,* the conclusion of the twenty-four hour continuous fast of the Day of Atonement when the demands upon a cantor's voice are greatest.

With his facility of movement he combined a diction that made every word which emanated from his lips stand out as though it had been carved with a fine instrument. He never missed a syllable even in the most tortuous, tongue-twisting passages. His clear enunciation enabled him to speed up the tempo of his recitation of that part of the ritual on which he did not elaborate musically. As a result the holiday morning services were usually concluded at the Ohab Zedek around 1 P.M., which was reasonable compared to the time schedule adhered to when other cantors of note officiated.

In addition to his fine diction my father had an almost perfect sense of pitch. Owing to the prohibition against the employment of musical instruments on Saturdays, he never used a tuning fork or whistle when officiating on these days. Yet he never went off key. It happened, on the other hand, that the choir, notwithstanding the fact that the directors had no qualms against employing tuning aids on holy days, wandered off the register and that my father, without any instrument, set them right again.

To conduct a choir with Yossele Rosenblatt was relaxation for the directors. It was never necessary to rehearse with him, because he could read the most difficult score the first time it was presented without previous coaching, and do it with the proper interpretation and emphasis. This was another one of his hidden talents which the outside world hardly suspected in a man who looked so much like the type of old-fashioned *chazan*. In this respect he excelled the most cultured modern cantors of the old world and the new.

The uniform color of his voice from the lowest tones of his baritone register up to the high C of his upper tenor notes was a marvel that critics often commented on. But it was his well-developed falsetto and the tricks he was able to do with it that made the masses go into ecstasy.

I recall vividly how on one Friday evening after he had winged his way through one of those breath-taking florid passages of his *Omar Rabbi Elozor,* in which his pianissimo rose first to the dizziest heights ever ascended by a coloratura soprano and then descended into the depths of a basso cantante, the worshippers, breaking all rules of synagogue etiquette, burst out in a round of applause which took some time to quiet. I remember also how on another occasion, when services were over, Sholom Aleichem (Rabinowitz), the outstanding humorist of Yiddish literature, who had just then arrived from Europe, walked up to the *Bema,* where my father was still standing, and kissed him. So moved was he by the performance.

This was no small compliment, for the Jewish Mark Twain was not a religious man in the conventional sense of the word, although he had a nostalgia for the ritual of the synagogue. To inspire a man of his sophisticated taste required more than ordinary ability. Yossele Rosenblatt apparently had it, and a warm friendship developed between the guileless *chazan* and the fastidious author, which was terminated only by the latter's premature death two years later.

My father's detractors, in an attempt to belittle his art as a singer, sometimes disparagingly referred to him as Yossele *Baal Tefillah*. That is, denying him the virtuosity usually ascribed to gifted cantors, they conceded to him only the ability to declaim in the traditional chant the prayers of the synagogue. In reality, far from derogating from his stature, they were hereby paying him a great compliment. For the faculty of making the ancient Hebrew text of the Jewish prayerbook comprehensible by means of his music was another facet of Yossele Rosenblatt's accomplishments as a cantor. When he pronounced the words "O my God, the soul Thou gavest me is pure," one could, so it was said, by the melody and the pathos alone picture a soul pleading with the Almighty for its life. And when he called upon the Creator to "Look down from heaven and behold His people's humiliation" whoever was in attendance felt the sorrow and the anguish of those for whom he was imploring the heavenly Father's compassion. His deep penetration into the meaning of the ancient litanies more than once evoked from an auditor the remark, at the conclusion of a service: "Reb Yossele, you are ready now to begin the study of *Chumish*, because as far as the prayerbook is concerned, you have mastered it" ("Weil davenen kent ihr shoin").

Non-Jews as well as Jews often experienced a sort of sacred awe when they heard him chant Hebrew liturgical selections. "Such singing could have been done only in Jerusalem to the words of the psalms of David" was the reaction of Assistant Bishop Hugh of Syracuse to his rendition of *"Elokay Neshomoh,"* while another high church dignitary who had been present at one of his recitals remarked: "There was a depth of feeling in your voice and a sense of tragedy in the music that led me to think that I was listening to the agelong cry of Israel, personified in you." It was no wonder, for he himself usually felt inspired, carried away with his praying. "Do you know," he once confided to an interviewer, "when I stand before the *Amud,* I do not worship like a *chazan.* I pray as though I were one of the congregation who has paid for a ticket of admission. I pray and listen to the prayer."

16

Life In New York

If my father had been one of those dictators whose lives are constantly in jeopardy, he would not have had to fear for his personal safety, because he was always accompanied by a private bodyguard on his way home from the synagogue after services on Friday evenings and Saturday mornings. This retinue, which would be made up of members of the choir, colleagues, admirers and just ordinary hangers-on, did not only take him up to the door of his apartment. They even followed him inside, regardless of whether they had been officially invited or not, participated in the *Kiddush,* very often remained for dinner or lunch and sometimes stayed as guests over night. My parents were both very hospitable. They were the kind of people who couldn't say "No." We always had open house, and I don't remember the time when our family sat down to a meal without some strangers at the table.

On Friday or holiday evenings there were often as many as twenty persons seated in our dining room. How my mother managed always to have enough food on hand, without an electric refrigerator to keep edibles fresh, is still a mystery to me. And I marvel even more at her energy in providing for so many mouths with no more help than a single Polish maid. Our pantry was generally well-stocked. We always ate well, and our food, while not the most expensive, was invariably wholesome and appetizing.

My father's total earnings should have sufficed to pay for the upkeep of even so large and hospitable a household, were it not for other items that always received priority. He had a standing rule that no hand outstretched for help must be turned back empty. If a beggar came to the door, he was sure to get a quarter if not half a dollar. A more respectable and higher class *schnorrer* could count on five and even ten dollars. And then there were our relatives in Europe who were a perpetual drain on the exchequer. A letter informing him that this niece or that nephew was going to be married was enough to send my father scurrying for funds to meet the demands.

And so his hands were constantly in his pocket—for people other than his immediate family—and he never got around to giving my mother a regular weekly allowance in order that she might be able to pay cash for the groceries and other articles of consumption. As a result the bills owed to the tradespeople kept growing continually and we were always behind in our payments. Because it was so hard to keep track of what we actually owed over an extended period of time, the unscrupulous among them would take advantage of our negligence and slap on charges for merchandise that had never been delivered.

Of all this the outsiders and strangers who made themselves at home at the Rosenblatt menage knew nothing or pretended not to know. There was, of course, no mention of monetary matters at the table on Friday nights or Sabbath mornings, which were always festive occasions.

Since all the male members of our family as well as my sister Gertrude were musical, the singing of *Zemiros* either in unison or in several voices was a regular feature of every Sabbath and holiday meal. Besides the traditional tunes we chanted melodies that had been specially composed for the occasion by my father. The most tuneful and popular of his Sabbath melodies, which still enjoys great favor in Israel today, is that to which psalm 126, recited before the grace after meals, is sung. He also composed music for *Sholom Aleichem*, the song of welcome for the Sabbath, *Menuchoh Vesimchoh, Kol Mekaddeish,* and *Yoh Ribbon,* all of which have the typical Rosenblatt swing and movement.

If the Friday nights and Sabbath mornings at our home were veritable song fests, the *Seder* ceremony initiating the festival of Passover was a concert worthy of a price of admission. The conductor and chief soloist was, of course, my father. Seated at one end of the long dining-room table attired in his white satin robe and mitre and reclining on the pillow placed on the left arm of the arm-chair on which he was sitting, he looked like a king holding court. But even more impressive than his regal appearance was the soothing sweetness of his mellow, resonant and robust tenor voice as he chanted the text of the narrative, telling the story of the exodus of the children of Israel from Egypt, in the traditional sing-song.

The Jewish celebrants of Passover are usually very hungry on the first night of the holiday, having virtually fasted during the day preceding. There is, therefore, a great deal of truth in the assertion that most people prefer the *Kneidlach* to the *Haggada.* In this instance, however, the twenty to thirty attendants at our *Seders* enjoyed the latter at least as much as the former.

The high point of the evening's exercises was reached when the narration ended and the singing of the psalms and the hymns began.

The melodies were of my father's own composition. One of them, a recitative for cantor and choir on the morning of the pilgrimage festivals, won the recognition of the renowned Ernest Bloch. It was a favorite with the Rosenblatt home choir on Passover eve and contributed greatly to the inspiration of the occasion.

It was on a hot day in August of the year 1913 that the only native American in our family made his entrance into the world. We were living at number 2 West 117th Street, in quarters a little more desirable though not more pretentious than our first apartment on 119th Street, when my youngest brother Ralph was born.

With eight children to raise and a large household to run my mother hardly ever had an opportunity to go out. I don't remember her having left the house even for relaxation before Ralph was old enough to take care of himself. She was too busy feeding and supervising the health of her offspring and attending to the needs of her husband to be able to participate in social functions outside of her own home. The theatre and the cinema might have been non-existent for all the use she made of them. The outside man of the firm was my father, whom my mother watched most lovingly, making certain that he was properly attired, rested and nourished.

From the time of his arrival in America, requests for the opportunity to hear him sing came in not only from institutions and congregations in New York, but also from many communities outside of the metropolis. His first appearance in New York's East Side took place on the Saturday after his election as cantor of the Ohab Zedek Congregation. By popular request he had been invited to officiate at the congregation's downtown synagogue. The impression upon the worshippers, many of them still recent immigrants, including relatives in whose home he spent the Sabbath, was indescribable. They went away from the house of worship fascinated. For weeks thereafter the topic of conversation among the Jews of the East Side was the new star that had arisen on the horizon of Jewish *Chazanuth* in America.

Throughout his life he remained the East Side's idol and not only among the frequenters of synagogues, but also among the actors of the Yiddish stage. The latter loved to imitate his style of cantorial music, just as he incorporated into his secular repertoire their theatrical airs and folksongs. Especially high was the esteem in which he was held by the writers of the Jewish press, whose headquarters are still located in that neighborhood. B. Kowner, in his column in the Jewish Daily Forward, prescribed a phonograph record by Yossele Rosenblatt as a sure cure of melancholy.

During the first five years of his residence in America, my father recorded exclusively for the Victor Talking Machine Company. These recordings helped still further to enhance his reputation. His name reached the ears of the Jewish banker and philanthropist Jacob Schiff. Mr. Schiff was at the time president of the Montefiore Home for Incurables, which was to dedicate its new synagogue in December of the year 1913, and he invited the recently arrived cantor to participate in the exercises. It was no small honor to receive an invitation from a celebrity of Jacob Schiff's calibre and my father accepted with alacrity. The next day brought him a letter of thanks from the Jewish Croesus. It stated that his performance had been "dignified to the audience and cheering to the inmates." From then on his concert for the institution became an annual event to which the patients looked forward with eager anticipation.

My father's functions in the synagogue were not restricted to officiating on the Sabbath and the major festivals. Whenever the eve of the new moon occurred in the middle of the week, a Minor Day of Atonement service was held, which he was often called upon to conduct. And then there was the week of *Chanukah,* the only occasion, outside of weddings, on which an orchestra of instrumental music could be used in the synagogue. His pièce de resistance at his *Chanukah* concerts was a musical rendition of *Bameh Madlikin.* The basic motif employed in this composition was the traditional chant of the students of the Talmud. It was introduced so skillfully, however, and with such variations that it never became tiresome.

Whether musical instruments were employed or not, my father was always assisted whenever he officiated by a full-sized male choir of men and boys. His first director, a competent enough musician, was a man with a rather negative personality. Even my father, who was usually so informal with his associates, found it impossible to become friendly with him. The result—he stayed only the first year. Then Herman Wohl, the conductor of the chorus of one of the Yiddish theaters, was recommended to him. When he was first presented to him, Wohl appeared to my father like a figure that had stepped out of the past. That handsome, round face with the piercing, black, kindly eyes,—it was so familiar. He had seen it somewhere before, only at that time it was adorned with earlocks. "Haven't we met previously, Mr. Wohl?" asked the cantor. "Of course, we have, Reb Yossele. Don't you remember? It was in Stanislav, at the home of Reb Alter Bauman. You were then nine years old and I was a young man of fourteen." The two musicians, cantor and choir leader, became fast friends, for notwithstanding the differences of outlook and mode of living between them, they had much in common. Wohl had retained the *Chassidic* fervor and swing of his youth, which was as pronounced in his compositions as they were in Reb Yossele's. It accounted for my father's fondness for Wohl's *Kedushot,* one of which has been recorded by him. Wohl, on the other hand, had profound respect for Reb Yossele's musicianship. They worked together harmoniously for an entire decade.

The adult contingent of the personnel of my father's choirs, some of the members of which later attained renown in the musical world, was drawn mostly from the chorus of the Yiddish stage. One or two of the boy-singers, especially those

who hailed from religious homes, were always quartered with
us over the Sabbath and on the holidays. All of them without exception loved my father and felt free to unburden
themselves to him. He used to treat them as equals, pinch
their cheeks as a mark of affection and joke with them. They
were, of course, proud to be associated with him, for some of
the lustre that attached to his name also fell on them. Thus,
for example, in a newspaper report of a *Yom Kippur Koton*
service given by him in Philadelphia in the fall of 1913,
mention was made of "the able support given the cantor in
the chanting of the sacred melodies by his choir of five men
and fifteen boys, all from New York."

17

War Breaks Out in Europe

Our family had just moved from its second apartment, where
its youngest member was born, to 100 West 114th Street,
when the first world war broke out in Europe. While most
Americans ranged themselves immediately on the side of the
Allies, the Jews of America, at the beginning at least, favored
the Triple Entente—not because they loved the Germans so
much, but because they hated Czarist Russia, which was Germany's adversary, more. Many erstwhile Jewish subjects of
the Czar were still toiling to gain a foothold in the new
world and had not yet forgotten the smarts and pains in-
flicted on their flesh by the *nagaikas* of the Czar's henchmen.
The memories of the bloodcurdling pogrom of Kishinev were
fresh in their minds. Nor had their native American brethren
been able to forgive the Russian government its affront to
their sensibilities and to their pride as Americans when it re-

fused to honor the American passports of Jews who had become citizens of the United States.

As for us former Germans, we were real rooters for the Vaterland and made no secret of our elation over the initial victories of the Kaiser's armies. I recall the frequent discussions I had with the old German janitor of our tenement house about German military strategy and tactics and the confidence with which we looked forward to Germany's winning the war. Little did we ween at that time how soon not only the Jews but other German sympathizers in America would change their minds and align themselves with the democracies that were arrayed against the Kaiser and his ambitions of world conquest. But that did not happen until two and a half years later, when Woodrow Wilson, who had been reelected president because "he kept us out of war," found that neutrality in the conflict was no longer possible and decided to throw in our lot with the Allies.

The effect of the war in its early phases upon my father was to stimulate his impulse for musical composition and cause him to write some of his most successful and popular recitatives. Deeply stirred by the sufferings of his brethren in the old world, he gave expression to his feelings in music composed for portions of the weekday service that spoke of Israel's age-old tragedy, rather than the Sabbath and holiday ritual which was preferred by other creative cantors. He used as his medium prayers like *Acheinu Kol Beis Yisroel, Shomer Yisroel, Habet Mishomayim Ur'eh* and *Elokay Neshomoh,* and gave vent through them to all the pathos and sorrow that filled the soul of the Jew. Never had these neglected byways of the traditional prayerbook been exploited as they were by him. Never had they been made so meaningful as when they were sung by Yossele Rosenblatt. This may have accounted to some extent for his acclamation on the occasion of his thirty-third birthday by the Yiddish press of

New York as "The greatest artist of the *Amud* in the world
. . . as one of the giants of Jewish music."

My father's own Bar-Mitzvah had, as we have had occasion
to observe, passed by almost unnoticed. In Eastern Europe,
where Jews were deeply attached to their hereditary faith
anyhow, there was no need to mark by a special celebration
the time when the performance of religious duties became
obligatory. It was different when twenty years later his eldest
son became of age in America. Here, on account of the wide-
spread laxity of Jewish observance, it was necessary to have
the event signalized by means of impressive festivities. My
Bar-Mitzvah was celebrated in such a manner. As the first
of Yossele Rosenblatt's children to be officially initiated into
Jewish manhood, I felt keenly the responsibility of upholding
the family honor by the way in which I performed the functions assigned to me in the synagogue on the Sabbath following my thirteenth birthday. I realized also that, as the first-
born, I would be setting the pattern for my four younger
brothers. I must have succeeded in the discharge of my obligations, for when the great day was over and all our guests,
from the rabbi down, commented favorably on my cantillation of the sacred texts, my father was very proud. He considered himself amply rewarded for the pains he had taken to
provide me with a thorough Jewish education.

Two weeks after this family celebration, apropos of my
father's thirty-third birthday, the following article by Asher
Selig Kramer appeared in the Jewish Daily News:

"Nearly thirty years ago when that great saint, the holy
Tzaddik of Tshortkov, married off a child of his, I made a
special trip to attend that royal wedding . . . The ceremony
took place late Friday afternoon. Immediately after I slipped
into a section of the large courtyard, where the rabbi of
Shtefanesht and his officials were stopping . . . I went there
to take in a *Minchah* service.

"Young as I was at the time, I was seized by a sort of holy awe as I listened to the ordinary weekday afternoon *Shemoneh Esreh*. They seemed like a breath of Paradise, which my mouth is not worthy of depicting—those delightful trills and that poured-out sweetness of the *Minchah Shemoneh Esreh*. I looked with envy at the little cantor—a little bit of a man, with a small white face, a little black beard, a semicircular tiny nose. It was Yossele Rosenblatt—his features, his figure and even his smile.

"When on Saturday morning, after the reading of the Torah, the holy rabbi was asked who was to be honored with the chanting of the *Mussaph* prayer, he pointed to the little man who had officiated at the afternoon service on the previous day. I stood beside him as he intoned the *Shemoneh Esreh* and felt as though I were chained to my place. The heavens seemed to open up. At the word '*Keser*'—a lightning bolt. At the phrase '*Mal'ochim Hamoney Maaloh*' something deliciously sweet was audible. And when the sentence '*Aye M'kom K'vodo l'haaritzo*' was reached—well don't ask me whether I knew where we were at that time. Over ten thousand human bodies stood as in a trance, enchanted, in a world in which angels were hovering about. One heard a kind of thunder followed by a 'still, small voice,' thirty stories up and then thirty stories down again—all in one breath. The little falsetto was working with machinelike efficiency. The vocal-cords spiralled and turned . . . I looked intently at his throat in order to find the orchestra or band that was apparently hidden in it. But there was nothing of the kind. Even Herman Wohl wasn't there.

"Such a person was that little cantor—an emanation from the Temple of Song, smothered in balm, adorned with spiritual delight, producing an elevation of the soul through the sweetness of the mouth that made pleasant melody in the purity of holiness. Yes it was Yossele in appearance, stature and voice.

"When Yossele arrived in America I recognized 'him' at once. The face was the same. Why it was right alongside of him that I had been standing. So I asked him: 'Don't you know me? I recognized *you*.' Smiling and laughing Yossele cleared up my mistake for me, for he was altogether 33 years old at the time of our first meeting. The man I had reference to must, therefore, have been his uncle Gedaliah, not *he*."

It was about this time that the gentile world of America, that was to take so much notice of him later on, began to learn about Yossele Rosenblatt's existence. The first non-Jewish periodicals to pay attention to him were the German language newspapers. One of them, after a concert of Jewish music given by him at the Washington Irving High School, compared his coloratura singing to that of the Italian bel canto school of vocal music.

A year later, in April 1916, non-Jewish America had another opportunity to make his acquaintance. The occasion was a concert given under the auspices of the Hadassah Organization at Albaugh's Theatre in Baltimore. The musical reviewers of the Baltimore Sun as well as of other periodicals ran out of adjectives in praise of him. One of the critics, commenting on "his wonderful rendition of the old ritualistic improvisations" stated: "One rarely hears so splendid an exposition of pure singing. The flexibility of the voice and Mr. Rosenblatt's remarkable control of it, his skillfully produced pianissimos and the color and variety of the musical sequences he presents are a thing apart." Such notices in the general press were, however, comparatively rare. My father's national celebrity was still a thing of the future.

The title of "king of cantors" was bestowed rather freely in the Yiddish press of the United States of those days. Even more than at the present exaggeration was an American characteristic; and Jews were here, as they were elsewhere, quick in assimilating the traits of their environment. There was not a precentor of the synagogue, not a "reader of prayers"

who officiated only on the High Holidays, however mediocre
his voice or musical ability, who did not claim to be the
greatest and best, the possessor, in short, of all the qualities
and virtues one would look for in an "emissary of the community" on such occasions. Yet when the Yiddish *"Wahrheit"*
on Sunday May 21, 1916, shortly after my father's 34th
birthday, in announcing a *Lag B'omer* concert at the Warsaw synagogue in New York, described him by that epithet,
it knew that it was not using that word in vain. The audience
of some 3000 people, that filled the house of worship on that
occasion, stood in the aisles, on benches and even on the steps
of the *Bema.* Thousands were turned away and the crowd
outside was so large and unruly that police reserves were
called to maintain order.

Meanwhile our family had moved again, this time only
half a block. In our new location we occupied the whole of a
four story private row-house. The additional space had become indispensable as the children were growing up. Besides, my father then cherished the plan of establishing a
school for cantors. On account of the war, which had cut off
the supply from Europe, there was a real shortage of *chazanim* in America. What became of the scheme eventually I
do not remember. The one thing certain is that many now
famous singers of the synagogue owed their first start in
their career to him, and that some, like Samuel Malavsky,
even boarded with him. He remained throughout his life a
friend and patron of men of talent and ability, and a loyal
colleague to all members of his profession.

His interest in the well-being of his fellow-cantors was but
one example of my father's sensitivity to public needs and
his espousal of all worthy Jewish causes, especially those that
had to do with the rehabilitation of Jewish religious life and
the national rebirth of the Jewish people. He gave expression to his intense love for Zion in his rendition of such
liturgical selections as *V'lirusholaim ircho* and the part of

the grace after meals that commences with the entreaty *Rachem no*. His life-long wish was to die in Palestine. Not that he did not like America. America was a wonderful country, a land of liberty, in which pogroms were not tolerated. He was proud of his American citizenship. But Palestine was the home of the Jewish people, and of the religion of the one God. Moses wanted to go there to die. That was why he, Josef Rosenblatt, also desired to end his life on its sacred soil.

The Zionist movement, which aimed to give practical realization to the longing voiced in the prayers of the synagogue for Israel's return to Zion, struck a very responsive chord in my father's heart. Most of all did he feel drawn to that phase of it which strove to rebuild the Jewish national home in the spirit of Jewry's religious traditions. I still have a vivid recollection of the day when my father took me to the headquarters of the Mizrachi Organization of America that had just then been opened up on Second Avenue, and introduced me to Rabbi Judah L. Fishman (Maimon), later to become the first Minister of Religion in the Government of Israel, who had then been exiled by the Turks from his home in Palestine.

The acquaintance of Rabbi Meir Berlin, the builder of the American Mizrachi, I had made the year previous. My father always had a high regard for this gifted man whom he had come to know in Hamburg in the year 1911 when the office of the world Mizrachi was opened there.

Another Mizrachi leader, whom he admired greatly, was Wolf Gold. He considered him the foremost orator among the Yiddish-speaking members of the rabbinate, just as he looked upon Dr. Stephen S. Wise as the first tribune of the Jewish people among those who used English as their medium. "To judge by the veneration with which this representative of Reform Judaism in the American pulpit spoke of Jewish tradition," my father would often remark, "one would imagine that he was the most orthodox of the orthodox."

To this day I marvel at the critical sense which a person like my father, who had had no training whatever in rhetoric and had received no formal education in any language, displayed in his estimate of speakers and his pithy manner of characterizing their performance. There was a certain preacher, an otherwise eloquent man, who had the habit of rising on his tiptoes when he delivered his discourses. Asked for his opinion about the man's oratorical ability one time, my father replied, "It seems to me that he danced his sermon" (Er hot obgetanzt a Droshe). His critique of another pulpiteer, who was subject to frequent coughing spells, was that he had coughed up a discourse (Er hot obgehusst a Droshe).

These facetious references to externals must not be construed as blindness to inner values or failure to recognize the worth of the contents of a message in spite of a defective delivery. Far from it. My father entertained the highest reverence for the gentlemen of the cloth. He would never turn down a request made of him by a member of the clergy. Especially devoted was he to the pedigreed descendants of the *Chassidic* saints, many of whom benefited materially from the concerts that he gave on their behalf. There was hardly a *Chassidic* rabbi in the United States, to whatever dynasty he might have belonged, who was not at one time or another the recipient of my father's favors.

On November 21, 1916, the aged Emperor Francis Joseph I of Austria, which was on the side of Germany in the World War, passed away. The United States was at that time still a neutral, and, when several months later she did enter the fray, the Austrian monarchy was not her chief enemy. However it be, in the fall of 1916 there was as yet nothing unpatriotic about public expressions of sorrow on the part of his former subjects over the death of a genial monarch who had on numerous occasions shown himself to be a friend of the Jews. And so a memorial meeting was arranged at

Cooper Union by Jewish New Yorkers of Austro-Hungarian provenance, and Yossele Rosenblatt was invited to chant the *El Mole Rachamim* in honor of his departed sovereign.

A crowd of some 10,000 persons stormed the great hall and fifteen policemen had their hands full in a vain attempt to separate those that had tickets from those who had not. "Inside," reported one of New York's dailies, "Mr. Rosenblatt, who had a closer connection with the dead emperor than many, stood while there was read a letter to him from Francis Joseph complimenting him on a song he had written in eulogy of the Emperor on his 80th birthday. Then Mr. Rosenblatt and his chorus sang the song, and it took a great deal of exhortation from the chairman and the ushers to suppress the handclapping—for this was a memorial meeting."

Several months rolled by. Then, one evening in February of the year 1917, a very stormy meeting was held by the board of directors of the First Hungarian Congregation Ohab Zedek. Tempers flew high as dignitaries present, most of them hard-headed businessmen accustomed to dealing with their employees in an arbitrary manner, accused each other of responsibility for what had happened. The cause of the tempest was Yossele Rosenblatt's resignation from Ohab Zedek. He had concluded a deal whereby he was to receive, for chanting the services on the High Holidays alone, the sum of $6,000—two and a half times as much as the total salary Ohab Zedek was paying him for an entire year. Besides that, he would be free for the rest of the twelve months to do as he pleased. This was made absolutely clear in the ad published in the Jewish Morning Journal.

"It is all your fault," one board member berated the chairman of the religious service committee. "You should have granted Yossele the increase he asked for. It wasn't so much and he was well worth it to us. Now we may jolly well go whistle."

"Do you really think he will go through with the deal?"

broke in a trustee. "Maybe it's just a ruse, a trick whereby
he hopes to extract from us what the traffic will bear. If I
know Yossele Rosenblatt, he is not going to officiate in a
hall on the *Yomim Noroim,* whatever the remuneration
may be. And what synagogue could afford to pay him the
price of $6,000 for just three days?"

"I am not so sure," commented a third. *"Die Noth bricht
Eisen.* Necessity has forced many a man to break with his
principles. Besides I have it on good authority that the contract with Felshin is genuine. I have spoken to people who
have seen it. At all events I wouldn't take chances on it's
being a phoney. There is too much at stake for the congregation."

"Well, what would you advise us to do?" asked several
of the congregational leaders. "How do you propose to stop
him, if what you say is correct? Will Uri Felshin, who is not
in this game just for the glory of it, release him merely because we, the Ohab Zedek, make the request?"

"I dare him," one of the officers joined in the debate,
"give up a synagogue like our for the sake of a dance hall,
and you'll see what we will do to him. We will come out in
the press. We will tear that mask of piety from his face. All
the world will then know that his religiosity was only a sham,
a means of pulling the wool over people's eyes."

"Now, let us not get excited," cautioned one of the calmer
spirits. "Let us not allow our passions to run away with us.
Vilifying Reb Yossele, who is so universally beloved and
has friends in the press who would take his part, is not going
to do us any good. There must be other ways of solving
this problem."

"Do you imply perhaps that we should bow our heads to
a mere cantor, we the Ohab Zedek, the leading orthodox
congregation in America, by yielding to his exorbitant demands? And suppose he asks us for $6,000 a year? Shall we

empty out our treasury and give it to him? And maybe even that will not satisfy him."

"No, gentlemen. You have me all wrong. No such thing ever entered my mind. My plan is that we request our rabbi, Dr. Klein, to take a hand in the matter. I know Yossele has a great deal of respect for him. I am sure Dr. Klein will set him straight."

Some of the board members quizzically shook their heads. Nevertheless the majority thought the plan was at least worth a trial and they voted accordingly.

The next day my father received a call from Dr. Klein and he immediately repaired to the latter's home. "Reb Yossele," said the patriarch, after greeting my father warmly, in his friendly, paternal manner, "I have something very personal to speak to you about. I would have hesitated had I not known the kind of man you are. About that contract you made for the coming High Holidays, are you sure that it would be befitting a *chazan* of your calibre and reputation?"

"Believe me, Dr. Klein. I didn't want it and my heart isn't in it. I would much rather serve a congregation like Ohab Zedek. But they simply forced me to take this step. The cost of living has gone up. My needs have increased. The congregation can afford to pay me more than it does. A portion of what is donated on the High Holidays alone would take care of it. Yet they have consistently refused to augment my salary."

"True, you have not been treated as you deserved, Reb Yossele. But money isn't everything," replied Dr. Klein. "Suppose you will pocket the $6,000. Then what? You will be like certain other individuals who possess the ability to sing, a *chazan* without an *Amud,* a sort of gypsy. People won't think of you anymore the way they used to. You won't be the same Yossele."

"It isn't only that, Dr. Klein," retorted my father. "As far as salary is concerned, I think a happy medium could be struck and I am not so greedy for money as to hold out on account of a few dollars more or less. What I resent most— it is positively an outrage—is that every time I officiate outside of the Ohab Zedek they not only deduct the $50 a week they are paying me but fine me another $50 besides. How will I ever be able to get ahead under such conditions?"

"If that is the chief bone of contention between you and the congregation, I believe it can be ironed out. I myself will see to it. As for the rest, you must have a little faith in God."

Dr. Klein was as good as his word. In return for cancelling his agreement with Rabbi Felshin, the congregation awarded my father a new contract for the next three years with an increase in salary from $2,400 to $2,600 per annum. This was afterwards raised to $6,000 and later to $10,000. It was furthermore stipulated that he was to officiate only twice a month instead of every week. That too was to be commuted in the end to one service a month on the Sabbath announcing the new moon. Most important, however, was the elimination of the penalty deductions for services rendered outside of Ohab Zedek. He was now free to keep for himself all the profits he would reap by his talents without giving an accounting to anyone.

18

For the War Sufferers

Dr. Klein's parting words to my father, on the day on which he had that intimate talk with him, had been that he should not be concerned about the future. "God will help." And

God did help, and very soon. A world catastrophe, that brought destruction and ruin to countless of his fellowmen, was indirectly the catalytic agent responsible for Yossele Rosenblatt's advancement. On the month after my father's differences with the Ohab Zedek had been patched up, President Wilson, with American patience at an end, declared war on Germany. With the entrance of the United States into the fray the European war reached global proportions, and the needs for the relief of its Jewish victims were greatly increased. It was particularly in Eastern Europe, where millions of Jews had been dislocated, that suffering was intense and the sums required to sustain life were enormous.

The only segment of Jewry the unfortunates could look to for help was that in the United States. It was to them that Israel Zangwill of England directed the appeal:

> "Jews of the great Republic,
> Clasped to her mother breast,
> Nestling so warm and peaceful
> Within that bosom blest,
> Turn to our tortured Europe,
> Hark to the myriad moan
> Of parched lips white with hunger
> That stiffen as they groan,
> And remember in these wan creatures
> Runs the blood that is your own."

But the amounts asked were fantastically high. No Jewish community had ever been requested to donate sums even remotely approximating them. How were the hearts of the Jewish masses of America, until then totally unaccustomed to such efforts at generosity, to be reached so that they would make the unusual exertions required of them? What would be the most effective means of making known to those who were so far removed from the scenes of horror all the woe and sorrow of their coreligionists living on the other side of the Atlantic?

Various schemes were proposed for achieving the stagger-
ing goal. One of them was to involve my father in a very
tangible and concrete manner. The author and promoter of
the plan was a modest insurance agent who happened to be
a member of the Ohab Zedek Congregation.

In the opinion of Morris Engelman there was no more direct road to the Jewish heart than the prayers of the synagogue. It was this tie that had kept alive among Jews the
feeling of the unity of their race, of their common aspira-
tions and destiny. Now no man had in his estimation interpreted these prayers better than Yossele Rosenblatt. When,
for example, he sang his *Acheinu Kol Beis Yisroel,* it would
move a stone. Couldn't this talent be utilized in bringing
about large gatherings of Jews wherever there were sizable
Jewish communities in order to appeal to them through song
and speech? Yes, a concert tour of America under the auspices of the Central Relief Committee, with Yossele Rosenblatt as the chief attraction, could not fail.

The voluble, restless, persuasive Mr. Engelman broached
the plan to Reb Yossele to enlist his cooperation. The idea
had a great deal of appeal for my father, who was eager to be
of help to his suffering brethren. However he was skeptical
about the success of the venture. He had sung in synagogues
that were packed to the ceilings. But to fill up a place like
the Hippodrome, which Mr. Engelman thought of engaging,
took a great many people, and it would require a lot of
promoting to entice them there. Could Mr. Engelman afford
the risk? Did he have enough experience with the mechanics
of such an undertaking to make a go of it? Who would be
his backers to underwrite a possible deficit?

"Leave that to me," said the optimistic, enthusiastic Mr.
Engelman. "I know whom to approach." And so after having gotten my father's consent, he went to the officers of the
Central Relief Committee and worked on them until they
too were convinced. What would they lose? If the first ex-

periment turned out successful, it would be an incentive for successes to follow. If not, they could drop the scheme before they had sunk too much in it. So they too gave their acquiescence and the groundwork was laid for the first concert in New York's Hippodrome, on Sunday, May 6th. What happened when that date came around is a matter of history.

Every seat in the giant playhouse was occupied. The audience included not only the Jewish rank and file, but also a very goodly representation of the moneyed aristocracy and the intelligentsia of New York Jewry, leaders of business and industry, professional men and public officials, in addition to the most distinguished members of the rabbinate.

The chairman of the evening was the philanthropist Nathan Straus. The addresses were delivered by Judge Otto Rosalsky and by the popular Jewish pulpiteer Zevi Masliansky. A total of $240,000 was realized.

But the drawing-card, that had in the opinion of most observers brought the crowd together, the sugar-coating that made the pill palatable, was the musical program. "JEWISH MUSIC STIRS 6,000 IN HIPPODROME" read the headline of an English weekly, and a Yiddish daily commented, "Yossele Rosenblatt entranced the audience with his magnificent voice and his masterful rendition of the prayers *Elokay Neshomoh, Velirusholayim, Atto Yotzarto, Uv'nucho Yomar* and *Zorea Zedokos.*"

And how did the non-Jews who were in the audience react? "Some of us," observed the critic of one musical magazine, "had misgivings as to the interest-sustaining qualities of a full Jewish liturgical program. Three hours later we left the Hippodrome converted. Cantor Rosenblatt is quite deserving of the advance reports which have filtered into music circles . . ."

"Israel's music finds a powerful interpreter in him. What Ernest Bloch has accomplished in the symphonic glorification of Hebrew tradition, Rosenblatt, this unique composer of the Temple, may achieve in spreading abroad the propaganda of his ancient art and belief."

Most lavish and generous in their praise were the German-language newspapers, the New Yorker Staatszeitung and the New Yorker Herold. "Everything that goes into the making of the cultivated Italian opera singer," observed the former, "is to be found in Rosenblatt's singing. . . . However impressive other cantors may be in their performance, from the standpoint of the art of singing Yossele Rosenblatt has hardly a rival among them." The New Yorker Herold said, among other things: "Rosenblatt is in his stature insignificant and hardly looks like a tenor in his long full brown beard. But when he begins to sing, when he ascends to the high notes, especially when he causes his headtones and the extraordinary trills of his Jewish music to be heard, this little man assumes the proportions of a giant who compels his audience to listen with amazement and can even make them weep."

The Hippodrome success exceeded all expectations. Mr. Engelman had won his first round. But what assurance was there that equal efforts put forth in the provinces would produce similar results? After all the Jewish potential of New York was without parallel. In a community of more than a million Jews getting together a crowd of 6,000 was comparatively easy. Would it be possible to repeat this performance in Chicago and Philadelphia and the small centers with Jewish populations nowhere near that of the metropolis?

Mr. Engelman was confident. During the summer that followed the initial undertaking at the Hippodrome, he made all the arrangements for the concerts to be given during the fall in the large Jewish communities of America outside of New York. He cleared the dates with the Ohab Zedek Congregation and immediately after the Jewish holidays the tour began.

A visit to the Jewish provincial centers of America was no

novelty for my father any more. He had officiated in Cleveland. He had been as far West as Omaha and St. Louis. This tour, however, was different from his previous jaunts across the wide open spaces of the U.S.—different in its extent and magnitude, in the lavish manner in which it was publicized and the nature of the performances.

The first stop was Philadelphia. The impression of his appearance at that city's Metropolitan Opera House was such that he had to promise to return for a *Chanukah* concert at the Arch Street Theatre. When he had finished singing at that second visit, men, it is related, emptied their pockets and women pulled the rings off their fingers and threw them into the baskets that were passed around.

In Scranton, his next station, the inclemency of the weather did not in the slightest affect the attendance at the Strand Theatre.

The Toronto Mail and Empire deplored the absence of gentile music lovers who, it said, "missed a rare musical treat at Massey Hall."

Buffalo Jewry was moved as deeply by his generosity as it was fascinated by his music. "As Yossele Rosenblatt warbled like a canary at the words 'child of my playing,' it seemed to me," testified a dignified old gentleman, "as though a child in distress, a little orphan, were pleading imploringly for a piece of bread."

"It is also worth noting," so ends the report of his Buffalo appearance, "that Yossele Rosenblatt is not greedy for money, but that he shares the beautiful gift that God has given him as a philanthropist divides his riches with his Jewish brethren. In addition thereto he is the first to make a sizable contribution from his pocket at every relief collection."

This freedom from greed on the part of my father was all the more remarkable when one considers the perpetual need in which he stood for money. Jacob M. Singer of Philadelphia, who together with Max Romm managed his concerts in the East when he sang for the war sufferers, related the following incident which was quite characteristic of my father's customary behavior. It happened after the first engagement they secured for him in Philadelphia. He had been promised $100 as compensation for his services. When the money was handed him, he took out of the wad of bills a ten dollar bank note and gave it to Mr. Romm. "What's that for?" asked the manager. "That's for the 'cut' you had made of the photo I had sent you. It was my face, wasn't it? Hence it is my obligation to pay for it." One of my father's passions —one of the few vanities he had—was to have himself photographed.

Not many years later, Mr. Singer recalls, my father received from him and Mr. Romm as much as $1500 for one engagement. He was happiest when an enterprise proved successful and the share that fell to the managers was large. The more they profited, the more was he pleased. On the other hand, if for one reason or another an undertaking did not turn out in accordance with the expectations, he did not insist upon his due according to the terms of the contract, but was most indulgent and cooperative with the unsuccessful sponsors.

Once a concert was scheduled at one of the Brooklyn theatres for the benefit of the Peretz School of the Jewish National Workers' Alliance. The place was filled to capacity but the sale of tickets had not produced enough revenue to pay the artists who had been engaged. When their turn on the program arrived, the violinist and the woman opera singer refused to appear on the stage until they had been paid in full. My father, on the other hand, did his part without a word of protest or unkindness. He gave the audience all he had and was recalled several times for encores.

At the conclusion of the performance the chairman went up to him and said: "Reb Yossele, we lost money on this venture and didn't have enough cash on hand to pay everybody. The others we were compelled to compensate immediately. May I ask you to be patient and wait till tomorrow when I will bring you what we owe you." My father, so this informant narrates, gave him that benign look of his, and said: "Well, when a man puts it that way, I have to take his word for it," and therewith he left for home as cheerfully as he had come. He received the remuneration agreed upon the next day, to be sure, but he had taken a chance, for his sponsors might have defaulted.

Liberality was bred in my father's nature. But neither those who commented on it nor my father himself had any conception of the proportions that his generosity towards his benighted brethren could reach. As it turned out, the royalties of 5% produced for the twelve months of the year 1918 by his recording for the Victor Company of *Eili, Eili,* the proceeds of which he had dedicated to the Jewish War Sufferers, totaled no less than $10,000. A photograph of the check of $2400 for the first installment was published in the Jewish Daily Forward. And this was not his only direct contribution to the great cause.

Thus my father's mission of mercy on behalf of the Jewish victims of the World War continued. On Sunday, February 3rd he was in Newark, and on Saturday night, February 16th at Camp Gordon, Georgia. On March 6th he appeared in Milwaukee and on March 10th in Kansas City. In between he participated with his colleagues of the Jewish Cantors' Association in a concert at the 14th Street armory in New York.

The tour came to its official close with a highly successful recital at the Monument National in Montreal on May 6th. The most important of all his appearances, however, important because it marked *the* turning point in his career, was the one in Chicago on March 17th. It was the concert he gave in the Auditorium Theatre of that metropolis of the West that brought him fame and fortune and caused his name to become known throughout the gentile as well as the Jewish world. And it wasn't due to the fact that his performance there was so very much superior to the account he had given of himself elsewhere. The concert was, to be sure, well publicized. In addition to the regular paid advertisements and announcements in the press, special feature articles were published in the Jewish periodicals. They played up Yossele Rosenblatt's voice. They dwelt on the excellence of his phonograph recordings. They spoke of his popularity and the magic of his name.

The result was that the affair was very well patronized. "Long before the concert actually began," reported the Chicago (Yiddish) Courier, "the Auditorium was overcrowded. Hundreds were compelled to turn back disappointed, and scores who were ready to pay as much as ten dollars for a seat in the gallery were unable to obtain it. The streets around the theatre were black with people who for hours had been streaming from all corners of the city towards the Auditorium. Jews came by streetcars, elevated trains and automobiles. From the number of autos that arrived at the theatre one might have thought that the socialites of the city were coming to attend a gala performance of the opera."

19

$1,000 a Night to Sing in Opera

The artistic success my father scored in Chicago was a real achievement in his role as a *chazan*. In the long run, however, it would have meant but little to him. Like his previous triumphs, it would have left the general tenor of his life undisturbed, were it not for an incident that turned the entire tide of his fortunes. That incident was the fact that seated in a box in the theater, listening to him was Cleofonte Campanini, the General Director of the famous Chicago Opera Association. Campanini's presence was not entirely accidental. He had come at the invitation of Mr. S. Neveleff, the Chicago Jewish communal worker, who had arranged the affair. The discoverer and sponsor of such outstanding opera stars as Rosa Raisa and Amelita Galli-Curci, Campanini was constantly looking around for new talent with which to adorn the personnel of his company. He was rarely mistaken in his appraisal of a voice, and once he made a discovery, he would not rest until he had added his find to the roster of his virtuosos. The voice as well as the unusual figure of the singer on the platform before him attracted the great impresario. He could envisage him in certain roles for which, without any change in appearance, he would be a natural. As soon as the concert was over, he requested an introduction and came straight to the point.

"Mr. Rosenblatt, I had the pleasure of hearing you sing this evening and I was deeply impressed with your voice. I feel fully convinced that you have the makings of a very great opera singer and would, therefore, like to engage you for my company, to play the role of Eleazar in Halévy's 'La Juive.' Your fee will be $1,000 for each performance, which I trust will be satisfactory."

My father was completely taken aback. Not in his wildest imaginings had he thought that his talents could carry him to such heights. The offer was extremely tempting. It meant fortune, fame, admiration, applause, new audiences, new worlds to conquer—all the things an artist dreams about. For a moment he was carried away, ready to yield. But very soon the incongruity of a man like himself playing a part in an opera struck him. And an inner voice said to him "Yossele, don't do it. Do not give up the *Amud* for the opera stage." The words of his father, uttered a quarter of a cen-

tury earlier, when Dr. Bloch of Vienna had proposed training him for the opera, echoed in his mind. "He was born for
the *Amud,* and at the *Amud* he will remain!"

Campanini, sensing the conflict by which my father was
torn, to reassure him and put him at ease, continued: "There
is no reason for you to be embarrassed, Mr. Rosenblatt,
and certainly none to be frightened. Your joining my company will not necessitate your giving up your religious principles. You are free to remain the devout Jew you have always been, and as for your beard, there will be no need for
you to touch it. I will assign to you roles that will enable
you to appear as you are."

As my father still seemed unconvinced, he added: "And
if you feel uncomfortable about having gentile women as
your singing partners, it can be arranged that your associates
on the stage be Jewish ladies like Rosa Raisa and Alma
Gluck . . . Furthermore you may at my expense stop at
hotels where kosher food will be prepared for you. And if
that isn't sufficient, I will have it stipulated in your contract
that you are not to appear on Saturdays and Jewish holidays
. . . anything you want. I am prepared immediately to draw
up an agreement for seventeen performances a year at $1,000
per engagement, totalling $17,000 besides travel expenses."

My father listened until Mr. Campanini had finished.
Then he replied with his characteristic modesty:

"As far as I personally am concerned your proposal is quite
acceptable. We could, I imagine, work out a modus operandi
on the basis of the conditions outlined. But I am not entirely
my own master. My contract with the Ohab Zedek Congregation is not due to expire until two years from now, and I
am not, Mr. Campanini, the kind of person that would break
his plighted word."

This imaginary obstacle that he held out as a possibility
was of my father's own making. He presented it in order not
to give an immediate rebuff to so generous an offer made in

such good faith. For as far as the leaders of the Ohab Zedek Congregation were concerned, it is doubtful whether they would have raised objections, had he been satisfied. They would probably have been very proud to have as their cantor a man whose gifts were recognized by the highest musical authorities. It was he himself who felt from the start that he could never go through with the project.

However Campanini was not in the habit of giving up so easily. If all that stood between Josef Rosenblatt and his engagement for such roles as that of Eleazar in "La Juive" was the Ohab Zedek Congregation, he figured, it should not be difficult to overcome the impediment. And so he immediately dictated to his stenographer the letter addressed to the president of the Ohab Zedek Congregation, in which, contrary to the later popular distortion of the facts, he made all the concessions to my father's religious scruples enumerated above.

CHICAGO OPERA ASSOCIATION
(Incorporated)
Auditorium Theatre
Chicago

Cleofonte Campanini
General Director

Herbert M. Johnson
Business Comptroller

March 21st, 1918

Mr. Morris Newman,
President, First Hung. Congregation,
Ohab Zedek,
18-22 West 116th Street,
New York City.

Dear Sir:

I heard Mr. Rosenblatt during his recent stay in Chicago and was so impressed with his voice and his art of singing that I made him an offer to sing, with the Chicago Grand Opera Company, the part of Eleazar, in the opera THE JEWESS, by Halévy.

I suppose the story of the opera is familiar to you. It is a glorification of the Jewish religion, and the role of the Jewess will
be sung by Rosa Raisa, who is a Jewess, a native of Odessa.

I offered Mr. Rosenblatt three performances in Chicago, with
an option of an additional one in New York and an additional
one in Boston, each to take place two to three weeks apart. He
would have to be in Chicago only one week for rehearsals prior
to the first performance. For all other performances he would
only have to come to Chicago for each performance. His salary
for each performance would be one thousand ($1,000) dollars
and railroad fares to and from Chicago.

Mr. Rosenblatt personally has agreed to this proposition,
under the condition that his congregation will allow him to
accept. There will be no performances for him on Friday or
Saturday, nor would he, in any way, have to take off or cut his
beard, and there will be nothing in the performances, or his
appearances upon the operatic stage that would in any way be
a reflection upon the Orthodox Jewish faith. Mr. Rosenblatt
has also given us an option on his services for the season of
1919/1920.

I expect Mr. Rosenblatt to make a great success in opera, as
he did in his concert appearance here.

Hoping to have a favorable answer at your early convenience, I am,

Yours very truly,
Cleofonte Campanini
General Director

The publication of Campanini's letter created a sensation
not only in the Jewish but also the non-Jewish world. Never
in history had it happened that a person so thoroughly unprepared as my father was for the opera stage, and a pious
singer of the synagogue besides, should have been caught up
so eagerly and been given so amazing an offer for a single
role. For a moment the war and its horrors were forgotten,
as Jews as well as non-Jews went agog over the cantor who
had overnight reached the highest rungs of the ladder of

musical art. But even more sensational than the opera director's offer was the refusal of it by the president of the congregation at the instigation of him to whom it was made.

"Your letter of March 21st," wrote Mr. Newman in his official reply to Mr. Campanini, "in which you express your desire to have the services of the Rev. Mr. Rosenblatt for the Chicago grand opera, 'The Jewess,' was before our board of trustees. Our board agrees with you that there is no objection to this opera from a Jewish standpoint, but we feel that the Rev. Mr. Rosenblatt's sacred position in the synagogue does not permit him to enter the operatic stage.

"We have, however, no objections to his singing at concerts, whether sacred or otherwise. We are greatly pleased to learn that you were impressed with his voice and art of singing, and we wish to assure you that we regret most sincerely our inability to comply with your request in this instance.

"However, we hope that your future requests will be of a nature that they will meet with the entire approval of our board of trustees."

The effect produced by this last letter was electrifying. From Maine to Florida, from New York to the West Coast the Jewish as well as the non-Jewish press carried the story of the cantor who had refused $1,000 a performance to sing in the opera on purely religious grounds. "Some Courage" was the title of an article in the Jewish Monitor of Fort Worth, Texas, commenting upon the deed. "If what we read is true, this man is a true Maccabean. We have heard of . . . cantors who have given up their profession because of financial strain; this is the first time that we have heard of a refusal of such an offer on the ground that it would interfere with religious duties."

The Yiddish humorous weekly Der Groisse Kundess (The Big Stick) of New York featured a cartoon of my father in his silk hat running away from a siren in a gossamer gown called Grand Opera who was pursuing him. "Come, Yossele," she beckons, " a thousand dollars a night." But Yossele, with his prayerbook in hand, emitting the martyr's cry of "Shema Israel," heads straight for the synagogue.

The Jewish journalist, L. Jach, was inspired to indite a poem in my father's honor entitled "Chazanuth and Opera."

Another writer devoted an entire dissertation to him under the heading of "Art and Money." "It is hard to believe," he wrote. "Money has on account of the Jew's insecurity so often played a dominant role in Jewish life" that few have been able to withstand its allure. "It is, therefore, a deep source of satisfaction to know that the non-Jewish world will now get the surprise of its life when it notes that a traditional, orthodox Jew had the courage not to permit his head to be turned by money, fame, success, big advertisements and favorable reviews in all important newspapers, but instead threw away an opportunity that so many are daily seeking."

The musical weekly "Musical America" in its issue of June 22, 1918 commented: "In these days of stern materialism it seems almost incomprehensible that any one would so recklessly discard gold and glory for a belief, a mere tradition. Nevertheless such was the case with Cantor Rosenblatt. Money holds no charm for this man in the face of faith and principle."

The news of how Yossele Rosenblatt had sanctified the name of God and of the Jewish people leaped across the Atlantic Ocean to England and Germany. "Some Chazan" was the caption of an article in the London Jewish World. After dwelling on his rejection of the offer to sing in the opera and foregoing a fee of $6,000 for the High Holidays in order to officiate for much less in his own synagogue the writer asks: "How many *Chazanim* are there with such a record? We doubt if there ever has been another since the first *Chazan* was known."

Perhaps the best summary of the significance of my

father's act of renunciation was that contained in the obser-
vations of the American Jewish Chronicle. "Though Cantor
Rosenblatt," its editorial stated, "is by no means a rich man,
he refused the offer of a thousand dollars a week made to
him by the manager of the Chicago Opera Company, because he thought that his sacred duties as a cantor are in-
compatible with those of an opera singer. By refusing to accept this generous offer, Mr. Rosenblatt has not only taken
an attitude which is much credit to himself, but he has also
conformed with the pride of the synagogue. Cantor Rosenblatt has proven once more that one is not a cantor just because one could not become an opera singer and that there
still are singers in Israel who, devoted to their religious duties, appreciate their sacred position more than wealth and
worldly fame. Cantor Rosenblatt has upheld the honor of
the American synagogue and what he has done is really *Kiddush ha'shem*. Needless to say, he has done a great service to
his own colleagues by strengthening their position."

Although the letter of Mr. Campanini had stated in unmistakable terms that by joining the Chicago Opera Company my father was not to be called upon to violate any of
his religious principles such as removing his beard or appearing on the Sabbath or the Jewish holidays, the impression got around that it was the apprehension of these even-
tualities that prompted his rejection. In reality it was not so
at all. My father trusted Campanini well enough. A person of
his calibre could be relied upon to live up to his promises.
The objection was more deep-seated. It was that the entire
atmosphere of the opera—its pantomime, its make-up and
make-believe, the mingling of the sexes—was out of character
with his type of life and with his calling. He could not see
himself, the sincere and earnest pleader for "sanctification by
God's commandments" as a Pagliacci, a playboy. He might
perhaps, in the course of time, have succeeded in shaking off
the onus of his past and in getting used to this completely

new mode of existence. Others had done it, apparently without too much difficulty. But his instincts pulled him in the opposite direction. His entire being rebelled against such a course. He knew very little about romantic love, and to embrace a strange made-up woman who was not his own legally wedded mate, even as an act, was unthinkable to him.

He could not tell this to the gentile world for fear of not being understood. All that he felt free to state for non-Jewish consumption was that he "did not think it dignified for a cantor of the orthodox faith to appear on the stage." But why should it not have been dignified? Isn't the opera the aristocrat of the theatre, the noblest form of entertainment, the type that is freest from the shortcomings with which the members of the acting profession are usually charged? That was something that was never made quite clear to the non-Jews. It was only to Jewish interviewers that my father revealed the reasons that had actually motivated him.

"Tell me, Reb Yossele," asked S. Dingoll of the Jewish Daily News, "why really did you reject Campanini's proposal? After all a thousand dollars a night isn't a sum to be lightly dismissed . . . and your beard would not have had to be touched . . . and 'Eleazar' is such a beautiful, moving role, just made to order for a Jew."

My father went to his desk and pulled out from one of the drawers a photograph. "Do you see this picture?" he said. "It is that of Reb Joel David Strashunsky, the Vilner Baalebeisel. As long as he served as cantor of the great synagogue of the Jewish community of Vilna, he had his voice, greatness, fame. He wanted for nothing. Once, however, he went away to *them* . . . sang for a countess or whoever it was . . . yes, sang *Kol Nidrei* for her, and didn't notice when his cap fell off his head—or somebody pulled it off—and so he sang *Kol Nidrei* bareheaded, how did he end? . . . He lost his voice and then his reason, and wound up by dying a stranger

among strangers sans voice, sans honor, sans a congregation
. . . an alien Joel David!"

Then he continued: "You know, there is no alibi that
would completely satisfy the Orthodox Jewish world. Our
younger generation may not understand this. It is true that
I was granted the privilege of observing my Sabbath and that
my beard would have been left intact. All good and fine! But
the Jews who are bound to the synagogue cannot come to
terms with the opera. There is a barrier that divides them,
that separates them from each other. It cannot be expressed
in so many words. One has to feel it.

"Even if my congregation had permitted it, and though I
felt flattered by the offer and for a moment I was inclined to
yield, I could never have gotten myself to carry out such an
impulse. A voice within said to me: 'Don't go! The path is
fraught with danger.' "

"You may assure the readers of the Jewish Morning Journal," he said to another interviewer, "that I will never deviate
from my ideal, even for millions. I never cared for monetary success, and I have certainly no desire to obtain glory for
myself at the hands of aristocratic non-Jews who might come
to the opera to see for themselves how a Jew forsakes his
God and forswears his religion and his people on account of
money. When I am warmly received by the officials of my
congregation, I value it more highly than thousands of dollars and the applause and flowers that might be showered
upon me on the stage. If I am destined to increase my earnings and be deserving of emoluments, it may as well be as a
Jew, in the capacity of a cantor of the synagogue. It is possible to reap in that field the same renown that Caruso
achieved in the world at large as star of the opera. It is high
time for Jews to begin to appreciate their own artists and
develop their own art."

When I think, in retrospect, of my father's decision, in

spite of all the blandishments of the opera, to remain the
precentor of the synagogue, it seems to me to have been
dictated by the highest wisdom. It is, of course, difficult to
say whether he would have met with the fate of the Vilner
Baalebeisel. He might equally well have turned out to be
the great opera singer for which, in Campanini's opinion,
he showed so much promise. One thing is certain, however.
He would never have been as unique in that field as he was
as a *chazan*. Of opera singers of ability the world had a
plenitude. Cantors of the type of Yossele Rosenblatt, however, were few in number.

It must not be thought now that his firm resolve to remain loyal to his first calling and dedicate his talents to his
own people made my father turn his back upon the rest of
the world to become a musical recluse. On the contrary, his
gesture of renunciation served only to enhance his reputation
and to cause his services to be more in demand than theretofore.

Two days after Mr. Campanini had paid him the extraordinary compliment of asking him to sing for the Chicago
opera, he was invited to entertain the soldiers at Camp
Grant in Rockford, Illinois. He was proud of the fact that he
was announced not as the "Russian" or "German" but as
"the Jewish tenor." About a month after the sensational
news of the Campanini offer and its rejection had spread
throughout the country, he was selected from among all Jewish cantors then in America to lend tone to a monster Jewish
patriotic meeting held on behalf of the Liberty Loan at
Cooper Union. A picture of him purchasing a liberty bond
from Judge Aaron Levy in the presence of "some of the best
citizens of the East Side" was featured in one of New York's
great dailies.

A week later he was heard performing on the steps of the
New York Public Library on 42nd Street and Fifth Avenue
on behalf of the War Savings Stamp campaign. A crowd

running into tens of thousands, composed of non-Jews as well as Jews, assembled to hear him. When he had finished singing the Star Spangled Banner, the audience was so vociferous in its applause that he had to repeat it. Among the artists present was the great Caruso, and when my father concluded the next number, which was *Eili, Eili,* with the word *"Echod,"* the king of operatic tenors was so moved that he came up to him and kissed him. Cries of "bravo" greeted the promise by the chairman Michael Kley to invite Mr. Rosenblatt to sing again. And he did indeed appear for the same cause in City Hall Park at the special request of Mayor Hylan, to whom he later dedicated a patriotic song for which he had written the music. He gloried in the opportunity to do his bit for his adopted country and it mattered not where, whether it was the Hippodrome, an armory or even a street corner. His loyalty to America won the recognition of all representatives of the government who came in contact with him. "You are the greatest asset the Jewish community has in New York" was the tribute paid to him after one of the patriotic functions to which he had lent his talents.

My father's renunciation of the opera was not a complete loss financially either. Paradoxical as it may seem this was one instance in which adherence to principle proved rewarding. The mere compliment paid him by Campanini caused his earning capacity to sky-rocket. Overnight his fees for concerts doubled, as managers vied with each other to secure his services. The very same people, who, for all their admiration of him as a cantor previously, had compensated him for his efforts with hundreds, were now ready to shower him with thousands.

20

A Cantor on the Concert Stage

Hitherto his musical programs, even those rendered in theatres at non-religious functions, had consisted almost exclusively of Jewish liturgical music, most of it of his own composition. He might have thrown in a Jewish folk-song or an
aria from the Yiddish theatre here and there. Outside of that
and the national anthem, however, the selections from the
Hebrew prayerbook constituted the bulk of his repertoire.

Now that a Campanini had indicated that he was good
enough for the opera and he was going to give concerts to a
mixed clientele, he found it necessary to enrich his programs with specimens of the musical genius of other peo-
ples. He had had no formal training whatever for the singing
of operatic music or the recital of other non-Jewish melodies
appropriate for concert purposes, and there were only three
weeks within which to prepare himself for his debut in New
York's musical Holy of Holies, Carnegie Hall.

Someone else in his place might have been frightened by
the prospect of facing the critical audience and the still more
critical critics that were ready to pounce upon any novice
who presumed to invade the sanctuary of music without the
necessary qualifications, but not Yossele Rosenblatt. What he
lacked in technical schooling he made up in natural assets.
In addition to self-confidence, he possessed a voice that was
naturally placed correctly, so that what it took others years of
hard effort and conscientious study to acquire, he was able to
do almost automatically and without difficulty. He also had,
as has been mentioned previously, a perfect sense of pitch

and could read the most difficult score practically at sight. Furthermore he had made a careful study of the methods of tone production of that master of the opera Caruso, whom he greatly admired, by playing the latter's phonograph recordings. And so, with the help of a professional coach who taught him the style and manner of the presentation of operatic selections, he felt confident of being in fair enough shape to face his audience without becoming subject to mockery and derision.

The vocal teachers whose advice he sought and whose services he engaged over a period of years reflected the kaleidoscopic character of the American melting pot. There were Professor Duberta, a Dutchman, F. Rogers, a typical Yankee, H. Spielter, who came from Germany, and Espinal, of Spanish ancestry. None of them—so they all confessed—were able to do much to improve the beauty of his voice. Their contribution to my father's musical development lay chiefly in the finish and polish they gave him.

They were all well paid for their pains and proud of their pupil. Only one of his coaches, in my recollection, ever caused my father real trouble and annoyance. That was due no doubt to the fact that he was a frustrated, unsuccessful individual, whose only means of making a livelihood was to mulct, as long as his victims would permit, soft-hearted persons like my father who had once engaged his services.

As for the languages in which he was to sing, my father never had the time to learn enough about them to be able to understand what he was saying. Since I happened to be the linguist of the family, the task of teaching him the text was mine. He would enter the foreign words phonetically in Hebrew characters in a little black loose-leaf note-book that he always carried with him. I often wondered what would have happened if, by some fluke, he lost this sine-qua-non of his concert equipment, but that never came to pass.

While he was thus busily engaged in grooming himself for

his debut as a concert artist in the presence of the chief
potentates of the musical world, my father had his first opportunity to meet the Jewish operatic star who had been suggested as his singing partner had he consented to play the
role of Eleazar in "La Juive" for the Chicago Opera Company.

His encounter with the big, handsome, buxom, dark-
eyed Italian-trained Jewish contralto from Bialestok, Rosa
Raisa, took place quite by accident. The diva of Campanini's
Chicago Opera Company happened to be a guest at a musi-
cale in New York and expressed a desire, prior to her departure for the operatic season in Argentina, to visit a synagogue. She wanted particularly to hear Cantor Rosenblatt
conduct a service. Her wish was soon to be gratified, because
on the Sabbath of that same week my father was scheduled
to officiate in the synagogue of the *Chassidim* of Lubavitch,
on Watkins Street, Brownsville. The house of worship was
crowded as it had never been before. Despite the fact that
the price of admission was $1 and over, upward of 1,200 per-
sons had found their way inside, some without tickets of admission.

On Friday evening it was only when my father, assisted
by his choir under the direction of Herman Wohl, began to
sing, that order and quiet prevailed. The decorum was much
better on Saturday morning. But around eleven o'clock,
when the reading from the Torah had been concluded and
the *Mussaph* service was about to commence, there was
again a terrific hubbub and commotion among the worshippers. It was occasioned by the fact that Raisa, the star of the
Chicago opera, had just arrived at the door of the synagogue,
accompanied by a gentleman and three lady escorts and
asked to be permitted to hear Yossele Rosenblatt *daven Mussaph.* Under ordinary conditions the officials of the congregation would have felt highly honored to comply with a request
made by such a celebrity. But there wasn't an empty seat in

the house and even the aisles were blocked. However Miss Raisa wasn't a bit perturbed. She was determined to hear the little *chazan* who had made so deep an impression on Maestro Campanini, even if she had to stand throughout the service. And stand she did—in prominent view in the women's gallery, with the eyes of a large part of the large assemblage glued on her as she followed every note of the cantor's recitation of the *Mussaph* prayer.

When the services were over, the street outside the synagogue was blocked with people. As she came out Miss Raisa received an ovation such as she had seldom gotten in the opera house. When somewhat later my father, too, emerged, the enthusiasm of the crowd could no longer be contained. Shouts of "Rosenblatt" and "Raisa," "the greatest cantor" and "the greatest singer" rent the air of Brownsville and the applause and noise were heard for many blocks. Miss Raisa warmly pressed the cantor's hand and in a fluent Bialestok Yiddish, which her years in the opera had not made her forget, said to him: "*Chazan*, you touched my heart with your prayers. I shall never forget the spiritual pleasure you have given me."

To the average person it may have seemed an inconsistency that, after having renounced the opera, my father should have invaded the concert stage. As he saw it, there was nothing incongruous about this decision on his part. On the concert stage he could appear as he was, without costume or make-up, without the necessity of gesticulating or playacting. He could be what he was and sing what he pleased, all of which would have been impossible in the opera. Besides he was anxious, as he expressed it, "to convince the public that his artistic possibilities" were not "confined to sacred music only." He aspired to be to the Jews what Harry Lauder was to the Scotch and John McCormack to the Irish.

It was a mild and pleasant spring day—that Sunday of May 19 on the afternoon of which my father made his first real appearance on the concert stage. Carnegie Hall, which seated close to three thousand persons, was almost completely filled. Although the majority of the audience, that had assembled impelled by curiosity, was Jewish, there was also a goodly representation of non-Jews in its midst.

When the little *chazan* with the long jet-black beard, dressed in clerical garb, his head covered by the never-failing skull cap, came into view on the platform holding in his hand his little black note-book, there was a quizzical look on the faces of many of those not accustomed to a spectacle like this in such a setting. But once he began to sing, they "who came to scoff, remain'd to pray." The audience was uproarious in its applause not only after the rendition of his own liturgical compositions, but even when he finished singing such operatic arias as "Questa o quella" from Rigoletto. As for the critics, the following is a sampling of their reactions.

"Time was," said the reviewer of the New York Post, "when opera singers of all altitudes, so to speak—from basses and tenors up to altos and sopranos—indulged in vocal acrobatics; that is in the rapid runs and twirls and trills and tripping staccato scales or arpeggios collectively referred to as coloratura singing. In the course of time this sort of thing was relegated to the singers of the feminine persuasion; gradually, indeed, the contraltos (who still held their own in Rossini's 'Semiramide,' for example) were neglected, and the sopranos had the field almost to themselves.

"But now, lo and behold! comes along a tenor who warbles like a canary bird. He isn't even an operatic tenor. From the synagogue he comes, straight to the concert stage. Josef Rosenblatt is his name, cantor his profession, and his New York debut was made yesterday afternoon in Carnegie Hall before a large and frantically enthusiastic audience . . . On his programme there were airs from Meyerbeer's 'L'Africaine,' Bizet's 'Pecheurs des Perles,' and Halévy's 'La Juive.' In this dramatic music the cantor displayed a voice of rare beauty and penetrating power . . . rising at times to almost Carusoan opulence, and nearly always true to pitch.

"What the audience enjoyed particularly was the cantor's singing of two numbers to which his own name was affixed, airs as Hebrew, as Oriental, as their names: '*Elokay Neshomo*' and '*Omar Rabbi Elosor.*' In these Andre Benoist, who supplied excellent piano accompaniments for the rest of the programme, was silent much of the time, while Mr. Rosenblatt sang alone, somewhat like a Mohammedan muezzin on a minaret; sang coloratura of unmistakable Semitic origin; sang with a falsetto voice that rose to Eiffel Tower altitude. By this the audience was so entranced that it broke in with applause several bars before he had finished."

Other reviews were equally enthusiastic. "He turns handsprings of coloratura," commented the New York Tribune, "that Amelita Galli-Curci or Maria Barrientos might well envy. His trill brought one back to Melba." "To hear him sing Jewish folksongs is like hearing McCormack sing 'Macushla,'" remarked the Morning Telegraph. "Such a display of florid execution has not been heard here since Edmond Clement," was the opinion of the Evening Globe, while Max Smith of the American, who headed his article "Jewish Tenor Triumphs in Concert" wrote among other things:

"The famous Jewish tenor's first public appearance since he refused a tempting offer from Cleofonte Campanini, director in chief of the Chicago Opera Company, attracted a great many enthusiasts from various parts of the city. Nor did the golden-voiced singer of synagogal chants fail to evoke thunderous approval in music that wandered far afield from the paths he was accustomed to tread. . . . It must be confessed however, that Rosenblatt was heard to best advantage in the exotically Oriental exuberances of his own '*Elokay Neshomo*' . . . and '*Omar Rabbi Elosor*' . . . In the plaintively melancholy cadence of this music, which asks for the lachrymose portamentos, the sobs, the strong dynamic contrasts and the fine-spun semi-falsetto coloratura, that are characteristic of his technique, he was quite in his element and sang with convincing freedom and fervor.

"His strict adherence to pitch in long and complicated passages, unaccompanied on the piano, was surprising. Extraordinary, too, was his dexterity in florid melody, which he sang in the most delicate and tenuous head tones. On one occasion in the 'Omar Rabbi Elosor,' for example, he trilled like a soprano, and with startling precision and ease on high C and D natural. For a moment he even touched the lofty F natural above."

In short it was generally agreed that in his own cantorial music his mastery was supreme. There was a division of opinion only in regard to the orthodoxy of the methods and style he employed in the singing of operatic arias. How now did the artist himself react to the criticism of the critics? When the question was put to him, he replied with his characteristic chuckle: "Peculiar people—these critics. First they say the most wonderful things about my voice. Then they turn around and find fault with me because I don't know the so-called professional tricks. They claim that I pay no attention to style and that I am not aware of operatic tradition. But they don't realize that I learned my entire operatic repertoire in less than three weeks, not knowing one word of French or Italian. That's what I would call a real trick. As for style or tradition, I would suggest that some great operatic tenor learn to sing my 'Omar Rabbi Eleazar' or my 'Elokay Neshomoh' in three weeks; I should not look for style or tradition."

To be honest, the dissenters were not entirely wrong. My father's singing of the non-Jewish portion of his repertoire had not been in accordance with the operatic tradition. Steeped in the ideology of the Orthodox Jewish past, in which eroticism had no place, he could not possibly inject the emotion and feeling into the French, Italian or Spanish lovesongs, the context of which was completely foreign to him, that he put into prayers of the synagogue in which he was so much at home. All the less was he capable of giving to the former the appropriate interpretation, however musically perfect his reading of the score may have been. I recall seeing in his anthology of musical selections a Mexican ballad that he was fond of singing on account of its catchy melody. It begins: "Una noche de placer m'encontre con mi bella Maria" (On one night of pleasure I met my beautiful Marie). He included it in a concert he gave before a very conservatively religious Jewish audience one time. Fortunately neither he nor his listeners, who enjoyed the music very much, knew what the song was about, or some faces would have been very red.

In spite of all this Josef Rosenblatt had passed his examination with flying colors. He had proven to the world, the larger world without, that, whatever his shortcomings might be, he was a first class vocal artist of universal appeal. The judges of the supreme court of the American republic of music had heard him. They had noted what he had to offer as a singer, and pronounced it good. What was the man of the street to do but accept their verdict? If there had been doubt in any manager's mind before as to whether Josef Rosenblatt was a box office attraction, there could be none anymore now. The man had drawing power. Any undertaking that featured him on its program was sure to be a success.

More engagements consequently began to come his way than he could possibly fill. Of course not all the calls for his services were for profit. To charitable organizations he continued to render them gratis or, at best, in return for a very modest fee, as had been his custom theretofore. But this much is certain: everybody wanted Rosenblatt. When the

Israel Orphan Asylum of New York decided to dedicate its new building on Second Avenue, Yossele Rosenblatt had to participate in its program. When the Kesher Israel Synagogue of Harrisburg, Pennsylvania, was opened, it was Yossele Rosenblatt who was engaged as the chief attraction to assure the financial success of the affair. The reason why he was invited to inaugurate the War Savings Stamps campaign in Baltimore was, to quote Governor Harrington of Maryland, that he could "think of no one better qualified to rouse Baltimore's Jewish residents."

Sometimes the officials of eleemosynary institutions in distress would turn to my father for advice and help. He would counsel them to arrange a concert toward which he would lend his talents, and usually enough money would be realized not only to meet the immediate obligations but even to show a surplus.

Like the fees for his engagements, the price of his phonograph recordings now, too, went up. The Victor Company began paying him advance royalties of $1,000 per record. America's foremost inventor, Thomas Edison, was then still alive and active at his laboratory in Menlo Park, New Jersey. One of the officials there thought he might be interested in meeting the cantor whose voice had become so familiar to him. So my father was presented to the white-haired wizard and, after greeting him, he pronounced upon him the special Hebrew blessing reserved for men of genius. Edison was deeply moved by this mark of esteem with its religious note. To show his appreciation he took a graph of my father's voice and informed him that it had the largest range of any that had ever been recorded. His phonograph records were, by my father's own admission, his best teachers. By listening to them he was able to discover his faults and correct them.

One of the rewards of renown is to be sought out as a subject of discourse by writers of articles for the press and other organs of publicity. Representatives of all kinds of periodicals, non-Jewish as well as Jewish, musical magazines and newspapers in general began to visit us at our home. They were surprised—I still do not know why—that the singer of the synagogue, who had swept the patrons of Carnegie Hall off their feet, led a normal family life; that in spite of his patriarchal appearance, he had a young-looking wife whose features did not at all correspond to the so called Semitic type that they had carried in their minds. It was a matter of wonderment to them that the Rosenblatt couple should have been blessed with eight children. One reporter was quite taken aback to learn that the cantor, whose artistic rendition of the prayers of the synagogue had afforded so much spiritual pleasure to the frequenters of Jewish houses of worship, prayed even when he was not paid to do so, and that he would not lift up the receiver to answer a telephone call on the Sabbath, let alone desecrate the holy day by discussing business on it.

The story of his life, of his birth in Russia, of the early evidences of his talent, of his wanderings in Austria-Hungary as a boy-prodigy and of his cantorate in Munkacs, Presburg and Hamburg, prior to his coming to America—all this was given wide publicity in the press. Interviewers were anxious not only to get at the bottom of his motives for rejecting the offer of an opera career, but also to obtain my mother's view on the subject, the woman's angle, so to speak. They interpreted the sigh of seeming resignation in her endorsement of her husband's decision as an indication that she did not see entirely eye to eye with him in throwing away so marvellous a chance for achieving fame and fortune.

In short whatever went on in our household quickly became public knowledge. Fortunately there was nothing there that my father needed to be ashamed of and would, therefore, have wanted to hide. On the contrary, in that year, he, the erstwhile immigrant who had only recently become a

citizen of his adopted American fatherland, had reason to
be proud not only of his own artistic achievements, but also
of the scholastic record of his children. I was just then grad-
uating from high school and it was on account of my
father's celebrity rather than the prizes I won that my photo
got into several musical magazines. As for him his features
were already then known throughout the country. "Musical
America" included in its gallery of celebrities a drawing of
his head, encased in the outline of a five-pointed star, which
was identified as "Cantor Josef Rosenblatt, a New Star in Our
Musical Firmament."

The marked increase in his income, which resulted from
his being catapulted into a position of renown by the rapid
succession of breath-taking events in the spring of the year
1918, made it possible for our family, which up to that time
had led a rather frugal existence, to indulge in more gracious
and comfortable living. My mother was able, in addition to
our Polish maid, to take in a cook and she was thus relieved
of the burden of preparing food for a large household. Our
help was always well paid and treated with consideration.
That was the secret of their remaining with us until either
marriage or illness terminated their services.

The summer of 1918 also meant another step forward for
us. Our family rented a cottage for the summer season on
the seashore of northern New Jersey. For eight years, except
1923, the year of my father's first European concert tour, as
soon as the school year was over and the summer vacation
began, we would barricade our house in New York, and
move to Long Branch.

There was a lovely little synagogue in the fashionable resort, that was presided over by the aristocratic Mr. Garfunkel. My father would conduct Sabbath services at least
once during the nine-week period.

The annual exodus to and the sojourn in Long Branch was
a God-send to our family and contributed greatly to its

health. But while everyone else benefited from this rest at the seashore, it was an almost complete waste for the master of the house himself. My father had no more patience at the age of thirty-six than he had had as a child of six. He was constitutionally unable to remain put in one place for any length of time. After he had been in Long Branch for three days in succession, he had to pick himself up and leave for New York.

"Yossel," my mother would plead with him, "why don't you go down to the beach and relax? It is so balmy and restful there and a little recreation will be most beneficial for your voice. Since we are spending so much money for the rental of the cottage, why shouldn't you derive some benefit from it?" But no, she was unable to detain him. A meeting of the Cantors' Association was scheduled to take place and without him present nothing would be accomplished. The *Chassidic* rabbi of the Sadagora dynasty wanted a favor, and he couldn't refuse. It isn't really so hot in New York as she thinks. "The fans in the subway produce such delightful ventilation." That's why he liked to go there to cool off, "Chappen Luft" (to catch a breath of air). There's nothing like New York's subways for comfort.

And so when the summer was over and all of us returned from our vacation suntanned and fit, father, who had only at rare intervals taken his ablutions in the ocean, would by comparison seem wan and pale. Nevertheless when, following our first summer in Long Branch, every one of us, including my mother and the maid, came down with influenza, father remained untouched. Our home in New York for a while resembled the ward of a hospital, with all beds occupied and two nurses running from patient to patient. Fortunately every member of our household recovered from the malady, which had taken such a large toll of human lives throughout the nation.

Seats were always at a premium at the Ohab Zedek on the

High Holidays during my father's incumbency of the cantorate at that congregation. But they were particularly hard to obtain for the fall festival season of the year 1918. "When Cantor Rosenblatt sang the services for his congregation" during the holidays that had just passed, Musical America informed its readers on October 5th, "the scale of prices for seats ran from eight dollars upwards. The demand for tickets was so heavy that many were turned away and a handsome amount was netted for the support of the synagogue."

The holidays, including the Feast of Tabernacles, which follows on the heels of the Day of Atonement, were no sooner over than the concert season began which was destined in that year to take my father all the way to the West Coast. His trips across the length and breadth of the United States of America brought back memories of the wanderings of his youth as a boy-prodigy, except that he now travelled in much greater comfort. The porters on the Pullman trains, which served as his hotel on many a night and the schedules of which he remembered better than the railroad employees themselves, came to know him. They catered to his needs and often would refuse to accept gratuities from him for services rendered, although he always tipped handsomely for attentions shown him. "Bless mah haht, if dis ain't de famous Cantor Rosenblatt, hisself!" was the exclamation of pleasant surprise with which he was often greeted by these faithful of America's hotels on wheels. They quickly familiarized themselves with the limited menu that his observance of the Jewish dietary laws allowed and, without having to consult him, they would bring to his compartment ice-cream and milk and sardines and salmon and the choicest of fruits and other such edibles as his religious scruples permitted. They wanted to make certain that he would not starve so long as he was in their care.

21

Touring America

The opening recitals of this, my father's first secular concert tour, were given, as was to be expected, in New York itself. The first was held at the Hippodrome, the scene of one of his previous triumphs. Although the violinist, Sasha Jacobson, who was the other attraction, had also given a good accounting of himself, it was "the singing of Mr. Rosenblatt," as the critic of the New York Herald stated the next day, "which was the feature" at this concert. "The enthusiasm of the audience of 5000 was unbounded, sometimes verging on the rhapsodical." Nor was it any wonder, for the "performance was as unusual as it was remarkable." "Gradually," so another reviewer began his account, "the great American public is being familiarized with the beauty of Jewish melodies . . . 'Eili, Eili' is a bit of lyric music that needs not the voice of a Joseph Rosenblatt to reach an audience's fount of tears. But given a voice of this unusual quality, singing a song so pathetic, and he or she who will not succumb must be a person without feeling."

To satisfy the large number of music lovers who had been unable to obtain seats in the Hippodrome, another concert had to be arranged for two weeks later in Carnegie Hall. This time the attendance was considerably smaller. In fact it "no more than peppered the auditorium." Musically, however, it was a great success. "He never has sung better in New York" was the Herald's comment. "He used his voice like a virtuoso would his violin and made it do phenomenal things, especially in his own compositions. One of these was akin to an operatic aria, and with the accompaniment elaborated would be a show piece for a Caruso or a Martinelli, though neither could match Mr. Rosenblatt's falsetto or coloratura." Even his rendition of the secular part of his program met with the approval of the critics.

As my father journeyed, beginning with the fall of this year, from city to city, Stuart Ross replaced Andre Benoist as accompanist. Ross gave exceptionally sympathetic support, not only in the secular music with which, as a professional musician, he was very well acquainted, but even in the Hebrew liturgical selections which had, up to the time he met my father, been terra incognita to him. Within a very short time he came to know all my father's personal habits and daily routine, including the minutiae of religious ritual.

It was most amusing to hear this tall dapper Irish Catholic tell curiosity seekers, who were anxious to buttonhole my father at the hotel or in his Pullman compartment, that Cantor Rosenblatt was not to be disturbed "because he was busy saying *Shemoneh Esreh.*"

My father managed quickly to make himself at home on the train. He felt no embarrassment, when the hour for the morning service arrived, about donning his prayer-shawl and phylacteries. Nor did he hesitate about removing his shoes and reciting the prescribed dirges if he happened to be on the road when the Ninth of *Ab,* Israel's black fast, came 'round. And if *Purim* surprised him en route and he was unable to leave the train in order to hear the book of Esther read in a synagogue, he would take out his own scroll and chant the text to himself according to precept.

The young Jewish musician Abe Elstein, who later became my father's permanent accompanist, happened to be with him on one such occasion. "Whenever the name of the arch-villain Haman, occurred in the course of the reading," so he relates, "Yossele expected me to give it the noisy reception with which the children were accustomed to greet that name in the old-type synagogues. Truth to tell, I was a little bashful, at the beginning, about doing it. But when Yossele Rosenblatt, having reached the word 'Haman,' gave me one of those knowing side-looks, I had to do my stunt. So I stamped my feet and rapped with whatever was within reach of my hands."

Once my father was travelling with the violin virtuoso Jasha Kanevsky, who starred together with him on a number of concerts. Kanevsky, a Greek Catholic, had the highest regard for my father's religious scruples, with some of which he became quite familiar. It happened one time that he was nibbling on a ham sandwich as my father was entering his compartment. Knowing that my father never ate bareheaded, he quickly pulled out his hat, put it on, and continued eating. He never did find out the cause of the guffaws that this gesture of his provoked among his Jewish companions.

The first lap of my father's tour outside New York was restricted to cities located in the eastern portion of the United States. Beginning with a recital on Tuesday, October 22, in Hartford, Connecticut, his route covered Waterbury, Providence, Newark, Cincinnati, Pittsburgh, New Haven, Boston, Rochester, Harrisburg and Milwaukee. Whether the audiences were large or small, he was well received wherever he appeared. But it was in Boston, America's oldest center of culture, that he scored his greatest triumph.

The Boston Evening Transcript carried a long article, headed "Strange Mr. Rosenblatt." It spoke about the "fleetness, piquancy, ease and exactitude" with which he sang the "florid ornament of his operatic airs." "From no woman's voice in these days," declared the writer, "has the like of this floritura been heard in our concert halls." Most laudatory and lavish in its praises was the Boston Traveler. "Those who were fortunate enough to get into Symphony Hall yesterday afternoon," declared its music critic, "enjoyed a concert to be treasured. Joseph Rosenblatt, the famous Jewish cantor, was the artist. After hearing this celebrated artist sing Hebrew ritual hymns, operatic airs and lighter music, one does not wonder why the Chicago Opera Company was eager to secure his services.

"One could have shut his eyes and well imagined he was listening to Scotti, the famous baritone; Caruso, the tenor; and Galli-Curci, the great soprano. Mr. Rosenblatt apparently has three voices, all beautifully used and all without the slightest apparent effort. His audience could easily have wished for a more varied program if for no other reason than to ascertain if this remarkable singer has any limit to his vocal abilities."

After his appearance in Boston's Symphony Hall my father was scheduled to sing in America's most famous opera house, New York's Metropolitan, at one of its Sunday concerts. The Metropolitan's own famed orchestra was to accompany him, and Frieda Hempel, the celebrated operatic coloratura soprano, to share the program. This was an honor that had not yet been bestowed upon any cantor. Unfortunately sudden illness prevented him from taking advantage of it. However he was given a chance to appear in the Metropolitan at a later date.

The following week he had recovered sufficiently to be able to sing to a large audience at the Regent Theatre in Paterson, New Jersey, and to bring to a glorious close the most eventful year in his life.

After a recess of several weeks, he was off again on his travels. This time the general direction was west. On January 21 he gave a concert at the Odeon Theatre in St. Louis. On the 23rd he was scheduled for a recital in Cleveland, on the 26th in Louisville, and on the 28th in Toronto, on February 2 in Chicago, on the 4th in Winnipeg, on the 9th in Seattle, on the 11th in Vancouver, and the next day in Portland, Oregon. He appeared twice in San Francisco, and once in Los Angeles. On March 5th he sang in Denver for the benefit of the Jewish War Sufferers, but not until he had entertained the patients of the Denver Jewish Ex-Patients Home. His entertainment of the unfortunates did not exhaust his generosity as the following letter from them reveals.

"Honored Cantor Yossele Rosenblatt,

"What a pleasant surprise it was for us to receive your ten records. You really proved to be more than an ordinary visitor who carries back with him trivial insignificant, superficial impressions. During the short time that you spent with us you managed to imbibe into the depths of your soul and spirit the misery and the pain of the sick, whose image you did not forget and the recollection of whom you will long carry with you.

"Ten records—what a world of music! How many patient sufferers confined to their bed by illness, despondent and despairing, will, on awaking from their horrible dream, be able to open wide their weary, dim eyes and breathe in into their shrivelled breasts your dear voice, the sweet tones of your Jewish religious prayers and songs that express so well the Jewish woe.

"For all this, for the deep friendship that you have evinced for us by giving us the concert which we shall never forget, and for the lovely gift of ten records which you sent us in time for the holidays, it has been moved at our meeting of the 'Patients' Mutual Assistance Society,' held on October 14, 1919 to enroll you as an honorary member of our club.

"We hope you will accept the membership in the same spirit in which it has been bestowed.

Martin Cooper, Chairman
R. I. Louis, Secretary"

After Denver he was heard in St. Paul, Minnesota and Columbus, Ohio. His out-of-town concert season was terminated by a recital at Montreal's Monument National.

Thanks to the advance publicity, released in several instances months before his appearances, and the eagerness of

the public to hear and see him, my father sang nearly everywhere to packed houses. In San Francisco, the cultural center of the Far West, the audience that greeted him was so
large and so many who sought admission were turned back,
that he had to give a repeat performance. The verdict of the
critics was for the most part a repetition of what had been
said about him by the reviewers in the East. J. Vion Papin
of the St. Louis Republic thought he had three voices. Herman Devries of the Chicago Evening American credited him
with four.

It was agreed by everyone that he was at best in his own
Hebrew musical compositions. Although there were some
critics who still had flaws to pick in his method of singing
opera, there were others who found him most competent
and adequate in this field also.

Strange as it may seem the most violent disagreement
with this chorus of praise was encountered in Jewish circles,
among his own people. An article in the Canadian Eagle of
Montreal, for example, took him to task for making unau-
thorized use of his falsetto in the singing of opera arias and
for finishing on a robusto note.

Another Jewish critic did not like the change from Yossele
to Josef Rosenblatt. The concert stage, he felt, was the
wrong place for the popular and greatly beloved interpreter
of the prayers of the synagogue who was known by his coreligionists as Yossele. Opera was not his role.

One Jewish musical reviewer, however, in a dissertation on
"Artists of the Amud" (the Day, November 16, 1918),
went much further in his disparagement of my father's art.
On the basis of having heard him sing two times, he had
reached the conclusion that Yossele Rosenblatt possessed
many of the "qualities that a cantor ought to have in order
to satisfy the average Jewish connoisseur: a soft, appealing,
little lyric tenor voice (very little), a falsetto and a passable
coloratura. He read Hebrew fluently and apparently under-

stood the meaning of the text. In addition thereto he was, by cantorial standards, a pretty good musician. Yet he was still far removed from that category of artists of the *Amud* who are capable of influencing the lesser cantors and of nourishing them in the manner of a Pinie Minkowsky, a Kwartin and a Birnbaum." The writer went on to say that my father was lacking in voice culture and that in Europe he would be considered only second-rate. As for his liturgical compositions, though they gave evidence of a certain amount of talent, they stood in need of rearrangement by a real musician.

This criticism contrasted sharply with everything that non-Jewish critics, who had heard my father, had said about him, and with the respect that musical geniuses like Ernest Bloch expressed for such compositions of my father's as his *Uv'nucho Yomar* and his *Halleluyah* (Psalm 113). Only two months after the appearance of the derogatory critique, Richard L. Stokes of the St. Louis Post Dispatch reached diametrically opposite conclusions. He credited my father with a "range of no less than four octaves and a minor third." He looked upon his falsetto as an astonishing vocal curiosity. He described Rosenblatt's normal voice as "a superb tenor, ringing with power, beautiful of quality, dramatic of timbre."

"Though self-taught," he said, "Josef Rosenblatt had found out for himself many sound principles which others often cannot acquire in many years of tuition. His free and facile emission of tone" was "almost ideal, and his skill in breathing no less than phenomenal. Not only was there no inflation of the chest, no heaving of the shoulders; it was difficult even with close watching to perceive his taking breath at all. Everyone has beheld singers visibly mustering up every resource of lungs and muscles for an attack upon a high note; Rosenblatt seemed to take such tones without the least preparation, and held them with an effortless volume and duration giving rise to the fantastic thought for a moment that he must be supplied with mechanical bellows, like a pipe organ."

Is it a wonder that my father's friends were incensed at his disparagement by a fellow-Jew and that one of them published a full-length refutation in the columns of the Day?

Because of the kind of life he had led and the strict views that he held, the usual pastimes of the road were not open to Yossele Rosenblatt. He didn't play cards, rarely indulged in drink, and he never contracted the smoking habit. How then did he occupy himself during the long hours of enforced idleness spent on trains between one station of his long itinerary and the next? In reality there was no problem. The seclusion and separation from the tumult and distractions of public life, which his confinement to the narrow limits of a pullman compartment made possible, afforded him opportunity for meditation and thought. Since mentally he lived in the world of music, especially that of the synagogue, he now had a splendid chance to resume his work of composition that had been interrupted by his coming to America and his being thrust into the maelstrom of American Jewish life. Left alone unto himself he had time to think and write, to try out and jot down new tunes and melodies. And indeed he never returned from a journey or tour without a new creation, giving musical expression to some neglected portion of the Jewish prayerbook.

Parts of these compositions would be scribbled on the margins of newspapers, on backs of envelopes or even on the cuffs of his shirts, if nothing else happened to be handy. Thus were born several of those selections of his that have won for themselves a permanent place in the musical tradition of the synagogue and are familiar to every Jew who knows anything about Jewish religious music. His *Habet Mishomayim Ur'eh, Rachem No* from grace after meals,

Elokay Ad Shelo Notzarti from the silent devotion of the Day of Atonement, *Shir Hamaalos* chanted before grace, and *Rom v'nisso* from the morning service, saw the light of day in this manner.

His strict adherence to the dietary laws made it impossible for him to take his meals in the hotels. He was, therefore, compelled to seek out, wherever he happened to perform, those of his coreligionists who observed the precepts. Before going to a strange city, he would make arrangements to eat at the home of the orthodox rabbi, of a synagogue functionary or a family that was recommended to him as observers of *kashruth*. Till this day I meet people from all over the country who pride themselves on the fact that my father slept or ate at their home. It was, of course, considered an honor to entertain a celebrity like Yossele Rosenblatt, and his hosts were often rewarded for their hospitality by a free dress rehearsal of the concert about to be given. Besides the guest was invariably, as he had been in his childhood, delightful company. Completely unaffected, he usually had amusing stories to tell and witty comments to make, and he was never niggardly in regaling his hosts with samples of his talent. Above all others did he cultivate the society of what he called *Jewish* Jews; those who clung to the traditions.

Stationed one day in Pittsfield, Massachusetts, where he had been invited to give a concert in the auditorium of the local high school, he noticed three Jewish patriarchs standing in a huddle after the performance. They greeted him most cordially, of course, and very timidly asked him whether he would be willing to spend a few hours in the home of one of their number to celebrate the birth of a child. They hesitated because they realized that he might perhaps feel obligated to show his respects to the people who had arranged the concert and brought him to Pittsfield. To their surprise and amazement, he accepted their invitation, stating that he preferred to be in the company of Jews who were not ashamed of their religious convictions and who had impressed on their faces "the image of God."

Even far away from home he never missed an opportunity, if he could only help it, to fulfill a *Mitzvah*, that is, a Jewish religious rite however trivial. Once on a Saturday night in Youngstown, Ohio, he made a special trip in a heavy downpour from his hotel to the home of the town's ritual slaughterer merely in order to participate, by eating a mouthful, in the meal of the outgoing of the Sabbath called *Melavah Malkah*. If the day on which he was scheduled for a concert in a locality happened to coincide with the Jewish new moon, he would make every effort to join some congregation in prayer rather than pray privately. Once on such an occasion he entered a prayer-chapel in Toronto. The worshippers, seeing Yossele Rosenblatt in their midst, took advantage of his presence by asking him to conduct the services. Since, according to the Talmud, such a request by a congregation could not be turned down, my father complied. However, instead of giving those who were assembled and eagerly looking forward to it a few samples of his art, the unwilling precentor plowed through the service like an ordinary lay reader. When at the conclusion of the services his listeners voiced their disappointment over his performance, his reply to them was: "I just wanted to prove to you that I was capable of reciting my prayers in the manner of a layman and not only like a cantor."

It was not always necessary for my father to "look for his brethren." Often they would come to him and make themselves known as his kith and kin. Even before he had settled in America, he had been aware of the fact that he had relatives there who had preceded him. He also had a general idea of who his kinsmen were and where they resided. However with the growth of his fame the circle of his blood-relations seemed to widen. Wherever he stopped on his migrations east or west or south, a new crop of cousins blossomed forth; cousins of the first, second, third or fourth degree of whose existence he had never been told.

How authentic the relationship was was often difficult to determine. At times the claims of affinity, even though genuine, proved a little embarrassing. For he could not refuse the offer of hospitality made by a relative. But he was not always certain whether those that posed as his kinsmen were trustworthy so far as the *kashruth* of their homes was concerned, and to be invited to partake of a meal and not to eat was worse than not to have accepted the invitation altogether.

In addition to newly found relatives there were also friends from the Old World upon whom he chanced in the course of his wanderings. He would never fail to visit them when he was in their vicinity.

One effective means of *wiping* out friendships, so it has been remarked by a clever punster, is to *sponge* on them. My father never liked to take advantage of the kindness and hospitality shown him by his many admirers. He preferred to be a dispenser rather than a recipient of gifts, and always insisted on paying for his board, especially when those who provided him with it had to go to inconvenience and trouble. And if they refused to accept compensation—which happened most of the time—he had other means of expressing his gratitude. A present of his own records was always deeply appreciated.

Once he stopped in Omaha, Nebraska with friends whose little daughter's canary had suddenly become mute. The parents of the heartbroken owner tried every expedient possible to induce the feathered warbler to break his silence. They had a veterinarian treat him. They changed his diet. They got him a mate. But all to no avail. Not a note came forth from the canary's throat. Then a set of Yossele Rosenblatt's records arrived, including his *Omar Rabbi Elozor,* with its florid coloratura passages. The trills seemed to touch a sympathetic chord in the bird, for as soon as he heard the stream of melody pouring forth from the phonograph, he began, by mimicking the sounds as it were, to sing again. The delight of the child was beyond description. The most valuable gift could not have been more satisfying.

Thus his first real cross-country jaunt brought my father into personal contact with thousands of people who had theretofore known him only through his recordings. But it was the concert he gave in New York's Hippodrome on Sunday, April 27, that was responsible for a syndicated article, topped by an Underwood photo of him in prayer-shawl and mitre, entitled "Jewish Tenor's Fame Is Growing." The story was featured by many leading newspapers of the country, in such diverse places as Cleveland, Pittsburgh, Minneapolis, Trenton, Chicago, Reno, Seattle, New York, Atlanta, Chattanooga and Erie. Being so well known, my father was a natural choice as the chief musical attraction of the Jewish Organizations of New York Victory Loan Demonstration of the night of May 6, 1919. His part at this event, which was addressed by many notables and attended by some 40,000 persons, again brought him a most laudatory letter of appreciation from Michael Kley, the chairman.

The chief effect of the world war that had come to a close in November, 1918, so far as the United States was concerned, was to bequeath unto the nation an indebtedness of unprecedented proportions which loans such as the Victory Loan were designed to absorb. The American mainland had remained untouched and the only casualties suffered were those of soldiers killed or wounded on overseas battlefields.

Quite different was the situation for Europeans and particularly for the Jewish masses living in Eastern Europe. Concentrated as they had always been along the frontier, the Jews were directly in the path of invading armies and, consequently, more exposed to attack than any other part of the population of the lands of their residence. The losses sustained in property as well as human lives, particularly in Poland, were enormous. But the trials of these first victims of war did not end with the cessation of general hostilities. There followed in Russian Poland and the Ukraine, where most of the Jews of Europe had their homes, a series of pogroms perpetrated by the wild hordes of the White Russian generals Kolchak, Petlura and Denikine. Jewish blood flowed like water and the governments stood idly by and did nothing to check the massacres.

The four million Jews of America reacted to the terrifying reports, as they had on previous occasions, with huge demonstrations of protest and indignation. On Wednesday, May 21, 10,000 Jewish war veterans marched in New York, the largest Jewish community in the world, in a heavy downpour all the way from the East Side to Madison Square Garden. Accompanied by hundreds of thousands of Jewish civilians they carried banners bearing such legends as "We fought for justice and now we demand the same thing from Poland"; and "We fought for all small nations, Poland included, and now Poland is murdering our brothers."

Inside the vast auditorium the 10,000 delegates and 15,-000 onlookers were addressed by speakers representing every section of American Jewry as well as the elite of non-Jewish America.

"But," asked one observer from the Jewish Daily News, "what did all the speeches delivered by these notables amount to over against the old Jewish *El Mole Rachamim* sung by *Chazan* Reb Yossele Rosenblatt? When he uttered the words: 'On account of the souls of the martyrs that were slain and massacred and murdered,' a wail could be heard on all sides simultaneously. War-hardened soldiers shed tears. The aristocratic old Mr. Straus wept; so did also the Zionist leader Barondess and the Socialist Olgin. Ambassador Elkus wiped his eyes. In the stillness of death that accompanied the dirge one could sense the sorrow that filled the entire assembly. Reb Yossele Rosenblatt's *El Mole Rachamim* had touched all hearts and evoked tears from everyone's eyes." Even an Irish policeman who watched the proceedings could not help being moved to tears. "In Yossele Rosenblatt's singing the deepest emotions of the Jewish soul found their true expression."

22

Invading Forbidden Sanctuaries

One of the advantages of genius is that it leaps across boundaries, that it knows no barriers, that no doors remain locked before it. It can penetrate the thickest walls and enter into places which to others less gifted would be forbidden territory.

Among these sanctuaries that my father was to invade in 1919 was the Great Hall of the College of the City of New York. I was a freshman at the college at that time. It was the custom then to have certain days set aside when the campus organizations would act as hosts for the entire student body. On May 29 it was the Zionist Society's turn. Eager to present to their non-Jewish fellow students and faculty members the best that Jewry had to offer, its officers very timidly asked me to prevail on my father to be their feature artist. They were very hesitant about making the request, because they had nothing to offer as compensation except the prospects of an appreciative and intelligent audience.

My father did not require too much persuasion. The education I was receiving at the college, whose scholastic standards were very high, was worth a concert and more. He deemed it a privilege to sing in the famous auditorium, whose vast vaulted ceiling and parabola in the front for special sound effects made it an acoustical paradise for musicians of all classes. Besides, there was the additional inducement of being accompanied by Professor Baldwin, one of the foremost organists in the country.

It was an historic occasion when my father in his customary attire appeared on the platform of the Great Hall of City College that May 29. Never before had the walls of this assembly room beheld in their midst a vocal artist of his type or appearance. But neither had there ever been such a turn-out as then.

"It is doubtful," wrote the Campus reporter in the paper's June 4 issue, "whether the hall could have held another person. Every seat was taken long before the artists made their bow, while the side aisles were jammed and some even had to stand upon the slender backs of the benches. Mr. Rosenblatt's voice is so colorfully changeful," he continued, "it is like a chameleon. It can be piteously imploring, thunderously denouncing, despairingly pathetic." "But whether his voice seemed to lay over the audience like the wings of an invisible angel, or seemed to tremble high in the infinity, there was no outward sign of strain on the singer's part. He appeared to run the gamut of the scales without effort."

The Methodist shrine of Ocean Grove was another sacred enclosure into which Josef Rosenblatt penetrated in 1919. A small community just outside of the New Jersey summer resort of Asbury Park, Ocean Grove was a stronghold of Wesleyan Methodism. The Christian Sabbath was so strictly observed there that no vehicles were permitted to enter the town on Sundays, nor was it possible to buy as much as a soft drink on the Lord's day. During the twenties and thirties of the present century, Ocean Grove's most important asset was its mammoth auditorium, which was used not only for revival meetings but also for popular concerts of a high order. Enrico Caruso and other opera stars frequently gave recitals in it, and symphony orchestras and outstanding instrumentalists were wont to perform there.

Here my father was invited by the Hotel Association to give a concert on Saturday night, August 16, in conjunction with John Philip Sousa's famous military band. It was another one of his firsts, and he apparently acquitted himself well, for on the Monday after the concert the usually restrained Shore Press of Asbury Park made the following comment: "Josef Rosenblatt, the cantor tenor, introduced a new kind of music in the great building. He sang several chants from the Hebrew ritual and . . . other numbers. He sings with unmistakable devotion and religious fervor. At times his tones sounded like a soprano singer, and though soft, were clear and true. His tenor tones were powerful and gave evidence of control and excellent expression . . ."

For quite a number of summers thereafter, the Josef Rosenblatt concert at the Ocean Grove Auditorium was attended by capacity audiences. At the second appearance, when he was the sole attraction, he was said to have been even better than the first time, but always he was a favorite.

However the most memorable event of the season was our visit one Sunday to the country home of the philanthropist Nathan Straus. I don't know whether this savior of New York's babies and sponsor of Palestinian health centers habitually cultivated cantors, but it is certain that he must have had a warm spot in his heart for Josef Rosenblatt. I remember the beautiful, well-kept grounds, the spacious house of many simply and yet tastefully furnished rooms, and the distinguished audience of some 130 guests whose names represented what might well be regarded as the social register of New York Jewry. I see my father seated at the piano, serving as his own accompanist as he sings songs in Hebrew, English, French, German and Russian, his head tilted slightly backward, and drawing applause after each number. Vivid also in my memory of that day's experiences is the delicious luncheon, that was served us in the cool bright dining room of the house, in the new blue-colored china that had been gotten specially to satisfy my father's religious scruples. We, that is my father and mother, Leo and I, had our hosts, Mr. and Mrs. Straus, all to ourselves, and we had a most delightful time with this genial couple.

The marks of attention shown my father by people like the Strauses did not go to his head. After being entertained by them, he went straight back to the East Side to sing for the pleasure of the Jewish masses living there as he had been accustomed formerly. Certain gentlemen of the Yiddish press saw in this fact signs of the beginning of a new trend. "It rarely happens," wrote one of them as he announced my father's appearance on September 10 at the Second Avenue Theatre, "that a great artist should come to the East Side. The rule is for those who are anxious to hear a good concert to go to Carnegie Hall. However times are changing." The real reason, however, was that fame did not affect Yossele Rosenblatt as, alas, it often does other persons who achieve renown.

On the High Holidays of this year my father's voice sounded to the representative of a Yiddish daily who attended his services at the Ohab Zedek, "more beautiful, more colorful and deeper than ever."

The singer himself explained this as follows: "As I officiated, I felt the woes and sorrows of our brethren in Russia, Poland and Galicia. I had before me a mental image of the pogroms and the persecutions to which our people is subjected. That may be the reason why my service this year was, as you put it, so appealing and moving."

"From all the indications," concluded the writer, concurring in the explanation, "the worshippers in the synagogue felt as Yossele Rosenblatt did. And if there were any who did not feel that way, they were made to do so by him. It wasn't the singing of the choir nor the competence of the director Mr. Wohl, notwithstanding his musical ability. It was solely the . . . noble, sincere tones of Yossele Rosenblatt, these and these alone that worked like a charm on everyone present."

His audience in Baltimore's Lyric reacted in precisely the same fashion when on November 2nd they heard him render for the first time his *Habet Mishomayim Ur'eh,* which he had composed during his recent travels to the West Coast. This prayer portrays in terse and vivid language Israel's utter helplessness, the contempt and derision with which it is treated by the nations of the world, its exposure to slaughter, destruction, injury and humiliation. It implores the Eternal's mercy on the ground that, despite its many trials, Israel has not forgotten His name.

One way to make certain that one's views will gain currency or one's efforts will win popular approval, the Talmud intimates, is to attach them to "the big tamarisks." In the musical world the best means whereby the work of a budding composer can be brought to the attention of the public is to have a prominent artist include it in his repertoire. Since my father now belonged to this category, and also constantly sought new material for his secular concert programs, Jewish songwriters of every description flocked to him.

Of course, not every melody submitted to him reached the concert platform. Although he was anxious to help anyone who appealed for assistance, especially musicians, he was professionally discriminating. However, when he detected real merit, he was ready to exert his influence to have it recognized. In this way he set many a gifted composer on his feet, while introducing something fresh and new to his concert audiences.

Yossele Rosenblatt at the age of 14 (P. 49)

Yossele Rosenblatt as cantor of Hamburg, Germany, at the age of 25 (P. 81)

Taube Kaufman (Mrs. Rosenblatt) at 17 (P. 58)

Kais. und kön. österr.-ungar.
General-Konsulat Hamburg.
Csász. és kir. osztrák-magyar
fökonzulátus Hamburgban.

Hamburg, *8. Mai* 191 *1.*

Zahl: *13817.*

Auf allen Zuschriften ist obige Zahl anzugeben.

Hochwohlgeboren

Herrn Oberkantor Josef Rosenblatt

H A M B U R G .

Das hohe k.u.k. Ministerium des Aeussern hat die
k.u.k. Botschaft in Berlin über Wunsch des Herrn Oberst-
Kämmerers Seiner k.u.k. Apostolischen Majestät beauftragt,
Euer Hochwohlgeboren für die Vorlage der Komposition
„Gebet für den Landesherrn" den Allerhöchsten Dank mit
dem Beifügen bekanntzugeben, dass dieselbe der k.u.k. Fa-
milien-Fideikommiss-Bibliothek einverleiht werden wird.

Ueber eine von der genannten k.u.k. Botschaft er-
haltene Weisung beehrt sich das k.u.k. General-Konsulat
Euer Hochwohlgeboren vom Vorstehenden in Kenntnis zu set-
zen.

Hochachtungsvoll

[signature]

k.u.k. Vizekonsul u.Gerent.

Letter of thanks for a prayer composed in honor of Emperor Francis-
Joseph's 80th birthday (P. 129)

Chicago Opera Association

(INCORPORATED)
AUDITORIUM THEATRE
CHICAGO

CLEOFONTE CAMPANINI
GENERAL DIRECTOR

HERBERT M. JOHNSON
BUSINESS COMPTROLLER

March 21st, 1918.

Mr. Morris Newman,
President, First Hung. Congregation,
Ohab Zedek,
18-22 West 116th street,
New York City.

Dear Sir:

I heard Mr. Rosenblatt during his recent stay in
Chicago and was so impressed with his voice and his art of sing-
ing that I made him an offer to sing, with the Chicago Grand
Opera Company, the part of Eleazar, in the opera THE JEWESS, by
Halevy.

I suppose the story of the opera is familiar to
you. It is a glorification of the Jewish religion, and the role
of the Jewess will be sung by Rosa Raisa, who is a Jewess, a
native of Odessa.

I offered Mr. Rosenblatt three performances in
Chicago, with an option of an additional one in New York and an
additional one in Boston, each to take place two to three weeks
apart. He would have to be in Chicago only one week for
rehearsals prior to the first performance. For all other performances he would only have to come to Chicago for each performance. His salary for each performance would be one thousand
($1,000) dollars and railroad fares to and from Chicago.

Mr. Rosenblatt personally has agreed to this
proposition, under the condition that his congregation will allow
him to accept. There will be no performances for him on Friday
or Saturday, nor would he, in any way, have to take off or cut his
beard, and there will be nothing in the performances, or his appearances upon the operatic stage that would in any way be a reflection
upon the Orthodox Jewish faith. Mr.Rosenblatt has also given us an
option on his services for the season of 1919/1920.
I expect Mr. Rosenblatt to make a great success in
opera, as he did in his concert appearance here.

Hoping to have a favorable answer at your early
convenience, I am,

Yours very truly,

Cleofonte Campanini

General Director.

Letter of Cleofonte Campanini, general director of the Chicago Opera
Association, offering Yossele Rosenblatt $1000 a night for the role of
Eleazar in "La Juive" (P. 143)

Josef Rosenblatt at the start of his first European tour, 1923 (P. 233)

In this cartoon Grand Opera is pursuing Josef Rosenblatt: "Come, Yossele
A thousand dollars a night!" (P. 145)

Two representatives of bel canto. The meeting of Josef Rosenblatt and Tito Schipa, March, 1925 (P. 263)

Cantor Rosenblatt eventually consented to sing for "The Jazz Singer," the first "talkie" (P. 290)

The Rosenblatt family, October 3, 1926 (P. 277)

Standing from left to right: Henry, Samuel, Leo, Marcus, Ralph. *Seated from left to right:* Gertrude, Taube (Kaufman) Rosenblatt, Josef Rosenblatt, Nettie, Sylvia

Charlie Chaplin welcomes the cantor to his Beverly Hills home, summer, 1927 (P. 290)

Cantor at Palace Puts
Abie in Trance

Abie the Agent thinks about Cantor Rosenblatt (P. 270)

Back to the Synagogue (P. 293)

Gaar Williams immortalized the cantor's theater performances (P. 259)

And the Jewish humorous weekly, The Big Stick, recorded the reception of newly imported cantors (P. 190)

Bornplatz Synagogue, Hamburg, Germany. Built 1906, demolished 1938 (P. 85)

Interior of the synagogue of the synagogenverband, Hamburg, Germany, 1906

The First Hungarian Congregation Ohab Zedek, as it appeared when Josef Rosenblatt was cantor (P. 109)

The Rosenblatt home, 50 West 120th Street, New York
(P. 197)

Tomb of Josef Rosenblatt in Jerusalem (P. 354)

Among Jewish songwriters who owed what renown they achieved to his use of their creations, the foremost perhaps was Mana Zucca, a little pianiste whose acquaintance my father made sometime in the fall of 1919. He was so carried away by her stirring Yiddish song *Rachem* that he put it on the program of his Philadelphia concert on November 16. It proved a tremendous success and its composer, who leaped into immediate fame, was able to advertise in the press that "Yossele Rosenblatt" sang her compositions. Another one of my father's discoveries was Rhea Silberta. Her *Yahrzeit* ending with the words of the hallowed requiem for the dead, *Kaddish,* was a favorite among his Yiddish selections. The most prolific among the creators of Jewish popular music whom my father sponsored, but who unfortunately was dogged by a miserable fate, was Solomon Golub. He was the author of such melancholy lieder as *Tanchum,* the unhappy Talmud student. His unsuccessful ventures cost my father many a precious penny. Another composer, whose song "The Wailing Wall" fascinated my father, was heavy-set, eccentric Platon Brunoff. Finally there was the conductor of the Yiddish theater, Sandler, whose *Eili, Eili,* which is still a classic today, owed its great vogue chiefly to the fact that Yossele Rosenblatt had made a recording of it and used it as an encore in many of his concerts.

On November 24 of this year my father had occasion to give a concert in Savannah, Georgia. Upon his return home he found the following letter from the mayor of that city:

My dear Mr. Rosenblatt:
    It was my privilege to be one of the audience that well filled the auditorium last night and enjoyed the wonderfully varied program that showed to such a great advantage the superb voice with which you have been gifted.
    The memory of the evening's entertainment, I am sure will long be cherished by all who were present. While we had been assured that you were a singer of rare powers I am convinced

that none of us had any conception of the enjoyment in store for us. Those who failed to attend certainly have reason to regret it.

There are today thousands of our people who, with praises of your singing ringing in their ears from friends and acquaintances, would welcome the opportunity to hear you. Those who heard you last night would equally be delighted to have a repetition of such an entertainment. I sincerely hope that it will not be long before you can accept a return engagement for Savannah.

> With best wishes,
> Sincerely yours,
> (signed) *Murray Stewart*

23

Charity's Cantor

The universal affection my father now enjoyed among his coreligionists was indicated by such announcements as one that appeared in the Jewish Voice of St. Louis. "Our dear Yossele Rosenblatt," so it read, "is coming to us and will charm us again." But more direct expressions of the esteem in which he was held were soon forthcoming. To show their appreciation for his many acts of human kindness, a group of his admirers decided to arrange a banquet in his honor. The prime mover was Judge Jacob Strahl, treasurer of the Bikur Cholim Hospital of Brooklyn that had often benefited from my father's generosity.

On Tuesday evening, December 23, some six hundred persons assembled in the Broadway Central Hotel to pay tribute to "Charity's Own Cantor . . . the greatest Jewish singer of our time, a Jew with a great heart and soul . . . a faithful husband and father." They constituted in their complexion a cross-section of the heterogeneous elements that made up the largest Jewish community in the world. The rabbinate, philanthropic institutions, the Yiddish and the English Press, the Cantors' Association, the musical and entertainment world and of course the Ohab Zedek Congregation, all of them were represented. A special message was sent by Jacob Schiff, American Jewry's leading philanthropist, and only illness and old age prevented Nathan Straus from presiding.

After the musical program, in which Mana Zucca and bandleader Edwin Franko Goldman, at whose open-air concerts my father had been a soloist on numerous occasions, participated, the speeches began. The speakers' list included Felix M. Warburg, Rabbis M. Z. Margolis, Bernard Drachman, Herbert S. Goldstein, and Moses Hyamson, and Judges Gustav Hartman and Jacob Strahl.

The address of the evening was delivered by the senior rabbi of Ohab Zedek, Dr. Philip Klein. Speaking in German, he compared the guest of honor to his biblical namesake Joseph, who bore the epithet of "the righteous." Just as Joseph, the son of the patriarch Jacob, was spoken of in the pentateuchal lesson of the week as having been "the ruler of all Egypt," so "Joseph Rosenblatt," said the speaker, "held undisputed sway in the realm of music." And just as the biblical Joseph had been a means of sustenance to many of his fellow men, so did this modern Joseph, by lending his God-given talent gratis to numerous charitable causes, bring succor to countless human beings in need of assistance. In this respect Josef Rosenblatt differed from many famous cantors who, though distinguished for their musical ability, were not so reputed for generosity.

What were the motivating factors responsible for making Yossele Rosenblatt the philanthropist that he was? How did he himself look upon the many acts of kindness that were his daily routine?

Some light is thrown on the subject by two articles that appeared in the press apropos of the dedication of the proceeds from his *Shoimer Yisroel* to the Jewish War Sufferers. According to the B'nai Brith Messenger, sympathy, heightened by a vivid imagination, prompted the gift of this composition, which was "the very essence of the appeal and pathos of a tragic people." "While I sat on the beach in Atlantic City," so it quoted the composer as saying, "the waves seemed to mutter the words 'O Guardian of Israel, save the remnant of Israel.' It was then that the idea occurred to me of dedicating the song to the suffering Jewish War Orphans, who are indeed the 'remnant' of our race."

Then, once he had made up his mind to devote his earnings from the sale of the song to the cause they were intended to aid, he felt like a person who had unburdened himself of a necessary obligation. "What I have done is not charity," he declared to the reporter of the New York Mail. "The Jewish law says that if you give and pronounce it charity, the *Mitzvah* is lost."

The year 1919 ended for Yossele Rosenblatt in a blaze of glory and 1920 opened as brilliantly if not more so. The critics, who heard him, whether at Symphony Hall in Boston or in Springfield, Massachusetts, or elsewhere, always marvelled at his falsetto. They saw in his rendition of Verdi's "Celeste Aïda" "a combination of what both Caruso and Murphy could do at their best."

Ernest Newton Bagg felt, after my father's debut in Springfield, that "not even Sirota, the famous cantor of Warsaw, when he sang some seasons ago in New York, could have made a more favorable impression upon a miscellaneous audience."

In January of this year he finally achieved the distinction of appearing at the New York Metropolitan Opera House, and of being accompanied by the Metropolitan's orchestra, under the baton of a Richard Hageman, in his own composition "Mogen Ovos." His debut in the famous temple of music was an historic event for his coreligionists who made no attempt to conceal their pride over the honor bestowed on their Yossele.

My father had often been mentioned together with John McCormack. Now chance was to give him an opportunity to meet his Irish counterpart and exchange compliments with him. It happened on a tour of the South, the first to take him to such distant communities as Houston, Dallas, San Antonio and New Orleans. The trip was hectic. He had hardly any time to rest between train and engagement, yet his voice seemed to show no sign of fatigue. By an interesting coincidence one of his specialties on this concert tour was the Irish folksong "Duna." He was singing in a Chattanooga theater when the mellow-voiced Irish tenor appeared among the crowd.

McCormack listened with fascination to Yossele's cantillation of *Omar Rabbi Elozor,* to his gliding up and down the scales of *Habet Mishomayim* and his imperceptible changes from robusto to piano. The concert was scarcely over when he ran up to the stage, and, grasping the singer's hand, exclaimed: "Hello, Jewish McCormack!" It was the highest tribute he could think of at the spur of the moment to express his admiration. But the cantor at once repaid him in coin by answering: "Hello, Irish Rosenblatt!" Next morning the Chattanooga newspapers appeared with headlines reading: "Hello, Jewish McCormack!—Hello, Irish Rosenblatt!"

Did the Irish Rosenblatt have an inkling of the strain under which the Jewish McCormack was laboring? I wonder. Somehow my father managed to keep in trim. As my brother Leo, who later on served as his personal representative and companion, recalled, his preparations for a concert were few and simple. He would review several of the more difficult numbers with his accompanist. Before a performance he would eat lightly to keep his diaphragm free, and would take along with him to the theatre a thermos bottle of black coffee, to ease his throat if it felt tired or husky. Tea, he found by experience, dried it too much. Whether it was really so is hard to say. Most likely the coffee affected him psychologically rather than physiologically.

In but two years on the concert stage my father attained an undisputed reputation as Jewry's foremost representative in the vocal art. After a recital by him in Milwaukee one of the periodicals remarked: "The Jews are not without their great singers, and none of them apparently foolishly take any pains to hide their nationality. There is Rosa Raisa, Alma Gluck, Sophie Braslau, Georges Baklanoff, and a host of others of lesser renown. All of these, however, have been 'denationalized' and made cosmopolitan either by their American bringing up or by their training. But Cantor Josef Rosenblatt, untouched by any non-Jewish influence, is the real national singer . . .

"Few of the many national singers the Jews possess have ventured to show their art to a cosmopolitan audience. For this reason it had been the belief of some that the Jews had no national music. Rosenblatt disproves this, and does the musical world an inestimable favor."

24

Meeting All Comers

Until this time, owing chiefly to the interruption of regular communications between the Old World and the New occasioned by the war, my father had the field of *Chazanuth* in America virtually to himself. This was so notwithstanding the fact that American Jewry already then harbored in its midst a number of precentors gifted with the power of improvisation and the interpretation of prayer. There was the massive Karniol, with his extraordinary coloratura, and the eccentric Ruttman, whose originality always impressed my father. Yet none of these presented any real competition.

The situation was radically changed when, after the end of World War One, the sea lanes were opened again. Among more than 119,000 Jewish emigrees from Central and Eastern Europe that landed on the shores of the United States of America, there arrived in the bumper year of 1920 some of the pick of European cantors and musicians of the synagogue. They came not merely "to sojourn," but "to stay" and make their fortune in this golden land of the West that had escaped the ravages of the war.

Outstanding among the newcomers in the cantorial field were Mordecai Hershman of Vilna, Sawel Kwartin of Budapest and David Roitman of Odessa. In the realm of Jewish liturgical composition the leading lights were Leo Liov of Warsaw, Pinie Minkowsky of Odessa and Seidel Rovner of Berdichev. The coming to America of such celebrities, each with a well-established reputation for ability, constituted a formidable challenge to my father's enviable position. According to the Frankfurter Zeitung, the voice of Hershman, when he uttered the words "Hear, O Israel!" resembled the eruption of a volcano. "It was overwhelming in its effect. It was the Jewish faith itself, that marvellous, heroic trust in the one and only God." Kwartin's majestic declamation of the prayers in his powerful baritone was, by my father's admission, unexcelled. Roitman's merit lay in such outstanding cantorial recitations as his soul-searing *Oshamnu mikkol om,* and his heart-rending *Rochel mevakkoh al boneho,* which my father had often sung before having met their composer. Pinie Minkowsky, again, had since his youth been his cantorial ideal, a master of the music of the synagogue who combined with musicianship a profound knowledge of the language and contents of the prayers. He always spoke with the deepest veneration about the great Pinie, who had known him as a child. And although the name of choir-director and composer Leo Liov was familiar to him only by hearsay, Seidel Rovner, who was then already past sixty, was more than a legendary figure to him. His own choir had sung the *Chassidic* composer's music for a good many years.

It seems, however, that in the opinion of the Yiddish press none of these contenders for the crown of royalty in the field of *Chazanuth* posed any real threat to Yossele Rosenblatt. The Yiddish humorous weekly Der Groisse Kundess (The Big Stick) of New York in one of its novel cartoons pictured my father dressed—or rather undressed—like a boxer, in *Arba-Kanfos*, shorts, boxing gloves and, of course, his never-absent skull-cap, standing in one corner of a boxing-ring, while stretched out before him lay one of the imported cantors. The caption beneath the cartoon read: "Battling Kid Yossele Meets All Comers."

Why were his competitors unsuccessful in dislodging him from his place of primacy? There were a variety of reasons. Pinie Minkowsky was too sophisticated an artist for the average American Jew. Besides his voice was limited in range and he had already passed his prime. Kwartin, though still in full possession of his powers, was not as versatile as my father. Roitman's voice did not have the quality. Hershman, the only true rival, lacked my father's delicacy. Furthermore he had offended Jewish communal leaders by his reluctance to lend his talents freely to charitable causes. But, whatever their merits might have been, the broad public missed in the newcomers that simple piety, that deep and sincere devotion to his calling that they found in my father and that colored so profoundly his entire manner of presentation.

My father himself never lost a moment's sleep because of the competition he was now getting. When asked by his zealous friends what he had to say on the subject, he would stroke his beard and reply with a smile: "I am not afraid of rivalry. It is only of God and the barber that I stand in awe. My beard, you know, is in constant danger of the hair-cutters."

He had a high regard for his distinguished colleagues, and to their credit let it be said that they reciprocated this feeling. At one of the gala concerts of the Cantors' Association, Hershman, so it is reported, after chanting a certain liturgical selection, was warmly applauded by the audience. Seeing Rosenblatt behind the stage, Hershman turned to him and said, provokingly:

"Nu, Berdenyu (Well, Beardie), do you hear how Jews clamor for me? Let's see, Berdenyu, what you will be able to accomplish after such an ovation!"

Then came Yossele Rosenblatt's turn to appear. When the president of the association announced him, Yossele turned to Hershman and said to him in a sing-song:

"Oy vet dir dos Berdenyu bald machen a Begrobenyu" (Oh, what a grave this Beardie will soon dig for you).

Then, when Yossele Rosenblatt finished his recitative, and the entire auditorium stamped and applauded ecstatically, Hershman, who just a moment before had good-humoredly teased him, ran to meet his rival, and, embracing him, said:

"Berdenyu, you deserve a kiss."

If the behavior towards my father of Mordecai Hershman, who was a rough and tumble sort of fellow, was a bit on the impudent side, that of Zawel Kwartin was always correct. Years after my father's death he wrote about his untimely passing in expressions of true sorrow. That he entertained this high regard for my father during his lifetime is evidenced not only by their appearance together at

many a joint concert, but also by the warm words of tribute
he spoke at one of the testimonials tendered my father, of
which we shall have more to say later.

The finest illustration, however, of my father's attitude toward other distinguished members of his profession is afforded by his experience with Seidel Rovner. That veteran
composer of Jewish liturgical music, which enjoyed particular vogue among East-European Jews of *Chassidic* provenance, was very conscious of his limitations as a vocalist. Hence he was, as a matter of principle, most reluctant
to share the spotlight with any cantor who would outshine
him by his voice. He must have been mindful of the story
related about Nissi Belzer, who, like himself, was more distinguished as a composer and choir director than as a singer.
A stranger hearing Nissi officiate one Saturday, assisted by
his famous choir, inquired of one of the officers of the congregation how much the choir cost them a year. On being
told that it entailed an expense of some 5,000 rubles per
annum, the visitor remarked: "If you can afford such a price
for a mere choir, you could for a few thousand rubles more
have engaged a good *Chazan* to go along with it."

To induce Seidel Rovner, who usually officiated when his
choir sang, to consent to appear on the same platform
with a cantor enjoying any sort of renown was regarded as
next to impossible. Nevertheless two very shrewd and enterprising young Jewish impresarios of Philadelphia, Max Romm
and Jacob M. Singer, whose acquaintance we have already
made, succeeded in persuading the jealous old Seidel to give
a Passover concert in Philadelphia's Metropolitan Opera
House together with my father on one of the intervening
days of the festival. He was to direct the choir and symphony orchestra, consisting of 60 artists, in his own compositions, while my father was to be the soloist in a selection of
his own well-known prayers of the synagogue.

The concert proved to be an overwhelming success. After

paying my father his share and compensating Seidel Rovner and his choir and orchestra, there was still a very handsome profit left over for the managers. My father was thrilled beyond words. Congratulating the promoters when the affair was over, he said to them: "You are miracle-workers, for you accomplished the impossible. It is said of marriage brokers, when they succeed in uniting in wedlock two families that seem very far apart from each other, that 'they have brought together two walls.' You have done something even more marvellous than that. In getting Seidel Rovner to consent to performing together with me you have brought together two beards. You deserve all the credit in the world —and the cash also—for being such clever manipulators."

In the spring of 1920 a quarter century had elapsed since my father's thirteenth birthday, when he had begun to function as a cantor in his own right. The attainment of such a milestone called for celebrations, a series of which now took place. They began with a concert in Carnegie Hall on April 27 and terminated with an evening restricted chiefly to professionals. His birthday itself, which happened to fall on a Sabbath, my father observed by officiating at the downtown synagogue of his congregation.

Of all these functions, the closing banquet at Abramson's Restaurant was the most interesting. Among the participants were the recently arrived Cantor Zawel Kwartin and his daughter, the Warsaw choir director Leo Liov, and Miss Rhea Silberta, the composer of *Yahrzeit*. Cantor Hershman, who was in mourning, sent a telegram. Zawel Kwartin, as the chief speaker, had many fine things to say about Reb Yossele's contributions to *chazanuth* as well as to the position of the cantor in the United States. The climax of the evening's program was the guest of honor's rendition of *Elokay Neshomoh* and *Shomer Adoshem es kol Ohavov*. "One had the impression, when Yossele Rosenblatt sang," remarked a listener, "of hearing angels make music."

The silver jubilee of a famous cantor was too important an event to be passed over in silence by the Jewish press. As was to be expected there appeared in a number of the Yiddish dailies of America appraisals of the work of Yossele Rosenblatt as *chazan* and of his place in musical art in general. Of these, the one drawn up by Aaron Rosen of the Jewish Daily News under the heading "Reb Yossele Rosenblatt, the Genius of the *Amud*," shows the deepest understanding.

After reviewing my father's career as a singer, the writer goes on to discuss his merits as a composer. "Reb Yossele," he says, "commenced to compose [Jewish liturgical music] when he was still a mere lad. He showed the writer of these lines an *Eshkol* that he had written for cantor and choir when he was fifteen years old . . . The people who had heard him chant it this year are unable to shake off the spell this prayer cast upon them.

"Reb Yossele's greatness as a composer and particularly as an author of oratorios, is first now becoming evident. The world war, the havoc wrought by it, had a deep impact on him. He looked for means with which to rouse the hearts of Jews to come to the rescue of their brethren, and he found them in the *Shemoneh Esreh* of the weekday synagogue service, the penitential ritual, the *piyut* of the festivals and the High Holiday liturgy. He has invested these prayers in his musical rendition with such depth and appeal that now all of America is stirred by them . . .

"He is now completing three important works. They are *Yishtabach,* an example of classical style, *Elokai ad shelo Notzarti,* a masterpiece of a confessional, and *Al Naharos Bovel,* which excels all the rest."

The fall of 1920, as B. Botwinik noted in the Forward, found four of the world's most popular cantors in New York, and all of them—Zawel Kwartin of Budapest, Don Fuchs of Vienna, Mordecai Hershman of Vilna and Josef Rosenblatt of America—officiated there during the High Holidays. He went to hear them, and each one had something to offer. But it was in the Ohab Zedek Synagogue that his yearning for the traditional in Judaism was most satisfied.

"I never had that sense of Jewishness," he confessed, "in the presence of the cantors of the old European congregations that I get from the American *Chazan* Rosenblatt, in the American synagogue of an American congregation. It is a real synagogue, with a real Holy Ark, with sincere Jews who pray devoutly. Reb Yossele Rosenblatt, with a young, fresh voice, interprets the text of the *Neilah* service in such a manner that it is like balm for the limbs of the body . . . He stands there, in front of the prayer-desk, with the full-length prayer-shawl drawn over his head, and a little boy of the choir sings in duet with him the time-honored litany of *'P'sach lonu shaar.'*

"In the synagogue there reigns perfect silence. The Ark is open. The cantor's tenor and the boy's delicate alto ring out high and pleasant. The innermost recesses of the hearts of all present were touched. One got a real *Yom Kippur* feeling."

25

Acquiring a Home

Eight years had rolled by since we arrived in America. My father was at the height of his powers and his fame. Yet he still lived in a rented house in a lower middle-class neighborhood. The block in which he resided boasted ten Jewish places of worship, a Jewish parochial school, shops catering to Jewish ritual requirements, and was noisy with children playing and delivery trucks passing through or unloading merchandise.

The cause for the rigid economy exercised by him in the satisfaction of personal needs was that so many other demands had to be given priority. The war had ruined even the self-sustaining relatives in Europe. If there were no more sisters to be married, there were the children of sisters, and without a dowry even the most attractive girl in the old country could not dream of matrimony.

One instance of mulcting by relations from abroad aroused my usually patient mother, who had always been overly modest in her personal demands, to unparalleled indignation. Aunt Gittel had by her persistent pleading wheedled out of my father $1200 to marry off her youngest daughter. Soon, however, the request was repeated. The money had been lost, and unless a like amount were to be forwarded, the poor orphan would, God forbid, forfeit her last chance at wedlock. That aunt Gittel should have come back for another handout was in itself not at all surprising. But how could so large a sum have suddenly disappeared? My mother insisted upon an accounting and it turned out that aunt Gittel's darling son Joseph, who combined with his talent as a singer a weakness for gambling, had lost the money at cards. My mother fumed and raged, but to no avail. Despite her protests the second $1200 was despatched, and that was the end of that matter.

At last the time came when my parents thought they could afford to live more lavishly. With the increase of his salary as cantor to $6000 per annum and the advance royalties of $1000 per record paid by the Victor Company, my father's regular income had risen sharply. Furthermore it was announced that during the season beginning with the fall of 1920 he was to give "more than fifty concerts in different parts of the country, going as far West as Denver, and

South to New Orleans through Oklahoma and Texas." He was also scheduled to appear several times in New York.

The wealth that had thus accrued to him enabled my father to purchase a four-story grey sandstone house on quiet, aristocratic 120th Street, directly opposite Mount Morris Park. Even then he was in no position to make a cash settlement. The most he could muster was $9,000, and he had to take a mortgage of $22,000. An additional $7,000 was spent on remodeling.

Though wedged in among others of the same size and general appearance, our home was commodious and comfortable and answered our needs. On the ground floor, two steps down from the level of the street, was our everyday dining room, a large kitchen, pantry and lavatory. On the story directly above it, which was accessible from the outside by a flight of stone steps, was the long living room, the ceiling of which my mother had decorated tastefully with gold leaf and the floor of which she covered with an exquisite Chinese rug. In it stood my father's grand piano and on its walls hung some fine paintings of Jewish scenes. Next to the living room was the large dining room, which was used on Sabbaths and festivals and whenever we had distinguished guests, while to the rear was my father's little writing room, where he kept his music, papers, mementos, old photographs and family archives. The large front room on the floor above, with the three dormer-windows, was outfitted as a library. It was separated from the master bedroom by two washrooms. On the top floor, finally, there were two large adjoining bedrooms for the younger children as well as rooms for the help.

The house had parquet floors from top to bottom. The walls were painted. The living room, main dining-hall, master-bedroom and library were provided with period furniture. Our home thus acquired an air of elegance in keep-

ing with the position held by my father in American Jewish life. It was a source of pride for my mother to be able
to entertain the celebrities who came to visit us, as well
as to show off her menage to the never-ending stream of cantors, rabbis, communal workers, lovers of *Chazanuth*, admirers and hangers-on.

Already prior to our acquisition of a home of our own,
the Rosenblatt residence was looked upon as a paradise of
schnorrers and my father as the redeeming angel of Jews in
distress. This applied all the more so now. At the beginning
of every Jewish month a regular pilgrimage to our home
would take place. Cripples and paupers of all kinds, real
and pretended, would ring the door-bell all day long, and
none ever went away without achieving his purpose. Certain
families were provided with milk. Others received shoes and
clothing, still others cash. For my father to give away the
last bit of silver he had in his pocket was not uncommon.
At times he would turn over to a panhandler in the street
the change he received at a wedding for taxi fare and use
the subway to ride home.

Sometimes the beggars, knowing my father's innate
goodness of heart and his absolute inability to turn back a
request for help, became brazen in their demands. One
morning a woman came to our door asking for a donation.
My father happened to be away at the time and all that my
mother had on her person was half a dollar, which she
promptly took out and gave to the beggarwoman. The latter, greatly insulted, indignantly threw the coin to the ground,
yelling "I am accustomed to receiving more." Whereupon
my mother—this is the only time I ever saw her react
this way—retorted: "If that's the case, you may look for
somebody else to sponge on. I have no contract with you."

Another instance of sheer impudence was that of a
would-be immigrant to America, a total stranger, who sent
my father a letter asking for steamship tickets to enable him

to come to the United States, with his family, or, if he wanted to save himself the trouble, to forward to him the sum of $1,000 so that he could purchase the tickets himself.

There was, finally, that supposed poor deaf-mute, who for years was accustomed once or twice a month to come to our house, either alone or with a friend, to peddle music. He always received a good meal plus some cash and was permitted to keep his music, even though he made a pretense by grunts and gestures to sell it. Once he paid us a visit when my mother's brother from Cracow was with us. Whether from experience or by native shrewdness, my uncle suspected that the deafness of the music salesman was not bona fide. By means of threats he got the beggar to speak. The impostor confessed that he was quite normal but claimed that he was compelled to feign his affliction in order to evoke the pity of his customers. This exposure did not stop my father from giving him hand-outs from time to time, but, of course, the mendicant did not come so frequently anymore.

A graphic picture of my father at home is presented in the following article by Jacob Kirschenbaum of the Jewish Morning Journal:

"I arrive at the home of Reb Yossele," says the writer, "early in the morning for an interview. The place is one that bespeaks Jewish aristocracy. On the wall hangs a *Mizrach* and a family-tree with many branches.

"I wait for Reb Yossele, who is still in the midst of his morning devotions. I have already waited an hour and a half. From the other room there issue snatches of song and melody. It is Yossele chanting his prayers, and I listen attentively. Finally Yossele emerges from the room:

" '*Sholom Aleichem*. Please excuse me. I happened to be praying when you called. Now let's sit down at the table and have a bite. I assume you have already said your prayers.'

"We wash for the meal and sit down at the table. Yossele

recites the blessing over the bread—and everything, even the blessing, is pronounced with a musical intonation. I get into conversation with him and tell him I want an interview. But he doesn't seem to understand what I mean by an interview.

" 'Tell me about your youth.'

" 'What can I tell you? I sang . . .'

" 'That's just what I want to know.'

" 'Well, what's there to tell about in that?'

" 'For example when you experienced your first urge to become a cantor.'

" 'God blessed me, and then, yes, at the Rabbi's table.' And he waxes enthusiastic as he describes the Rabbi's fervor and his outpouring of the soul. Then he calls a Jew in from the street so that he could recite the grace with a *Mezuman,* 'for not every day do I have the privilege of having a *Mezuman* at the morning meal.'

"As I left Reb Yossele that day I carried away a haul of material about the rabbinical courts of Sadagora and Tshortkov . . . and became acquainted not only with the cantor but the man, with the truly religious Jew, Reb Yossele. I had a chance to observe his way of living, and the atmosphere of his home, and the causes of his extraordinary success became clear to me. I obtained no interview in the usual sense of the word. But he did sing his compositions for me while his son Henry accompanied him on the piano. Leaving his house I hummed his melodies which I shall forever remember."

Within a very short time after we moved into it our new residence became known as the rendezvous of cantors, musicians and artists from all over the world. Joseph Schwarz, the handsome, white-haired chief baritone of the Vienna Staatsoper was a frequent visitor. Zawel Kwartin and his daughter often were guests. I still have in my possession an Elgin watch that was presented to my father by a colleague from

Australia, in appreciation for the courtesies extended him by our house during his stopover in New York on the way to Europe.

My father was not only a genial host, but also, without intending it or striving for such a position, a patron of the arts. Struggling Jewish artists—and there was always an abundance of them—knowing of his generosity, would apply to him for financial assistance. The only recompense of his kindness they could offer was the fruits of their labors. That is how we fell heir to the oil paintings depicting Jewish scenes and other objects of art that adorned our living room.

Then, one evening in December of the year 1920 Yossele Rosenblatt, the unsophisticated Jewish cantor, who had never received a formal education, musical or academic, found himself a "sponsor of prodigies." The plan of charging him with such a mission originated in the mind of the popular American Jewish novelist, Fannie Hurst. Since Josef Rosenblatt had himself been a boy-marvel in his youth, she felt certain that he would take kindly to the idea of giving encouragement to children of promise in the development of their talents.

So she assembled a score of them together with their parents in our home and had my father give them a private concert while my mother served as hostess.

The group, which had been selected on a non-sectarian basis, included pianists, violinists, cellists and dancers, ranging from the ages of six to sixteen. The youngest was Sammy Kramer, who was later on to attain considerable fame as a violin virtuoso. But the most interesting member of the party, for whom my father developed a particular fondness, was the recently arrived eight-and-a-half-year-old Polish Jewish chess marvel, Sammy Rzeszewski.

My father's first encounter with the somewhat precocious lad had been back-stage at the Brooklyn Academy of Music on the night of the concert sponsored by the B'nai Israel

Mizrachi Congregation. The boy had been asked by the chairman to appear before the public and refused.

"I can't see," said the determined little fellow, "what benefit the audience will derive from my making a fool of myself by showing myself on the stage." Even the pleas of my father, who was behind the curtain, that he do him a personal favor by acceding to popular request, failed to move him. "I would do anything for you, Reb Yossele," was his firm reply. "I would even play chess for you. But not this. I can't see the sense of appearing on the stage."

"Look here, Shmilekel," my father continued pleading with him. "I am older than you. Nevertheless, when people demand it, I don't mind showing myself, especially when I feel that I might thereby be of assistance to a good cause."

"How can I compare myself to you," was the youngster's immediate rejoinder. "You are a mature artist, while I am only a young boy." And so it remained. He could not be persuaded to ascend the platform.

My father thought Sammy mighty clever. The boy possessed in addition to other gifts a prodigious musical memory. He was able to repeat by heart all of my father's liturgical compositions, with the recordings of which he had become acquainted while still in Paris. This made for a close bond between the youngster and the cantor he admired so much. Another interest they shared was the game in which Sammy excelled. My father loved to play chess. It was among the very few pastimes in which he indulged and for an amateur he played rather well.

Shortly before his departure for the Holy Land, which occurred about twelve years after he had met Sammy Rzeszewski for the first time, my father participated in a game of chess, prior to a wedding he was to perform, and lost. As it was time then for the ceremony to go on, he was unable to reinstate himself. However he promised his opponent that he would, in the not too distant future, play him a return engagement and make up the loss. On account of his premature death the promise remained unfulfilled.

About ten years later the same gentleman was playing chess with a friend at a Jewish summer camp. While the men were immersed in their play, a youngster of fifteen, who was looking on, challenged the victor to a game. The older men thought it a bit impudent for a young whippersnapper to think he could match players who were his seniors by many years and much more experienced than himself. Nevertheless they decided to let him have his wish and thereby perhaps teach him a lesson. To their utter amazement, the boy, instead of losing, won several games in succession.

"What's your name, young man?" inquired the chastised veterans of the chessboard.

"David Rosenblatt," was the reply.

"Any relation to the late Cantor Josef Rosenblatt?"

"Yes, he was my grandfather."

A look of surprise lighted up the eyes of the older players.

"That evens the score for Yossele Rosenblatt. His honor as a chessplayer has been vindicated by his grandson."

Reference has been made several times already to Yossele Rosenblatt's innate charity, to his instinctive responsiveness to human suffering and misery. This sensitiveness to his fellowmen's lot, instead of being blunted by growing fame and fortune, became intensified thereby. If previously his philanthropic activities were confined almost exclusively to his own people, to Jewish hospitals, orphan asylums, homes for the aged, synagogues, schools and seminaries, they now began to cut across the barriers of race, class or creed. Thus, for example, we find him singing in January, 1921, at Madison Square Garden for the benefit of the striking tailors of New York, in whose ranks at that time already there were included many non-Jews as well as Jews. By lending his talents to that cause he was, as the beneficiaries of his generosity expressed it, "helping them in their struggle for a more abundant and better existence."

A month later he was given his first chance to bring a little cheer by means of his voice into the darkness of the lives of men sentenced to years of penal servitude in Sing Sing prison in expiation of crime. There were more non-Jews than Jews in the audience. Yet they were all visibly moved by the performance. The question still to be decided is who got the bigger thrill, the singer or those for whom he sang. For when father came home he remarked that by looking at the faces of these hardened sinners it was impossible to tell them apart from decent, respectable people, and his heart went out towards the unfortunates when he noticed the tears streaming down their eyes as he sang *Habet Mishomayim Ur'eh.* "And can they pack a wallop! I have never heard the like of it. I would still have been singing for them if they had had their way. Luckily the warden came to my rescue."

When in the spring of this same year a joint Jewish Passover and Irish Easter Relief was organized in Harlem, he agreed without a moment's hesitation to be one of the headliners of the program arranged at one of the local theaters. His answer to the query of the Home News reporter of how a busy man like him managed to take time out to participate in the function was: "It is hard to refuse to volunteer for two such noble causes."

Yet indiscriminating and generous as he was in the use of his gifts for charitable purposes the first place in his affections was still held by those men whom he had learned since early childhood to revere next to God. When receptions would be tendered to the leaders of East-European *Chassidism,* in the surroundings of which he had grown up, he would drop whatever he might be doing to show them honor. The teachings of his youth would reassert themselves and he would react accordingly.

These heirs of the glories of a past that was fast disappearing were then beginning to stream in considerable numbers to America. One of the most distinguished among them, who visited New York in May 1921 was the rabbi of Drohobycz. He was the first of the *Chassidic* rabbinical authorities of Galicia to endorse the Balfour Declaration and to settle together with his followers on the soil of the Jewish homeland. At the demonstration of homage arranged at the Roumanian synagogue on Rivington Street in honor of this head of Galician *Chassidism* Yossele Rosenblatt seemed in the opinion of the Yiddish press to be the right man in the right place. Certainly no selection could have struck a more fitting note to grace the occasion than *Al Hatzaddikim* as rendered by him there.

The spring of the year 1921, in which this reception took place, marked the end of my college career. I was to receive my bachelor's degree in June. In honor of the occasion my father was once more invited to sing in the Great Hall of my alma mater. Souvenir programs, bearing his picture, were distributed. Prominent visitors were invited to attend the function, and clubs that usually met on Fridays postponed their meetings in order to assure a full turnout.

The program was magnificently and inspiringly executed. My father was happy for the opportunity to do his little share for the institution in return for the many benefits his son had derived from it. He was even more pleased by my decision upon my graduation to enter the rabbinate. He would often remark later on with deep pride that his pedigree was higher than mine. For while he was able to boast of having a son who was a rabbi, I could only lay claim to a father who was a cantor.

Just before the fall school season opened, one of the most illustrious teachers of the Jewish Theological Seminary of America, at whose feet I had hoped to sit, Dr. Israel Friedlander, was tragically murdered by bandits while he was in the Ukraine on a mission of mercy. My father, who had been associated with Dr. Friedlander in the work of the Joint Distribution Committee, was called upon to recite the *El Mole Rachamim* at the memorial meeting held in his honor in Carnegie Hall.

26

Relatives from Abroad

The summer of the year 1921, like those of 1919 and 1920, meant the transfer of our menage from New York to Long Branch. The musical world knew where "the little Jewish cantor was vacationing" because the rotogravure sections of the musical periodicals carried pictures of him relaxing on the lawn or the beach with members of his family. Actually he did not spend more than two weeks altogether at his summer home, because his vacation was always interrupted by concerts, not only the one he would give in July or August at Ocean Grove, but in Denver or Jersey City or Binghampton or other such distant or stiflingly hot places.

This summer differed from its predecessors only in that the population of our cottage in Long Branch had been augmented by visitors from abroad. One of our guests was my father's brother Levi, who was then cantor in Groningen, Holland. A second was my mother's youngest brother Samuel, who had accompanied us on our way to America. They had come from impoverished Europe to rehabilitate themselves economically. Each was provided, through my father's mediation, with a high holiday position. Uncle Levi was able by means of what he earned thereby to pay his debts, and Uncle Samuel accumulated sufficient funds to marry and establish a household.

Uncle Levi bore a very strong external likeness to my father. Although no shorter than his older brother, he was less robust. His even blacker beard was of the same size as my father's, but not his voice, which was tinny and lacking in mellowness. He had retained in his singing the quaint mannerisms of the old-fashioned *Chassidic* precentors, of which my father had long ridded himself. And in general his demeanor and outlook were those of a provincial who had remained untouched by his urban surroundings. He appeared to me to represent what my father might have been if his voice had not been developed, and if he had not been thrust, when he was still a young man, first into the cultured milieu of Hamburg and afterwards into the unfettered environment of America.

Uncle Samuel was his direct opposite. Fairly tall and powerfully built, he had seen a good bit of the world and cherished no illusions about it. When the Russians invaded his home town of Brzesko and made a pogrom on the Jewish population, he had the presence of mind to disguise himself as a drunken Polish peasant and pretend to loot together with the mob. By putting on this act he was able to save his father's life and bring him to Karlsbad, where he remained until the war was over. Uncle Samuel was a bon viveur. But at the age of thirty he decided that it was time to settle down. When I saw him in the summer of 1922, he had grown a beard and was well on his way to becoming the official cantor of the devout community of Cracow. He had a high-pitched voice of considerable power, and not without beauty, although it occasionally went sharp.

Together with him on this trip came my mother's nephew Melech Kaufman, a tall, handsome, strapping fellow with a ruddy complexion and smooth, almost hairless skin. His voice was a sweet lyrical tenor, and with my father's help and a little training he developed very quickly into a very competent cantor.

All these relatives stayed with us in Long Branch over the summer and afterwards for the duration of their sojourn in America or, in Melech's case, before he secured a permanent position at our home on 120th Street. Their presence did not unduly tax our household. Since it rarely ever happened that less than twenty persons should sit down at our table to eat on Sabbaths or festivals, a few extras were hardly noticeable. Our Jewish cook, Esther, followed her regular routine, and serving half a dozen diners more or less made little difference to our Polish maid.

Thus the summer of 1921 came and went and the fall season rolled around. For us children autumn meant return to school, and we were all going to school that year. I had just enrolled in the Seminary. Leo was a sophomore in Columbia. Nettie was in her senior year at Hunter High School. Gertie was at Wadleigh. Henry was beginning his musical studies at Damrosch's Institute, while the three youngest were in the elementary grades of public school. I do not remember any one of us ever receiving help in our lessons from our parents or being told what school to go to and what courses to take. Father had no time to bother and, even if he had cared to, he could be of but little assistance since he had himself never received a formal education. It was enough if he paid the bills. Only in the matter of our religious training did he manifest real interest. We all learned to read our Hebrew prayers fluently. Father would promise the younger ones a dime or a quarter for saying the grace after meals or learning the *Shemoneh Esreh* by heart. Furthermore, all of the boys of our family were able, on the Sabbath of their *Bar-Mitzvah,* to chant, besides the *Haftarah,* the entire Pentateuchal portion for the week. In regard to other Jewish subjects our accomplishments varied, notwithstanding the fact that my father was more than willing to pay our private teacher, Mr. Weisbart, anything he would have asked for teaching us.

Father was never a stern taskmaster, but usually a most indulgent parent. One example of his tolerance goes back to my earliest childhood memories. I was then about five years old and a bit of a zealot. Leo, a year and a half younger, had forgotten to say his morning prayer, and I reported this sin of omission to my father. Instead of punishing the culprit for his dereliction, my pious father, to my amazement, said: "Well, we'll have to excuse him this time. After all he is only a little boy."

He never told any of us what kind of friends to have or not to have. At worst he would ask my younger brothers and sisters not to be seen in the company of people who were smoking on Friday nights lest outsiders get the wrong impression about his offspring. He would never reprimand any of his children's friends for violating the Sabbath. Once, however, when on a Sunday he found my youngest brother's buddies, who had not been sufficiently discreet in his presence on a Friday night, puffing away at their cigarettes, he remarked to them sarcastically: "You are not allowed to do this today. Only on Saturdays is it permissible."

He rarely ever spanked his children for their misdeeds. Mother was the disciplinarian of the family and even she was not too strict. It was not in her nature to be severe with anyone. One Saturday afternoon, my two youngest brothers were playing ball with their pals in Mount Morris Park, across the street from our home, keeping a sharp lookout for father all the while. Just when they least expected it, who turned up but father, in his Sabbath walking suit and high hat? And he did not scowl or frown. He merely tipped his hat in the friendliest fashion and walked away. Afterwards, when we were all seated at the table for the "third Sabbath meal," he suggested that henceforth, if his children had to play ball on the Sabbath, they do so in the backyard and not in a public place.

27

The Golden Era of Chazanuth

A Rosenblatt concert in New York or other large Jewish centers of America was in the year 1921 no longer a novelty. Though his audiences never tired of listening to him and packed the synagogues or concert halls in which he officiated or gave recitals, his appearances there had by this time lost the quality of the sensational. Quite different was the reaction of the inhabitants of smaller communities. These rarely ever had the privilege of having in their midst artists of the first magnitude, because they could not afford the fees. For that very reason, the enthusiasm of the audiences that had the fortune of hearing my father knew no bounds. The following article written by the Reading correspondent of the Philadelphia Jewish World, speaks for itself.

"He came, sang his part and left.

"With you this may be a commonplace. With you Jews who live in the large cities a concert by a celebrated cantor is an ordinary phenomenon. You have one every Monday and Thursday. Not so with us in the provincial towns. The only acquaintance we have with our world-famous cantors is through the phonograph. That is why Reb Yossele's coming here put us into a holiday mood.

" 'Will it really be *the* Yossele Rosenblatt that we will hear?' they asked one another. You see, the provincial audiences have lost confidence in the impresarios from the large cities. They have been fooled once too often by these fellows who promised them all sorts of things and seldom lived up to their words. And God only knows they don't deserve it . . .

"This time, however, was an exception. The real, great Yossele Rosenblatt, with his big black beard and fur coat, with his tuning-fork by means of which he struck the right note and his brief case armory containing his entire repertoire, came to us in person and sang for us. He sang and introduced us into a new world . . . The audience gave him a big ovation, and Yossele—I do not say it to his discredit—likes applause. The more he was applauded, the more did he sing.

"But it was first after his rendition of his cantorial selections, with which his listeners were acquainted through his records, that real enthusiasm manifested itself.

"The audience refused to let him leave the stage. They clamored for *Eili-Eili* and he acquiesced in return for a few more hundreds of dollars for the Sanitarium, for the benefit of which the concert had been arranged."

Such a to-do over a cantor was no rarity in the third decade of the twentieth century, which was the golden era of *Chazanuth* in America. Orthodox congregations were at that time still overwhelmingly in the majority, and as they were then constituted cantors seemed more important, answered a greater need and were paid higher salaries than rabbis. To understand and evaluate a rabbinic discourse properly, a person had to be a bit of a Talmud scholar. Only a small minority of American Jewry in those years could lay claim to such erudition. But to appreciate a *chazan* all that was necessary was a sensitive ear and acquaintance with the prayers of the synagogue. What father's son, with even a smattering of Jewish knowledge, did not possess that? Even the most ignorant among the Jews hailing from the orthodox colonies of Eastern Europe, if he knew nothing else, was at least able to read Hebrew.

A good cantor could serve many useful purposes. He could be an attraction to raise funds. He had the capacity of inspiring worshippers in the synagogue. He could provide the mood for joyous occasions and console his patrons in their grief with his soothing melodies.

Thus cantors played a significant role in the public as well as the private life of the Jew in those days. Their function was considered to be of sufficient importance to cause them to be talked about and compared with one another. Of course, there were cantors and cantors. Not every Jew with a voice who opened his mouth before a prayer-desk was deserving of a critique. Only the leaders of the profession merited discussion. But show me even one outstanding rabbi who was subjected to such scrutiny by the mass of American Jewry as were the personalities dissected in the article by B. Kowner? This columnist of the Jewish Daily Forward happened to attend services on a Saturday morning at the Beth Hamidrash Hagodol Synagogue when the young and diminutive Cantor Joseph Shlisky was officiating. And this is what he claims to have overheard:

"A Jew with a flaming red beard is all steamed up. 'Yossele Rosenblatt is what I call a cantor! Every word of his is a pearl, a polished diamond, full of sweetness. His prayers are worth your life! I heard him recite *S'lichos,* and I tell you . . .'

"But a Jew with a greying beard doesn't let him finish. Just as excitedly as the other he says: 'Yossele Rosenblatt you call a cantor? A fine cantor, indeed! If it weren't for his handsome beard and his beautiful face and his pretty little voice with his pianissimo, he might have done for a rabbi. A cantor in my language is Kwartin. Have you ever heard his *V'chol Maaminim?* You haven't? Then what's the use of talking? Kwartin, you must understand, doesn't try to pull off stunts. He is not a trickster. What he has to say—he says.'

" 'He may have been good once upon a time, not now anymore,' interposes a little Jew standing on a side, 'once upon a time, about fifteen years ago.'

" 'You are crazy, that's what you are,' retorts Kwartin's devotee. 'He is even better today than he was formerly, pro-
founder, more mature. He has more phantasy.'

" 'Phantasy, shmantasy! Who cares for phantasy, when . . .'

" 'You are all babbling arid nonsense!' a young fellow with
a mouth half full of gold teeth breaks in. 'A cantor, if you
want to know, is a man like Hershman! He is what one
could call a declaimer. When he recites a prayer, he takes
the insides out of you, he draws the marrow out of your
bones. There is no second to him and there never will be.'

" 'What's the good of all his declamation when everything
that he recites is second-hand, pilfered from other cantors.
Let him show his ability by reciting something original, that
he has composed himself. True he knows how to sing a Jewish folksong. That he does like an artist. But how does he
come to being a cantor? I wouldn't give half a dollar for his
praying.'

" 'If that's the case,' replies Hershman's partisan, boiling
with rage, 'you are as much of a connoisseur of cantors as I
am an expert on pearls! To make up for that, when Hershman takes a note and holds it, it is held! He does it so
smoothly, with so little effort, that it is just a delight. One
time he held a tone in Thomashevsky's theatre something
like three-quarters of an hour by the clock. It was so long
that he had to rest ten times perhaps before he was finished
with it. That's what kind of a tone it was.'

"All the bystanders burst out laughing, but the Hershman-
ist continued:

" 'And as for your claim that he doesn't sing his own compositions, that may be so. But where is it written that a cantor must always sing his own? As long as . . .'

" 'Say what you like, he doesn't come anywhere up to
Shlisky,' a lean little Jew with a thin nose interrupts him.
'Shlisky is "the boy." '

" 'Stuff and nonsense!' a fat little Jew with tiny eyes cuts

him off. 'He doesn't come near Shlisky because he doesn't
have his address. But what kind of a cantor is yours when he
doesn't even have a register, neither a high, nor a middle nor
a low register? And a cantor without a register can't be a cantor. Yossele Rosenblatt, you see, has all the registers, even
more than are required. I have all his records. As for Kwartin,
he has the middle register but lacks the upper . . .' "

The general public's appreciation of Yossele Rosenblatt
was fully shared by the members of his own profession. In
this connection the following incident related by the first
president of the Cantors' Association of America, with
whom my father often came in contact, is most enlighten-
ing.

"Yossele is sitting on a chair in the auditorium of the
Cantors' Association, where Rumshinsky is rehearsing with
three-hundred cantors in preparation for the concert that is
to take place the next day. Rumshinsky is dissatisfied. He
shouts excitedly, 'The concert is scheduled to take place tomorrow, and this is neither a rehearsal nor what one could
call singing!' He makes some cutting remarks about the cantors and threatens that he will not direct because he doesn't
like the soloists.

"Suddenly, Yossele runs over to me. He is pale and tired. I
go out into the street with him. Yossele pleads with me: 'I
am supposed to give my solo now. Could you perhaps persuade Rumshinsky to excuse me. He is very much excited at
present, and I am after all a cantor with a reputation and it
doesn't befit me to be insulted in the presence of the other
cantors.'

"However Rumshinsky was in no mood to excuse anybody. Yossele had to sing. When Rumshinsky saw Yossele's
handsome face and heard his voice, he smiled. 'With such
a soloist,' he said, 'the success of the concert is assured.' "

Another celebrated Jewish music director, Zavel Zilbert,
had a similar experience. It was his task to conduct the choir

of the said Cantors' Association at the Hippodrome. And a difficult assignment it was, far more difficult than getting ordinary singers to harmonize. "For what cantor does not look upon himself as an artist? Each tries to outshout the other. Nobody pays attention to timing, not to speak of shading, whether it be forte or crescendo."

In spite of Zavel Zilbert's tuneful *Habdalah* and his melodious *Boruch Eil Elyon,* the concert would have been a complete fiasco, were it not for the soloist. "The savior," remarked the Daily News, "was Reb Yossele Rosenblatt, who was in excellent voice and really warmed up in his *Elokai Neshomoh* and his new composition *Yehi Rotzon milif'nei Ovinu shebashomayim.*"

At the end of the first decade since his arrival in America my father was certainly, as the Pittsburgh Volksfreund recalled, a person of world renown. What that really meant was brought home to me by a trip I took through Europe in the summer of 1922. I had occasion to visit, in the course of fourteen weeks, eight different countries, and wherever I went I found the name of Yossele Rosenblatt to be a magic key that opened all doors. This applied not only to such communities as Hamburg and Presburg, where the memories of him were still fresh. Nor was his fame confined to places where kinsmen and childhood friends resided. His praises were sung in localities in which he had never set foot, by persons who had never seen him, knowing of him solely by reputation. The size or population of a place made no difference. I was received as cordially by Rabbi Meier Hildesheimer, the spiritual head of the Orthodox Jewish masses of Berlin, as by the leading family of the small Jewish community in Lucerne, Switzerland.

When I returned home just in time for the Jewish New Year, the newspapers were abuzz with another bid to my father to appear in opera. This time the fee offered for every engagement was $3,000, and it was the same Chicago Opera

Company that made the offer. However just like the first proposal this even more generous one was declined. "I do not find it anti-religious or anti-Jewish to sing operatic music," he explained to the representative of the Kansas City Jewish Chronicle who visited him in Long Branch. "What is more, 'La Juive' is thoroughly Jewish . . . Yet I could not accept the offer because, as an Orthodox Jew and cantor besides, I have too much respect for the Jewish tradition to allow myself to deviate from it in the least by going on the stage." He added that the late Enrico Caruso, after having heard him sing, had expressed regret over his refusal to appear in opera, especially in "La Juive," as he would have made such an ideal Eleazar. The Jewish world was proud of his persistent refusal to yield to temptation. "We wish we had more men," remarked the Detroit Jewish Chronicle, "ready to sacrifice themselves as he has done in an ideal cause. He has put Jewry in his debt by his decision."

28

Resignation and Reconciliation

Even more of a flurry than was caused by the renewed offer of the Chicago Opera Company was that which was engendered by a proposal of a different kind, one that entailed no compromise with religious scruples on my father's part. He was, namely, engaged by three Jewish entrepreneurs from Philadelphia to chant the High Holidays services at the unprecedented price of $15,000 or $5,000 a day. This was more than the celebrated Italian idol of the opera had ever been paid for a single performance.

The signing of the contract created a world-wide sensation.

It was featured not only in nearly every periodical of importance in the United States. Papers in London and Jerusalem
also carried the news. There was something of the inevitable about the event. Ever since he had risen to fame as a result of his encounter with Campanini, my father had been
dissatisfied with the niggardly salary he was being paid by the
Ohab Zedek. Even the $6,000 per annum that he had been
receiving since 1920 from the synagogue was out of proportion to the honoraria which he was now accustomed to obtain for individual concerts. His demands for a modest increase, to which he felt entitled, were turned down or
ignored. Nevertheless he long resisted the tempting offers
made him by congregations as well as impresarios anxious to
secure his services.

As early as May, 1922, there appeared in the (Yiddish)
Day of New York a rumor to the effect that he had declared himself willing to become the cantor of the Adath
Jeshurun Synagogue of Bluehill Avenue, Roxbury, Massachusetts, which was allegedly ready to engage him for life at
an annual salary of $15,000. The reporter was skeptical about
the consummation of the deal at such terms, because he
could not see any congregation assuming so heavy an obligation even for "the king of cantors." As it happened, he
turned out to be right. The negotiations failed, and on the
High Holidays of 1922 my father was still, to quote the Jewish Daily News, the "chief attraction in Harlem."

However hardly more than a week had passed since the
conclusion of the fall festival season than the "Rosenblatt
bomb" burst. The first periodical to publish the details was
the Jewish Times of Philadelphia. It reported in its October 25 issue that on the previous day my father had signed,
in the office of lawyer Joseph Gross, a contract calling for his
officiating in the Philadelphia Metropolitan Opera House
during the High Holidays of 1923 at a remuneration of
$15,000. A similar arrangement—the place to be determined

later—was purportedly entered into for the two following years. The fulfillment of the agreement would net my father, for the nine days in question, the unparalleled total of $45,000, leaving him free during the rest of the time to accept any engagement for synagogue services or concerts.

"As soon as the contract was signed," said the Jewish World of Cleveland, "Yossele Rosenblatt resigned from the Ohab Zedek Congregation."

The causes that led to his resignation this time were revealed by my father himself in a paid statement that appeared on November 19 in one of New York's Yiddish dailies.

"The managers with whom I signed a contract last week," it said, "approached me about four years ago, but out of loyalty to my congregation I hesitated to accept their offer. Besides, I thought that in staying with the Ohab Zedek I would have what one may call a permanent religious home where I could pray regularly for members of the same congregation. Of course, you know that the salary I was getting there for a whole year was less than one half of what I am now to receive for only three days of the High Holidays. Yet I was willing to continue at practically the same compensation, provided my congregation would give me a life contract, so as to enable me to devote all my time and energy to my work, instead of having to worry about tomorrow.

"When, however, it came to discussing the terms of my new contract, certain members of the congregation began dickering. They offered me a thousand dollars a year less than what I asked, and refused to extend my contract for more than a few years. They failed to appreciate the fact that for my first five years with the congregation of Ohab Zedek I had been paid only $2,400 a year and had to officiate every Saturday and holiday. They failed to see that a cantor whose art is appreciated, not only by his own congregation, but by others was entitled to greater consideration on their part. Besides, they would not appropriate a sufficient amount of money for improving the choir. When, therefore, the Philadelphia managers approached me once more with their proposition, I could not, out of justice to myself, and for other considerations of which I will tell you presently, decline the offer. Of course, my congregation is now very sorry and willing to give me anything that I ask to remain with them. But once having taken the step, I cannot and will not retract."

The other considerations were the opportunity to lead a larger congregation in prayer on the High Holidays— four thousand worshippers instead of fifteen hundred—and to serve communities all over the country and abroad. "The Jewish religious sentiment," he added, "will by no means suffer . . . It makes me feel happy to think that I shall now be able to devote more of my time to charitable activities."

If his resignation from Ohab Zedek might have brought my father material advancement and made history in the world of *Chazanuth,* it would, according to B. Shelvin of the Jewish Morning Journal, have been a calamity for the congregation. "With his departure from it, the very existence of that synagogue will be forgotten. One, therefore, wonders why the congregation permitted him to accept another position. He is certainly worth as much to it as to others."

It did not take very long before overtures were made by the officers of the Ohab Zedek Congregation to win my father back. Notwithstanding his declaration that his decision was irrevocable, he did return, on the promise of more favorable terms. He was now to receive a salary of $10,000, officiate an average of only once a month, on the Sabbath before the new moon, in addition to the festivals. He was given a new choir, under the direction of Meyer Posner. Also, in order to secure his release from the contract he had made with Messrs. Romm, Shubin and Singer of Philadelphia these gentlemen were to receive an indemnification of $5,000. This money, which was a sort of penance the congregation had to pay, was not so easy to extract, and all my father's wit had to be put to use to humor the managers until they received their due. On April 4, 1923, he wrote as follows:

Dear Friend Mr. Singer:

Your worthy letter is on hand. For the moment I do not know what to answer you apropos of the payments. It stands to reason that, if you, a businessman who is not so well known in the world, can be so much in need of funds, how much the more should this apply to a cantor like myself . . .

Oh I was so anxious to lay my hands on those fifteen thousand dollars (that you had offered me). But this crazy world won't let me. What am I to do to these people? Tie them up? Where can one find enough rope for such a purpose? To come to the point, I shall think about the matter and try to give you within this week a term-note more quickly redeemable than the one you now hold . . .

At any rate do not worry. All will be well as long as we remain good friends. My parishioners had insisted on not paying the $5,000. before the lapse of several months and by installments. Do you know what I said to them? "Nothing doing! If you don't pay at once, I go to Philadelphia." So they took fright and came across before Passover. I want you to know this.

Keep well and accept my best wishes. Remember me also to Messrs. Shubin and Romm. And tell Romm I want the check to be photographed so that the world might be convinced that this wasn't a bluff, God forbid, as certain envious individuals claim.

Your friend forever,
Josef Rosenblatt

If my penmanship is not so perfect, you must remember that we are now in the midst of the festival week on which Jewish precept demands that we modify our writing a little.

And so the matter ended. As a consolation to the Philadelphians, the managers offered them a concert during the intervening days of Passover. The program was to include many of the liturgical selections that my father would have sung had the arrangements for his appearance in Philadelphia on the High Holidays gone through as planned.

29

Enter the "Light of Israel"

Up to this point in his career my father's star had been continually in the ascendant. He had reached every goal to which a person in his profession could aspire. As far as fame was concerned, he was listed by an influential Anglo-Jewish weekly among the twelve greatest Jews living in America. His services as a cantor were remunerated more highly than those of any other known to history. The royalties from his phonograph recordings alone, which were being turned out in an endless stream, yielded an income of at least $8,000 annually. He was one of the best compensated artists of the concert stage at the time and it happened more than once that in order to release him for the performance of a wedding ceremony his managers had to be paid the entire price of a concert recital.

Whatever yardstick might be used as a gauge, Josef Rosenblatt was, at the age of forty, a success. Thanks to the popular favor that he enjoyed he was able at long last to extricate himself from the burden of debt that had until then held him in thrall. For the first time in his life his ledger showed credits instead of debits—this notwithstanding the prodigal-

ity of his charities and the higher standards of living to which
he and his family had become accustomed.

However it seems as though Fate, which had showered him
with so many gifts, begrudged him that measure of security
that such gifts are ordinarily expected to bring. Just when he
had accumulated a little money that might have been set
aside as a reserve, Satan appeared in the guise of several slick
promoters of an ill-fated newspaper venture and took it away
from him.

In a way what happened to him did not differ very much
from the fate of other members of his class and calling. Artists are as a species notorious for their lack of practical
sense. Wrapped up as they are in their art, they become easy
prey for connivers who are quick to take advantage of their
naïveté in worldly affairs and their inexperience in matters
of finance. My father shared these failings with his colleagues
of the artistic fraternity.

With the childlike simplicity of the average artist, however, he combined an intense devotion to his hereditary faith.
Although he was thoroughly opposed to the use of force or
violence, he had a passionate desire to do everything possible
to bolster Judaism in America by the gentle methods of encouragement and persuasion. He never regarded the request
made of him to sing gratis for the benefit of a Jewish institution of learning as an imposition. "The obligation (*Mitzvah*)
to spread the knowledge of the Torah," he would often reply to the officers of *Yeshivahs* or seminaries who approached
him, at times very hesitantly, for such favors, "is as much
mine as it is yours."

But it was above all for religious youth, for young people
who tried to be observant, that he had a tender spot in his
heart. Once on a Sabbath eve, which he was spending in the
Brownsville section of Brooklyn, he decided to say his prayers
in the local Young Israel synagogue. When the weekday afternoon service was over, one of the hardier spirits among the

youthful worshippers, knowing the wish that was in everybody's mind but which none of the others present dared to express, plucked up enough courage to suggest to the visitor that he chant the service inaugurating the Sabbath. "I know, Cantor Rosenblatt," he said very timidly, "that you are usually paid handsomely for performing such a service, and you are certainly entitled to a rest when you enter a synagogue just as a guest, but . . ." My father did not let him finish his sentence. "I deem it a pleasure and a privilege to officiate for so fine an organization as yours."

The charlatans who brought about his undoing were aware of this weakness and they exploited it to the utmost. The negotiations started some time in the fall of 1922. In the course of one of his visits to Montreal, Canada, two residents of that city, very suave and smooth-tongued gentlemen, accosted him for the purpose of discussing with him a grandiose idea which, they felt certain, ought to interest him. Their plan was to found in New York a 100 percent orthodox Jewish weekly, in English, Yiddish and Hebrew. Its aim would be to "perpetuate and strengthen traditional Judaism" in its true and undiluted form in the western hemisphere and combat heresy. And they wanted him, Yossele Rosenblatt, to head the enterprise. With his name and prestige behind it and because of his popularity with the Jewish masses the project could not possibly fail. Also he would have the great satisfaction of having been, by his sponsorship, the initiator of a Jewish religious rebirth in America. Finally, the periodical, which was to be called "The Light of Israel" in English and "Dos Yiddishe Licht" in Yiddish, would assure him an income that would enable him eventually to retire from the cantorate or, at least, slacken the pace of his activities.

My father's initial hesitancy in accepting the honor, on the ground that he knew so little about newspaper business, was quickly overcome. "That," said the experts, "need not stand in the way of your participation. We will take full charge of the business end of the undertaking. All that will be required of you as president of the company to be formed is to supply the financial backing." "In the meantime, Mr. Rosenblatt," they added, "we would advise you to observe the utmost secrecy. Even your wife must not be told a thing about what transpired between us until our plans are completed. She might raise objections—you know how women are—and our enterprise might come to naught."

One would imagine that only in a clumsy movie melodrama would it be possible for such a trick to be played on the hero. It seems so utterly preposterous, fantastic. Should not the very precaution of silence he was asked to take have aroused the would-be-victim's suspicions and put him on his guard? Should not ordinary common sense have directed my father, even if he was afraid to trust my mother's judgment, to at least consult his good friends about a matter fraught with such grave consequences for him? The only explanation I have for his strange behavior is that he must have been disarmed by the aura of religiosity assumed by his deceivers. He had such implicit faith in the integrity of persons, who were ostensibly scrupulous in the observance of every minutia of Jewish law, that it was inconceivable to him that they could harbor dishonest motives.

However, notwithstanding all the measures adopted to prevent a premature disclosure of the details, the secret leaked out. When a few small checks that my mother had drawn were returned because there wasn't enough money in my father's bank account to cover them, she immediately suspected that something was amiss. On the night of my father's return from his trip there was enacted between him and my mother a scene which I shall never be able to put out of my mind. Of all the children I was the only witness, as the rest had already gone to bed and were fast asleep.

I can still see my mother agitated, upset and my father nervous but defiant. "Yossel," she began, "haven't I been a faithful wife to you all my life? Have I ever crossed you? Haven't I always humored you no matter how unreasonable your demands may at times have seemed to me to be?"

"Why these questions all of a sudden?" was my father's rejoinder. "What are you driving at?"

"What I am driving at is that you have been withholding things from me of late. You have not reposed in me the confidence due to a partner that has been as devoted to you as I have always been."

"What do you mean? How have I been derelict in my duties? Am I not making a good living for you and the children? Don't you have a comfortable home, fine clothes to wear? Certainly you don't suspect me, God forbid of . . . ?"

"No, Yossel. I am not complaining about my personal comfort or lack of comfort, or your fulfillment of your conjugal responsibilities. But you have done me a great injustice by hiding certain matters from me, by harboring secrets that affect the well-being not only of yourself, but of our entire family."

"What are you talking about? What secrets have I been keeping from you?"

"Listen Yossel, what's the use of pretending? When you send me $6,000 to deposit in the bank and the checks I make out in payment of household bills come back marked 'invalid on account of insufficient funds,' something must be radically wrong. For if all is well, how do you account for the sudden shortage?"

"I am telling you, Taube, to stop worrying," replied my father angrily. "The shortage will be made good, and all will be well."

But my mother was not satisfied. She insisted on knowing what was happening. Seeing himself cornered and his usually yielding wife so persistent, my father finally broke down, making a clean breast of the whole story, of how he had been approached with a marvellous plan which, in addition to the services it would enable him to render to Judaism, would make him economically independent and permit him to relax from his strenuous labors—this last point was, I suspect, added, more for her consumption, than because he believed it.

My mother quickly realized that arguments to the effect that the prospects of security and ease held out to him were only a pipe-dream would not be very convincing to my father. So she tried another line of attack. "If the undertaking is really as wonderful as you claim that it is, why didn't you tell me about it as soon as it was broached to you? Wherein have I sinned that you should keep me in the dark when things of such importance are taking place?"

The only answer my father could give to this challenge was that, when it came to matters of business of this sort, women knew very little about it and the less they were told, the better. My mother sensed that these words were not his own. They were so unlike his usual trend of thoughts. Never before had he failed to confide in her. And if this time he was lacking in complete candor, it was because somebody had influenced him against her and put these arguments into his head. By continued prodding she learned that in the effort to launch the contemplated newspaper my father had, in addition to sinking all his personal assets, incurred obligations to the extent of $20,000 for which he was held personally responsible.

This was the last straw. When my mother realized how deep my father was already sunk in the morass from which he was destined never to be able to emerge, she wept like a child. "Yossel, what have you done? Don't you realize that this is economic suicide, taking the good fortune with which God has blessed you and throwing it to the wind? Can't you see how this will wreck the life of our family?"

"Then what do you want me to do?"

"Get out. Resign. Forget what the venture has already

cost you and start all over again. You still have your voice, thank God. In a year or so you will have worked off your debts and be a free man once more, owing nobody anything."

I, too, tried to rally to my mother's support by pleading with my father to sever his connections with the "Light of Israel." "Newspaper business is not your line, papa. You are a great cantor. You have made a marvellous success in your calling. To run a periodical, however, requires other talents and an experience you do not possess." Unfortunately my pleas made even less impression upon my father than my mother's tears. He dismissed my advice as childish, as the typical attitude of an unworldly scholar.

"Ridiculous," was his reaction. "Sheer madness. If I will add to my investment, I will retrieve what has been sunk in the undertaking hitherto. If I withdraw now, whatever has been put into the paper up to the present will be pure loss."

At this point mother was in complete despair. She became hysterical. Sensing with womanly intuition the abyss into which she and her family were relentlessly being hurled she made one last attempt, by feigning to do violence to herself, to ward it off. But it was all to no avail. My father remained adamant.

At a moment, when if he had but heeded the voice of prudence speaking through his wife he might have checked himself against committing the blunder of his life, the streak of stubbornness in him manifested itself and prevented him from recognizing what others saw so clearly. Perhaps if his father, whose orders he had always obeyed without questioning, had been alive, he might have influenced the son to change his mind. But Raphael Rosenblatt was gone, and so the former prodigy, who had had his own way in many matters for years, insisted on asserting his independence by refusing to listen to reason. His retaliation to my mother's threat was to resort to a device which he used on other oc-

casions when he was thwarted. That was to faint. Now, of
course, his health and mood, upon which his livelihood was
dependent, had to take priority over all other considerations.
And so my mother was forced to give in, and for the nonce
my father had won the battle. Unfortunately it was a Pyr-
rhic victory. The catastrophe that my mother had so clearly
foreseen was not to be staved off for long.

Amidst such circumstances, my father's credulity and
obstinacy and my mother's grave misgivings, the "Light of
Israel" saw the light of day. The first issue was released
on January 19, 1923. Just one day prior to its appearance
there was published in the Jewish Daily Forward an interview which presented Yossele Rosenblatt as a "record-
breaker." My father was preparing to leave for Chicago when
the reporter came to interrogate him and in his preoccupa-
tion did not immediately grasp what sort of records his interviewer had in mind. His first thought ran, out of habit, to
phonograph recordings, which, of course, did not make any
sense. Soon, however, he realized that it was the large number of his public appearances that was referred to. The fact
was that within a period of six weeks beginning with Friday,
November 24, he had given no less than thirty performances in different parts of the United States. The list of cities
in which he had appeared included Milwaukee, Chicago,
New York, Lawrence, Portland (Maine), Washington, Nor-
wich, Syracuse, Detroit, Brooklyn, the Bronx, Baltimore, Toledo, Utica, Scranton and Bridgeport. "And if a person permits himself the luxury of singing at so many places within
so short an interval of time to audiences totalling some 40,-
000," the visitor concluded, "doesn't he deserve to be called
'a record-breaker'?" Yes, my father was, indeed, a breaker of
records, not only by virtue of the volume of professional engagements filled by him and the amount of compensation received therefor, but also because he had less left from all his
earnings than any other artist in his class. And for *that* he

was chiefly indebted to the "Light of Israel." But he did not find it out until later on and he learned it the hard way.

In the meantime the periodical, which referred to itself as a "weekly" issued by the Ner Tomid Publishing Company, appeared more often at two-week intervals than every seventh day for a period of about two years. The editor of its Hebrew and Yiddish departments, who wrote most of the original articles, was II. Hirsh. A capable journalist, with a good Jewish and philosophical background, he had a somewhat uncertain religious past. But whenever aspersions were cast on his character, my father, who was deeply impressed —one might almost say "smitten"—with him, would reply: "Well, supposing that what is said about him is true, he is now a 'Baal Teshuvoh,' and we must accept him as such and not hold up to him his past misdeeds." The English department of the paper was given respectability by the contributions of men of impeccable character and reputation, such as Rabbi Leo Jung and his brother Moses, the Rev. Dr. George Bacarat and Rabbi Herbert S. Goldstein. They had no connection at all with the financing of the periodical.

But whatever the merits of the articles that appeared in the "Light of Israel" might have been, it was not they nor even the number of subscribers that the periodical was able to attract that could determine the financial success or failure of the venture. That was a matter that depended chiefly upon the management. And over that my father had no control. Even though technically speaking he was, as president, supposed to have a voice in the matter, newspaper business was to him a blind article in which he was completely at the mercy of the highly paid experts. One of these, who was drawing a rather large salary, when asked what his function was that merited such generous remuneration, replied: "Ich red mit Menschen" (I talk to people). That is to say, he was supposed to act as public relations counsel. How many of such functionaries the paper employed will remain a secret! One thing is certain—for a weekly that only rarely appeared every week it consumed a tremendous amount of money; and no matter how much of his earnings my father poured into it, there never seemed to be enough.

He was always short of funds. When Jacob Singer asked him to advance the indemnity of $5,000 due from the Ohab Zedek Congregation for releasing my father from his High Holiday contract with the Philadelphia managers, the best he could offer him was a promissory note for the amount. The reason why he was unable to give Singer cash was that he had invested whatever he had on hand in business—that is, the "Light of Israel"—and that he had not been successful in collecting from the people that owed him money.

The need for capital to feed the insatiable "Light of Israel," compelled my father to work harder than ever. But whether it was on account of his seemingly inexhaustible energy or the effortlessness of his singing, these exertions were not reflected either in his voice or in the quality of his performance. After his concert in Orchestra Hall, Chicago, on January 21, 1923, for example, Herman Devries, the music critic of the Chicago American, heaped lavish praise on him as on previous occasions. "To indemnify us for the departure of the opera company," he said, "Rosenblatt emptied the entire operatic bag of tricks, and became Lassari, Formichi, Schipa, Marshall, Mason, Galli-Curci and a few more thrown in for good measure.

"This is not a tenor, but a whole company. Rosenblatt could sing the entire score of 'The Barber of Seville'—Figaro, Basilio, Almaviva, Bartolo, Rosina and Bertha. Besides this, he is [sic] perpetually perfect pitch-pipe!"

As for the Jews of Chicago they were, according to the correspondent of the Jewish Morning Journal, "walking about as in a dream" after this recital, which drew as many enthusiasts as the Polish pianist Paderewski. Wherever one went, one stumbled up against persons "humming Yossele

Rosenblatt's tunes." To satisfy the hunger of his Jewish patrons in this city he had come back for several return engagements before the season ended.

Thus, while the "Light of Israel" was devouring his material resources faster than he was able to produce them, my father continued on his artistic merry-go-round as though nothing had happened. He solemnized socially prominent marriages, participated in banquets tendered to celebrities, sang for all sorts of institutions, and soloed for the United Hebrew Choral Societies of New York. There were many good voices among the members of this organization which was coached and directed by the foremost Jewish choir leaders. "Yet," as the "Big Stick," reported, "notwithstanding all the skill of the squadron of commanders (that is directors Leo Liov, Davidson, Leon Kramer, Weiner, Levin and Posner), armed with batons, in coaxing musical sounds out of a thousand throats, the person responsible for the success of the concert given by the Societies was Yossele Rosenblatt. He was the hero of the hour."

The secret of his continuing popularity was explained by the Day in an article discussing the quality of his phonograph recordings, which in 1923 enjoyed the best season ever. In addition to other accomplishments the writer mentioned that of perfect breath-control. "This enables Mr. Rosenblatt to avoid interruptions in the midst of his singing as well as to pass from forte to piano in a manner such as no other singer has ever succeeded in doing . . . And not only are his listeners pleased, even the technicians who manufacture the records are delighted whenever Rosenblatt has to make a recording, because they know that it will not be necessary for him to do it over again. One singing is sufficient, so perfectly does his voice record the very first time."

One day, when my father arrived at the laboratories of the Victor Talking Machine Company and was asked what selection he intended to record, he was unable at the moment to give a definite answer as the music had not yet been composed. However, being in a prayerful mood, he stated that he would improvise while the recorder was turned on. All that was necessary was for the accompanist to play a chord whenever he would pause in his singing. He happened to be particularly inspired that day, and the sound engineer in charge was highly pleased with the results.

Unfortunately there was a mechanical defect in the recording, so that the record had to be done over. But how was he to repeat verbatim a recitative that was pure improvisation and that had never been written down? My father thought for a while. Then he said to the mechanic: "Play that faulty record back to me." The record was played over to him several times, and by means of the notations he made he was able to reproduce the original recording without any flaws.

In April of this year the Ohab Zedek Congregation finally remitted the indemnification of $5,000 to the Philadelphia managers, and my father was released from his contract with the latter for the High Holidays. It was an exceptionally busy month for him, and May was even more so. In addition to officiating on a Sabbath in Philadelphia and conducting the Shabuot festival services in his own synagogue, the notices in the press reveal that he gave concerts during the three week period beginning May 2nd in eight different localities as distant from each other as Chicago and Bangor, Maine.

On May 24, 26 and 27 he sang once more in Detroit, Chicago and Cleveland.

His appearances in these three cities were sponsored by the Workingmen's Culture League. The incongruity of the engagement of a man of his type by a group whose philosophy of life was so far removed from all that he stood for evoked from the "Big Stick" the comment, "It would seem now that Yossele Rosenblatt takes the place of Karl Marx.

Our masses are becoming music and cantor minded, and have as little relationship with socialism as Abe Cahan has."

On the second day after his concert in Cleveland father was on his way to Europe for the first time since his settlement in America.

As early as January rumors had been circulated in the press of plans nurtured by Yossele Rosenblatt to tour the European continent and arrange to celebrate Passover in Palestine, the land of his hopes and dreams. His keen desire to visit the Holy Land was not fulfilled until a decade later. But as far as Europe was concerned, he did visit it this year. But why go to Europe, which had been impoverished by war, when America had so much more to offer? There were several reasons. One was that my brother Leo, who had just completed his pre-law courses at Columbia University, took over the direction of his father's affairs and he had a notion that a trip to Europe would be beneficial for his client. Secondly, travel was broadening. For a vocal artist to be able to say that he had sung with some measure of success in the cultural centers of the Old World had advertisement value in America. It made him an international figure, adding to his prestige. Furthermore the hot summer was usually a slack season in America, whereas in Europe the climate was much more agreeable. Finally, both my parents were anxious to come into personal contact again with their relatives whom they had not seen since 1912.

And so the six youngest members of our family were packed off to camp for the summer, while I made provision to combine study with ocean bathing in Atlantic City. On May 29 my parents and Leo set sail on the Mauretania for England. Friends, admirers and colleagues of father came to the pier to see them off and bid them God-speed. A snapshot of the travellers published in the Jewish Morning Journal bore the legend: "In return for the favor bestowed

on us by Europe in providing us with a continual supply of
new cantors, America has decided to return the compliment
by sending to the Europeans for a short time a cantor of its
own, and a really worth while one, Yossele Rosenblatt, who
left for Europe last week."

30

First European Tour

More than a month before his arrival in the British Isles,
where he was awaited with eager anticipation, a report on
the personality of the visitor from America was published in
the London Jewish Times (die Zeit). The article dwelled
on the position occupied by its subject in America, delineated
his features and described his ideal home life. It spoke of
his unswerving loyalty to his religion in spite of his artistic
achievements, of his sincerity, and of his unusual generosity. One would imagine that after such a build-up there
would not be one discordant note among the Jews of England
in regard to Yossele Rosenblatt's personal merit. However
unanimity of approval is perhaps more than any human being has a right to expect anywhere. About a week before my
father's first appearance in Great Britain, the following letter was addressed to the editor of the London Jewish Chronicle by the president of the *Chazanim* Association of England:

Sir:
  We note that the Rev. J. Rosenblatt, of America, is shortly to
visit this country and proposes to give a recital at the Queen's
Hall.
  Some years ago we expressed our opinion on the subject of

such recitals, and we beg once again to place before your readers our considered views concerning this matter.

If this gentleman visits England as a secular artist, the matter is no concern of ours, but if he visits us and advertises himself or is being advertised as 'Rev.' or 'Cantor' or *Chazan,* we shall feel that the holding by him of public concerts at which the recital of prayers is made on a concert platform is degrading to the position of a *Sheliach Tzibbur.*

We feel it necessary in the interests of the dignity of our calling to say this.

Yours very truly,
D. *Klein*

Fortunately the attack did not remain unanswered. Another colleague took up the cudgels in my father's behalf. "Is it degrading," he asked, "for Cantor J. Rosenblatt, one of the very few great *Chazanim,* who is well able to move one's heart and stir one's soul with his rendering of traditional melodies, to appear at a concert before a Jewish assembly, or is it degrading the dignity of our calling by having a colleague who can so ably demonstrate to the *Umos ho-Olom* our own exclusive Jewish art of *Chazanuth,* which has moved the hearts of even notorious antisemites and transformed them into friends and defenders of Jews—as I can easily testify?

"Should a man be berated for belittling his calling," added my father's advocate, "who had refused offers of $1,000 a night to sing in the opera because he was of the opinion that that was degrading to the dignity of a *Sheliach Tzibbur?*" Finally why should there be so much objection to a cantor's appearing on the concert platform in England when all the learned and pious rabbis of America with its Jewish community of 4,000,000 souls had never registered a word of protest against such a practice?

Whatever his motive may have been the reverend Mr. Klein's strictures failed completely in dimming the brilliance of Yossele Rosenblatt's success in England. Once the inhabitants of the island kingdom got to see and hear him, he won their hearts. The usually reserved British press indulged in lengthy encomiums, and he made many warm friends among British Jewry, particularly those of comparatively recent East-European provenance.

At his first public appearance in London on the evening of June 12 there was "scarcely a vacant seat. All Jewry was at the Queen's Hall to hear Cantor Joseph Rosenblatt." The audience, according to the Daily Mail, was "as piquant as the singer." There was a division of opinion among the critics about the orthodoxy of his methods in the singing of classical and operatic music, but no dissent from the universal acclaim that greeted his rendition of the Hebrew and Yiddish selections of his program. Greatest enthusiasm was, of course, manifested by his Jewish listeners, who understood him best. The Jewish Chronicle compared the "gymnastics he played with his voice" with Heifetz's virtuosity with the fiddle. A. Z. Romanovsky, writing in Yiddish, waxed absolutely lyrical in the account of his impressions of the concert. "We stood before an inexhaustible fountain of music," he said, "which God created for us human beings to enable us to lift ourselves up from this lowly world to that which is all good."

"Let us lift up our hands to heaven in gratitude," so he concluded his review, "for the fact that this musical genius was not lost to Jewry as were many other outstanding singers and artists, but that he is ours body and soul."

On the Sabbath subsequent to this inaugural concert, my father officiated in the Great Assembly Hall, Mile End Road, East. The Manchester Guardian, which, commenting on his performance, presented him as "a jovial person and a delightful raconteur," also told of plans he had to visit Manchester, Leeds, and Liverpool.

The divine services he conducted at the Leeds Town Hall

under the auspices of the Labor Zionists drew people from all over the city. Synagogues were closed to give their patrons an opportunity to hear him. His singing evoked the usual enthusiastic response. However the reaction to his chanting of the Sabbath prayers was surpassed by the impression of his recital on Wednesday evening of the week following. The Yorkshire Post pronounced that concert "in every way a notable success." "His ringing tenor notes," it said, "filled the hall as few other voices have done."

Similar to his reception in Leeds was that accorded him in Manchester, when he appeared there in the Free Trade Hall.

Lack of advance publicity accounted for the limited audience that assembled to hear him at the Brighton Dome upon his return from the continent in August. To compensate for that his appearance at Albert Hall in London on Sunday, August 19, attracted enough people in the words of one reporter "to fill Queen's Hall twice over." And "to attract an audience of between three and four thousand people to the Albert Hall on a Sunday evening in the middle of the dead season" was, in the opinion of the Manchester News, "a feat worth recording."

As for the reaction to this farewell recital in England: "You cannot talk about Cantor Rosenblatt's wonderful voice," said one critic. "That would be misleading. He has a series of voices. The lowest sounds like the bass tones of the cello. The middle one is a clear oboe-like tenor; and out of that he breaks straight into sweet, thin falsetto—a couple of octaves of it—for all the world like the voice of a woman soprano heard on the gramophone . . . His agility—he has a perfect trill—might make the most accomplished soprano leggiero jealous. Sometimes he begins a series of florid passages in his bass cello voice, continues in his tenor, and finishes away among his octaves of head-tones . . . And it is all wonderfully done; so wonderfully . . . that you find it difficult to believe in him as a flesh and blood singer. Only a robot, you feel, brought to extra perfection, should be able to sing like that. The audience at Albert Hall on Sunday night would have overflowed any other, and there was much enthusiasm."

Great Britain was the only important country in Europe at the time with a stable currency. Notwithstanding the huge toll in human life and substance that World War I had taken from it, the British Empire was still intact. The pound sterling continued to be, as it had been theretofore, the standard of value, and the Bank of England, that backed it, "as strong" financially "as the Rock of Gibraltar." Concertizing in the British Isles could, therefore, be remunerative. The situation was entirely different on the continent. Inflation had rendered its currencies virtually worthless. This was particularly true in Central Europe. I recall how in the summer of 1922 I had to wait half an hour in a Viennese bank for the clerk to count out the equivalent in Austrian guldens of ten American dollars. It required an entire brief-case to cart away the bills. Conditions were even worse in 1923. The German and Austrian banknotes weren't worth the paper on which they were printed and the amounts in circulation had reached astronomical heights. Under such circumstances any thought of a concert tour for profit on the mainland of Europe had to be dismissed. It was not to receive but rather to give that my father proceeded to the continent after his brief sojourn in England. He went to see what remained of his and my mother's families, so that he might alleviate their plight if possible. He was anxious, also, to renew bonds with the friends he had left behind when he departed for America.

Crossing the border from one country to another in continental Europe was at that time by no means a simple matter. Baggage was searched thoroughly at every boundary. The customs officials had no respect for even the most inti-

mate personal possessions of either man or woman. Every·
thing strange looking and outlandish was suspected as
contraband and subject to confiscation by the jittery servants
of the newly created states. Thus my father forfeited, as he
passed from Germany into Poland, the little portable phonograph he had carried with him to play his records. There
was no means of convincing the Polish guards of the harm-
lessness of the gadget and of its being my father's personal
property. It was a dangerous instrument, and he had no
choice except to surrender.

I shall not even attempt to portray the ecstatic joy of my
parents' relatives, including my eighty-five-year-old maternal grandfather, on seeing their Yossele and Taubshu again.
Eleven years had elapsed since my father and mother had
left for America to seek their fortune. They did not have
the least inkling of what the future might have in store for
them. Now they returned to the scenes of their youth as heroes, as adventurers who had taken a risk and made good.
Besides, the visitors had come bearing gifts. They paid
handsomely for whatever hospitality was extended to them.
In fact my father was so cleaned out during his stay in
Cracow that he had to borrow money to purchase a railroad
ticket for the short journey to Tarnow. But even when he
did not dole out cash, his mere presence was helpful. Thus,
for instance, it was through his mediation with his former
congregation in Hamburg, Germany, that his brother Levi,
who had been most anxious to give up his post in Groningen,
was engaged as cantor of the Synagogenverband. He held on
to that position for an entire decade until the advent of
Hitler. It was also after his visit with my mother's youngest
brother Samuel that the latter was chosen chief cantor of
the Jewish community of Cracow.

The World Zionist Congress was convening that summer
in Karlsbad, Czechoslovakia. My father must have attended
some of the sessions, for he was listed as one of the signa-

tories of the message of sympathy sent from that conclave to Mrs. Warren G. Harding upon the death of her husband, the president of the United States. He also visited Presburg. Two recitals were given by him in this city, one on Tuesday evening, July 31, the other on Wednesday evening, August 8. The proceeds from both were used for the benefit of the new Jewish hospital that was to be erected. Among the personalities that came to hear him in the Grosse Redoutensaal was his first vocal teacher, Professor Van der Staats, now aged and bent. The old man's eyes glistened with tears of joy as he heard his former pupil sing. With rapt attention did he follow every note, every nuance and shading of the voice, tapping with his cane to mark the rhythm. And when the singer had finished, he hobbled up to him, and threw his arms around him in deep emotion and kissed him. That mark of affection and admiration meant more to my father than the finest tribute that any critic could have paid him.

Among the enthusiasts that attended my father's Presburg concerts were also several students of the Hungarian *Yeshibot,* clad in long kaftans and wearing the traditional earlocks. Two of them, children of very poor parents, had come all the way from Galanta. With the irrepressibility of youth they sought out the artist at his hotel in Presburg, arriving just as he was going over his program with his accompanist. What followed has been related to me by one of them, Chazkel Schwartz, who is now living in Jerusalem.

"Reb Yossele, do you mind if we sit here and listen while you rehearse?"

"Of course not. Sit down and make yourselves comfortable!"

The two lads were delighted. It seemed to them from then on as though they had been transported to another world.

"How did you like it, boys?" asked my father when the re
hearsal was over.

"How did we like it? We never experienced such a pleas'
ure," and they kissed my father's hands.

"Do you have tickets for the concert?" By the nonplussed
look in their faces my father recognized that they did not.
He should have suspected that much. For the lowest admission charge was 35 crowns, which to these indigent *Yeshivah*
students represented a fortune. "Well, here is a pass for the
two of you and I hope you will enjoy it."

From that moment on the two youngsters, whom he had
received so warmly, followed my father around like two little lambs. Wherever he went, they went. They even accompanied him to the railroad station where he was going to take
the train for Tyrnau, the residence of his sister Gittel. "Is
that you, Chatzkele!" he exclaimed to my informant with
genuine delight, when he saw him at the depot. Then, turning to my mother he said: "Taube, look, my *Chassidim* are
here. On account of them I am going to travel third class,
in order not to put them to too much expense." As he rode,
he gave the young enthusiasts a private concert.

As the train approached Tyrnau, and his young admirers
were about to take leave of him, my father asked them:
"And where are you bound for?"

"Back to the *Yeshivah* in Galanta to study."

"Do you mean to say that you are not going to see your
parents during your vacation?"

"Our parents we can see another time. Reb Yossele comes
to us only once."

My father immediately understood that it was the expense
of the journey that kept them from going home. Without
saying a word he took out 75 crowns, the cost of the railroad
fare to Kashau, where the boys lived, handed them to the
conductor, and obtained from him two tickets. "Here you

are," he said to the youngsters. "Let it not be said that on account of Yossele Rosenblatt you were kept from fulfilling the commandment of 'Honor thy father and thy mother.'"

Another one of the mementos of this first European tour is that which has been preserved for us by Herman Swet, the Berlin correspondent of the Warsaw Moment.

"I met Rosenblatt for the first time in Marienbad five years ago," so he reminisced in 1928. "For the many Jews who gathered there from the four corners of the earth Yossele Rosenblatt's arrival was a great sensation, and his concert at the Kurhaus attracted an audience of more than a thousand persons.

"In the auditorium there sat two famous singers: the onetime favorite of Wilhelm II—his 'Lohengrin,' Hermann Jadlowker, and the most beloved of German tenors, Leo Slezak.

"Both these European artists listened with bated breath to Rosenblatt's virtuosity and artistry, and were fascinated by his supernatural falsetto and especially by his phenomenal coloratura . . .

"On the day after the concert we were with him at the home of the old rabbi of Belz. The *Tzaddik* received Rosenblatt very cordially, gave him his blessing and asked him to chant something. Rosenblatt responded with a *Y'hi Rotzon* from the new moon benediction and sang so touchingly that he brought tears to everyone's eyes.

"The *Chassidim* of Belz then made a circle around Rosenblatt and refused to let him go. Yossele did not need to be pressed too much. He sang with that inner joy that radiates from his entire being. I have never seen a person exuding so much joie de vivre as Rosenblatt. He knows nothing of melancholy or doubts or problems. He loves the world, music, *Chazanuth;* and the world loves him too and dotes on him as one does on a gifted child.

"The Jewish masses, the common people, always had their

favorite cantors . . . I recall well how Odessa esteemed its unforgettable and unequalled Solomon Rosumni. He was literally deified. But people were also afraid of him, as it were. There was always a sort of barrier between him and his fervent admirers . . . With Yossele, however, one feels completely at home, as with a close relative. He is the entire world's kinsman.

" 'What is really your name, Herr Oberkantor?' several German *Yahudim* asked Rosenblatt at the Marienbad railroad station as he stood there surrounded by hundreds of his admirers who had come to see him off. 'Yossele,' answered Rosenblatt. 'Isn't it Josef?' repeated the modernists. But the crowd of old-timers as one man corrected them: 'Not Josef, but Yossele.' He is their Yossele."

Distances are not great in Europe, and so it was possible for my father to reach Hamburg from Presburg before Friday evening, August 10, in order to officiate at the inauguration of the Sabbath. Mother and Leo did not accompany him on this trip. Leo had fallen a victim to the prevailing epidemic of paratyphoid fever. This compelled mother to remain behind with him in Europe while father returned to America in time for the High Holidays.

My father's presence in his former community caused quite a sensation. "Last Saturday," reported the Hamburger Familienblatt, "the frequenters of the Bornplatz Synagogue had a special treat in store for them. The cantor on that Sabbath was none other than Mr. Joseph Rosenblatt, whose *Chazanuth* is still well remembered by all. The mere announcement of his appearance had attracted many worshippers, so that the house of God was filled to the last seat. Everyone listened with rapt attention to the recitation of the service by Rosenblatt, whose chanting of the new moon prayer was most inspiring and elevating."

Even more enthusiastic was the comment on the concert given in the Conventgarten on the following Sunday morn-

ing for the benefit of the Jewish philanthropic institutions
of Hamburg. "An extraordinarily large congregation had
hastily assembled in order to hear the renowned cantor and
singer. And those who came were really not disappointed.
Vocal endowment and the most refined power of expression
and modulation are united in him. Whether he presented
German oratorios or appeared as an interpreter of lyrical
works or sang appealing melodies by Italian composers—one
always had to admire the absolute assurance he evinced and
his complete mastery of his assignment. All this, however,
receded into the background when Rosenblatt recited Yiddish or Hebrew selections. There his Jewish soul was revealed in all its richness, jubilation and grieving, longing
and rejoicing. How well he understands how to give content
and meaning to the simple words of the daily prayers, and to
fill with pulsating life the oft-repeated and commonplace.
It was a deeply religious experience. Symbolically enough
he concluded his recital, which was extended by many encores wrung from him by a wildly applauding audience,
with the Yiddish folksong *Aheim, aheim* (Homeward,
homeward). There may be differences of opinion with regard to details. The general impression, however, was most
favorable, as evidenced in the enthusiastic applause of the listeners . . .

"On behalf of the governing board of the German-Jewish
community Mr. Jacob Heckscher thanked the beloved and
highly esteemed guest for having so unselfishly dedicated his
talent to the service of the good cause, thereby indicating his
loyalty to his former congregation. He urged those present
to fill out the contribution blanks that had been distributed
and, emulating the example of Mr. Rosenblatt, to help meet
the needs of the forthcoming winter. A spontaneous ovation for the artist followed these words."

What a comedown for the once purse-proud community
that the cantor, who had to leave them because they would

not grant him the small increase in salary that he asked, now felt constrained to ask him to render his services gratis to help its institutions.

Between the time of his next appearance, which was in Brighton, and his farewell recital in London's Albert Hall my father took occasion to cross the English Channel to Antwerp. He went at the invitation of that flourishing Belgian Jewish community, which consisted largely of recent émigrés from Galicia, and which was thirsting to hear him. The concert he gave left, according to both the Flemish and the French press, a most favorable impression. It was very well attended. In the opinion of the critic of the Neptune the artist did not belie the great reputation that had preceded him. Even "persons hardest to please had reason to be completely satisfied."

Vladimir de Pachmann was in his prime one of the foremost pianists of the world, on a par with Paderewski and other such ranking musicians. He also had the unenviable reputation in his old age of being the world's number one grouch. So antisocial was this once celebrated virtuoso, that he would even shun the company of members of his own profession, shut himself up like a hermit in his hotel room or cabin, and avoid all contact, to the extent that it was possible, with his fellow men.

Josef Rosenblatt apparently broke through the crust of the old misanthrope's armor. No sooner did the eccentric pianist espy the little cantor on board ship as it was leaving Europe, than he took a liking to him. Though he rarely uttered a word to anyone else, he could be seen pacing the deck for hours talking with his newly discovered companion. And he had a great deal to say that was interesting, particularly on the subject of music and the musical art. When the steamer arrived in New York harbor and the two artists, the tall aged instrumentalist, de Pachmann, and the younger, shorter vocalist, allowed themselves to be photographed standing arm in arm, excitement in circles close to the former ran high. "What had come over de Pachmann?" they wondered. "Had the little singer of the synagogue hypnotized him?" The question remained unanswered.

A person who could please a de Pachmann had no difficulty in remaining in the good graces of more outgoing people. If there was any group of men that was happy to see Yossele Rosenblatt back again in America, it was the Ohab Zedek Congregation. For a while they had been greatly disturbed by a rumor, that must have originated in London, to the effect that their cantor had accepted an offer to tour the world. They were, therefore, very much relieved, when on the Jewish New Year they saw their *chazan* standing at his regular place on the *Bema* of their house of worship just as he had during the previous eleven years.

New York's gain was London's loss. "This year's High Holidays were spoiled for London Jewry," wrote the Jewish Morning Journal's special London correspondent, "and the person responsible for it is none other than your fellow-countryman Reb Yossele Rosenblatt.

"We quickly became used to him and we wouldn't believe that he would forsake us. We didn't want to think about it, but it happened anyhow, and it was with a heavy heart that we took leave of him at his departure. However it was first on the High Holidays that we felt his absence. London has had great cantors, but of course we don't have a Reb Yossele."

The great success my father had scored in Europe made people all the more anxious to hear him at home. When he officiated on the Sabbath of the intervening days of the Feast of Tabernacles—a sort of offday in the midst of the holiday season—in the Bronx, there was formed outside the synagogue building what the Jewish Morning Journal called the famous "Rosenblatt line." "It filled those who were forced

to stand in it with chagrin over their lack of foresight to provide themselves with tickets beforehand, while it made
speculators rub their hands in glee because of the chance it
gave them to fleece the public."

Such queues were to be encountered in various cities of
the East and the Middle West in which, according to Musical
America, "Josef Rosenblatt had been booked solidly for the
season,"—in Newark and Toledo and Johnstown, in Cincinnati and Philadelphia, in New Brunswick and Syracuse,
and of course, at any public function in his own New York
whenever it was announced that he would sing.

One of the most amusing experiences of my father in the
winter of this year was what happened to him when he sang
in Winnipeg, Canada. This third largest city of the vast British dominion to the North of the United States of America
had one of its not at all infrequent blizzards, and when my
father ventured forth, after a very successful concert, into
the subzero weather, his beard was transformed into an ici-
cle, which took some time to thaw out.

On his way home, he stopped off in Chicago. His chief
purpose was to scotch a rumor that had been circulated to
the effect that my sister Nettie was engaged to be married
to the popular Jewish lightweight champion Benny Leonard.

When the Chicago editor of the Jewish Daily Forward remarked to my father: "But what would be the calamity if
your daughter were to marry Benny Leonard? Isn't he an
honest person and has he not, by his clean living, reflected
a great deal of credit on the Jewish people as well as the
pugilistic profession?" my father replied:

"Yes, Benny is a very respectable young man, and I would
have had no objection against his becoming my son-in-law if
only his work had not compelled him to violate the Sabbath. As for his profession, that would have presented no
obstacle. For in a way I am also a fighter of a sort. My man-

agers are constantly fighting to secure more engagements for me, while I fight with them to get better prices."

Nineteen twenty-four would have been a good year financially as well as morally in my father's artistic career were it not for the ominous shadow cast by the ever mounting expenses of the "Light of Israel" that were consuming his capital and preying on his state of mind. His prestige as a cantor had never been higher. No Jewish public function, whatever its nature might be, was considered complete without him. Whether it took the form of a reception to Chief Rabbi Kook of the Holy Land or a rally on behalf of Jewish education, a benefit performance, joyous celebration or a demonstration of sorrow, it had to be graced by Yossele Rosenblatt.

His schedule of concert engagements was such that he had to zigzag across the United States several times in order to fill them. His route that year covered South Bend, New York and Buffalo in January; Raleigh, Savannah, Jacksonville, Charleston (South Carolina), Miami and Portland (Oregon) in February; and Seattle, San Francisco, Los Angeles and Denver in March. In May he sang in Chicago, St. Louis, Minneapolis and Omaha, and in June in St. Joseph, Kansas City, Plainfield, Hartford and again in St. Louis.

There were not wanting minor embarrassments and mishaps. Once in Miami the brief-case containing the music of his repertoire of secular music was stolen. As a consequence, sixteen-year-old Abie Elstein, who replaced Dr. Philip Friedman as his accompanist, was compelled to play the entire score by heart. The audience was completely unaware of what had happened. But what would the singer have done if his assistant had not been so competent?

Then again there was that time when he was forced to spend an entire Saturday in a town of Indians. The train that was supposed to take him from Florida to Portland, Oregon was late. There was no chance of his reaching his destination before nightfall on Friday, when the Sabbath

would begin. So he requested the conductor to let him off at
the nearest town with a Jewish population. The station at
which he descended was Pendleton. Among several thousand pure blooded American Indians there lived exactly
two Jews. They entertained him as well as they could by,
among other things, playing him some of his own records.
And so he whiled the time away until, at the outgoing of
the Sabbath on Saturday night, he was able to proceed.

All these inconveniences were more than made up for
by the crowded synagogues and theatres that greeted him
and the compliments paid him by the critics. Dr. John J.
Becker, the music director of Notre Dame University, acclaimed him as "a supreme artist." "No greater nor more
original artist," said he, "than Josef Rosenblatt is living in
America today."

Edwin Schallert of the Los Angeles Daily Times called
him "the ambassador of the literature of the Jewish people,
both Hebraic and in dialect, as it has been fashioned into
song." The Jewish Voice of St. Louis testified to the desire of
the Jews of that city to "hear the King of the *Chasonim* at
the pulpit." The wish was realized when he officiated at
the Shaare Zedek Synagogue in June.

Neither these tokens of esteem and marks of success
nor even the five-year contract awarded him by the Victor
Company—an unusual distinction for a singer over forty
years of age—were capable of giving my father any real
sense of security. The brilliance of his achievements was
dimmed more and more, as the months rolled by, by the
gathering clouds of impending doom brought upon him by
the "Light of Israel." To save costs the business managers
decided to buy machinery to produce their own type. This
meant additional outlays of money. Since no funds for
such purposes were on hand, they had to be borrowed. Now,
the only person connected with the publication whose credit
was good was Yossele Rosenblatt. Hence it was his name and

borrowing power that was exploited. He was sent to his friends and admirers to negotiate loans and all sorts of papers and promissory notes were put under his nose to sign, the import of which was often concealed from him. To quell his apprehensions and fears he was nourished with false hopes and vain illusions. A group of prominent rabbis, he was told, would soon take over the paper. So-called proof was presented to show that at any moment enough advertisements and subscriptions would come pouring in to cover the expenses. Thus several more thousands of dollars as well as endorsements were extracted from him. Finally came the crowning insult. We were again vacationing in Long Branch, but it was an uneasy and restless vacation for us. We felt as though we were living atop a volcano that was ready at any moment to erupt. We had to borrow the rent for our cottage and everything we ate was obtained on credit—all on account of the "Light of Israel."

The brain trust of the "Light of Israel" must have been aware of our state of mind and, in order to appease my father and retain his good-will, decided to present him with an automobile. So on a fine morning in July, lo and behold! a beautiful, shining, brand-new Chrysler pulled up in front of our cottage to the jubilation and delight of the children. Ah, what luxury, what comfort! You open the door and fall into the plush seat and order James to go to Asbury Park or Lakewood or Avon-by-the-Sea, as all our rich neighbors were wont to do. The only ones who weren't pleased were my mother and myself. She wouldn't go near the thing. She wanted no gifts from the managers of the "Light of Israel." Whose money was it that they were spending anyhow? It was that which her Yossele had earned by sleeping on trains and eating at irregular hours, by hustling and rushing restlessly in all kinds of weather from city to city, and town to town. He didn't have to wait for *them* to buy him an automobile. If he had felt the need of one, he could have gotten it himself. To present him with one out of the paper's funds was like taking money out of one pocket and putting it into the other.

Well it didn't take very long before it was proven how right my mother had been in her hostile attitude. A few days after the arrival of our gift-horse—the smell of newness had not yet worn off because it had not been driven much over one hundred miles—a summons was served to my father. He was asked to appear before the judge of the criminal court to answer a charge. The crime of which he was accused was that of being in possession of a stolen car. But who ever stole a car? How would a man like my father in his wildest dreams think of taking what was not his, he who was so ready to part with his own? Upon further investigation it turned out that the car had been purchased in my father's name but had never been paid for, because the treasury of the Ner Tomid Publishing Company was bare. Not having been paid for, it did not belong to him. Ergo it was stolen.

Of course we did not lose a moment in straightening out the mess. The car was returned at once. The colored chauffeur was paid for an entire month. There were to be no more pleasure rides in our own automobile for that summer. But the heartache and anguish, particularly of my poor mother, and the shame and disgrace that the incident caused my innocent father—these could never be eradicated.

From that time on whenever someone mentioned gift to us, we were on our guard. We wondered what sort of joker was attached to it.

31

Bankruptcy

My father must have been endowed with extraordinary reserves of spiritual strength to be able to carry on at all during the fall that followed this summer. How the man, who was acclaimed as "the only real contender the great Caruso ever had," whom B. L. Blaisdell of the New York Telegram and Evening Mail pronounced "the greatest American male singer" and who was chosen as the soloist at the Naumburg Memorial concert, was able to function on the High Holidays or participate in the testimonial affairs to comedian Eddie Cantor and to Arthur Lehman, the president of New York's Jewish Philanthropic Societies, is past understanding. For towards the close of 1924 even he, the inveterate optimist, realized that he had reached the end of the road, that it could go no further. His house was mortgaged up to the hilt. His insurance policies were impounded. He had no resources that could be turned into cash. Instead there was a huge mountain of debts staring him in the face. There seemed to be nothing left for him to do but declare himself in voluntary bankruptcy.

In a last ditch attempt to stave off the evil and keep his personal affairs, which had become so intimately tied up with the fortunes of the "Light of Israel," from being dragged into the open, Leo who, fresh from Columbia Law School, had taken over, called together the creditors to arrange for a settlement or at least a moratorium. He was made to realize very quickly that, no matter how favorably disposed people may feel towards those whom they had loaned money, they are not always ready to relinquish so easily their claims to what is legitimately and legally theirs. There were among the holders of the Ner Tomid Publishing Company's notes some who entertained for its president so deep an affection that they were willing to forget about what he owed them altogether. Others were agreeable to a postponement of the date of payment until such time as would be convenient for him. There remained, however, a hard core of inflexibles who refused to wait. "A man with his earning capacity—even according to the income tax report, which usually does not reveal everything—he netted during that year a total of $32,000—should be made to pay at once," they said. "His contention that he has no funds is merely a ruse. He is holding out on us and should be forced by law to make good his obligations."

The result was that after several futile efforts to keep out of the courts my father was at length compelled on January 14, 1925, through his attorney David W. Kahn, to file a petition in bankruptcy. His assets were listed as amounting to $32,859, of which $27,000 consisted of real estate—the house we lived in. His liabilities, due mostly to promissory notes endorsed on behalf of the "Light of Israel," were computed at $191,719.

As soon as the news was made public that "the golden-voiced cantor," fortune's child, had been "forced into bankruptcy" all sorts of wild rumors began to circulate as to the causes of the fiasco. People could not understand why so successful an artist as my father would have been reduced to a position where such an expedient should be necessary. The only way they could figure it out was that either he had lost his money on the stock-market or gambled it away on the race-track or overspent on his wife's jewelry. That it had been buried in a supposedly idealistic venture, from which he neither derived nor expected to derive personal profit, was something that needed clarification. And my father did make it clear in a series of public statements, the first of which appeared in the Yiddish press on February 17, or about a month after the filing of his petition in bankruptcy. In it he told the whole story of his involvement with the "Light of Israel," of the motives that had induced him to become connected with the periodical and the reasons that prompted his withdrawal. What hastened his resignation was, among other things, his inability to sanction the policy of attacks on the most important Jewish movements and institutions adopted by the paper's editorial board. These tactics on the part of the editors of the "Light of Israel" had caused him infinite embarrassment and put him in a very uncomfortable position. The general public did not know that he had no more to do with these matters than he had control over the business aspects of the periodical. The least that his former associates might have done, now that the partnership between them, from which they had benefited much more than he, was terminated, would have been to leave him in peace. Instead of that the "spreaders of light," after reducing him and his family to bankruptcy, in return for the services he had rendered to their cause and to them personally, added insult to injury by vilifying him in the press.

However what he was concerned about most was not the monetary loss; the fact that he woke up one morning to find that "everything that he possessed had gone up in smoke, that the earnings of many years of hard work would not belong to" him. What pained him was that the friends who had reposed so much confidence in him, "had been misled together with" him, that the savings of widows and other persons of modest means, that had been risked in the venture, had also been wiped out. His purpose in declaring himself bankrupt was not to default on his obligations, incurred on behalf of the "Light of Israel." It was intended rather as a device for gaining time to get back on his feet so as to be able to satisfy those of his creditors who needed their money the most.

"I have," so he concluded his statement, "commandeered the help of the only gift left to me, of which nobody can deprive me—my voice, my art, my ability to bring cheer and inspiration to Jews and non-Jews by means of song. I shall make use of this faculty to produce sufficiently large funds to enable me to free myself as quickly as possible from the burden of debt that weighs upon me.

"I hope that the Jewish masses, that have throughout the years evinced toward me so much veneration and love, will show understanding for the situation in which I am placed . . . That sympathy . . . will give me the strength to surmount the crisis which came upon me so suddenly."

The public did understand and on the whole was sympathetic. Most people believed the story as he had told it. They had faith in his honesty and integrity. "Don't worry, Yossele!" the Jewish humorous weekly, the Big Stick, consoled him in a cartoon, published a week after he had filed his petition, in which it pictured him roped in by a skein of promissory notes. "Wicked people have caused you to become entangled but your good angel will disentangle you."

Even the referee of the bankruptcy court, Seaman Miller, recognized that the defendant before him was not the type of person who could ever have entertained the thought of defrauding those who had confided in him. He, therefore, treated him with the utmost deference.

32

Entering Vaudeville

In spite of the necessity in which he found himself, because of the immediate circumstances, to declare himself bankrupt, my father had put himself on record, in his letter to the people, as having no intention of disavowing his debts even if he should be successful in being legally cleared of them. "In the course of time," he stated, "I shall make good every penny. I shall spare neither effort nor energy to fulfill my obligations."

But how were these noble resolutions to be carried out? What could he do with his voice to produce those increases in income that had to be forthcoming in order to pay back his indebtedness besides taking care of the needs of his family? Had he not reached the pinnacle in his career as cantor and concertist? Was he not the highest priced cantor in the world and one of the best-remunerated performers on the concert stage? And if these sources could not yield sufficient revenue for the purposes required, where else could he turn? What fields were there left for him to conquer?

Leo, who had given up school in order to devote himself entirely to his father's affairs, gave the matter some very serious thought and it occurred to him that there was still one province of the entertainment world that had not been invaded by my father, one hitherto untapped reservoir that might provide the needed dollars. That was the variety theatre. Classical concerts as money-makers had, as a matter of fact, begun to decline. People were unable to pay the high prices demanded. In October of this same year in which my father had filed his own petition of bankruptcy, his latest manager Sol Hurok, too, found himself insolvent. He owed the dancer Anna Pavlova alone a backlog of $40,000. Vaudeville, on the other hand, still had a great drawing power. Since the talkies had not yet been invented, it was necessary to supplement the eye appeal of the pictures with acts on the stage that would be pleasing to the ear. Lovers of music for whom the admission fees charged for regular concerts were out of reach—and that took in a large proportion of the American population—could quench their thirst for song and melody in the much more popular priced variety theaters. Singing on the vaudeville stage was well remunerated. Better-class entertainers drew pretty large salaries, because, if they possessed any merit at all, they could usually count on packed houses.

Vaudeville, therefore, seemed to Leo to offer the opportunity to my father to rehabilitate himself economically and eventually to crawl out from under. But there were also complications, serious questions that appearances on the variety stage posed, knotty problems that had to be solved before the plunge into vaudeville could even be contemplated by him. First, he was a vocalist pure and simple, without adornments or frills, and a serious one to boot. But the kind of music demanded by the patrons of vaudeville was the popular variety and those that sang it usually had to do a little acting besides. Would an artist of Josef Rosenblatt's calibre and appearance prove enough of an attraction for the frequenters of the variety theater, the overwhelming majority of whom were non-Jews? Secondly there was the matter of background and staging. It was beneath his dignity as a precentor of the synagogue to have anything to do with other acts or their performers, the chorines, jugglers or dancers, with whom he had so little in common. What could be done to keep his part on the program separate and apart from the rest? Finally there was the most difficult problem of all—that of the Sabbath. Most movie houses opened their new shows on Friday night and one of the most popular performances was Saturday matinee, at neither of which times my father would sing in a theater. Could the managers or owners of theaters be persuaded to accept him on such terms?

Leo gained the confidence of enterprising, dapper Ned Jaakobs, a young man well versed in all the secrets of show business. They went over the proposal from every angle, considering the risks involved as well as the potentialities offered. True there would be an initial outlay for advertisement, but Josef Rosenblatt had a large following, first of all among the rank and file of his own people, who had been willing to pay high prices to hear him; and, in addition, among music enthusiasts in general. In cities and neighborhoods with large Jewish populations his name alone should prove to be a great drawing card. Once the managers were convinced of his box-office power, they would not mind releasing him from appearing on Friday evenings and Saturday afternoons.

Ned Jaakobs felt satisfied. He immediately got in touch with Jack Loeb from whom he engaged the Fox Theatre in Philadelphia, a city boasting some 200,000 Jewish residents, for the period of one week beginning January 12. He saw to it that this, my father's first appearance on the vaudeville stage, was well publicized in the Jewish as well as the general press, leaving nothing to chance. The results of this first trial venture were overwhelming. They exceeded the wildest expectations of the entrepreneurs. All records were broken. In the Wednesday, January 21 issue of Variety Ned Jaakobs and William Morris, as exclusive managers for "Tenor-Cantor Josef Rosenblatt," were able to boast in a full-page advertisement:

JAMMED THE HOUSE FROM PIT TO DOME EVERY
DAY LAST WEEK—THE GROSS TELLS THE STORY

$24,633.85

Smashed Every Existing Box Office Record
at the

FOX THEATRE

PHILADELPHIA

Double Lines a Block Long—Waited Nightly in the Cold to Hear

THE INTERNATIONALLY FAMOUS

J O S E F   R O S E N B L A T T

THEY HEARD   THEY CHEERED   THEY ACCLAIMED

A cartoon by Gaar Williams, entitled "How to Keep from
Growing Old," presented a graphic picture of the crowd standing in line in front of the Fox Theatre ticket office for as long
as two hours in the cold in the hope of being able to hear
"Tenor-Cantor Rosenblatt." "Pardon me," said one fellow
who tried to muscle in, "if I just slip in here. I'm a little in
a hurry, see!"

The experiment had turned out to be a complete success.
Erno Rapee, managing director of the Fox Theatre, was
credited by Variety with having "pulled a sweet coup in
booking this feature. There was an element of chance in
the extent of his draw, but the jam Monday afternoon put
away all doubts. The gross was $7,000 and more above the
weekly average." Another theatrical newspaper predicted
that "Rosenblatt appears on the strength of his Philadelphia
performances to stand out as a most unusual attraction for
picture theatres in some of the bigger cities, and should be
a clean-up in New York, Chicago and Boston, where there
is a large Hebrew population, for he will draw them all and
get the real music lovers as well, possibly building up an unusual clientele for any house."

After this triumphant and record-breaking entree into
vaudeville the task of selling my father to the managers of
the variety theatres was a simple one. As early as January

16, that is before my father's first week's run at the Fox
Theatre was over, Ned Jaakobs received from Jack Loeb a
letter, dated January 15, confirming their verbal conversation. It stipulated that Josef Rosenblatt was to appear in
New York at three Fox theatres, namely the Audubon, the
Crotona and the Folly. His salary per week of seven days was
to be $2,000, with a fifty-fifty split of gross receipts over
$14,000. He was to sing no more than three times a day at
any one of the houses. The engagement for the three-week
period seems to have begun on February 1.

The Jewish residents of the neighborhoods in which the
New York movie houses were located did not disappoint the
hopes of the impresarios. They turned out full force to
hear their idol. According to the Home News, Manager
Moore of the Crotona Theatre had received so many requests
for reservations from Jewish organizations in the Bronx that
he found it necessary, in order to be fair to his patrons, to assign to each a different evening. Besides Jews there was a
goodly number of non-Jews in the audiences. Many had never
before seen a singer of my father's type on the stage, and just
as had happened at the time of his debut on the concert platform in Carnegie Hall seven years previous, so here the reaction to the first appearance of the—to them—exotic figure
was one of amusement. No sooner, however, had the unusual vaudevillian opened his mouth to sing than the snick-
ers of amusement were transformed into smiles of admiration. And when the second number had been rendered by
him in a virtually flawless English, those who had nudged
each other mockingly at the beginning wound up by applauding most enthusiastically.

Not only the patrons of the theatres reacted in this manner
to Josef Rosenblatt's performance. The personnel themselves
were affected by the impact of his music. The assistant
manager of the Crotona confessed to having been moved to

tears by "one of the sentimental songs used by Cantor Josef Rosenblatt."

After completing his New York engagements, my father proceeded to Newark, where he was again greeted by packed houses. "The feature picture" at the Branford, observed the Newark Ledger, "had already started, but the applause did not subside. The lobby was jammed to the box office and those near the doors kept as still as possible so as to catch the notes of the cantor inside." When Friday came, "Mike Cullen . . . was kept busy on the telephone informing people, in answer to queries, that Cantor Rosenblatt would not appear that night because of the Jewish Sabbath."

My father's programs in his vaudeville appearances were usually short. Two or three such favorites as "Eili, Eili," "The Last Rose of Summer" and "Duna" plus an encore was all that there was time for at a single performance. Since, however, he had to appear an average of three times a day for at least six days a week, his work was rather confining. And when thereto are added many chores that he tried to wedge in between the acts—for he abhorred idleness as much as ever—they total up to a rather strenuous schedule. But he did not mind the exertion. Whatever effort may have been involved was more than balanced by the compensations. Every time he pocketed a $2,000 pay-check for a week's performance, he saw his mountain of debt reduced. Secondly there was the broadening of the horizons of his activities that singing in vaudeville theatres afforded him, the enlargement of the audiences to whom he was able to bring his message. As Dean Collins of the Portland (Oregon) Telegram correctly appraised the situation, "out of the undeserved misfortune that befell Cantor Rosenblatt it comes to pass that hundreds of thousands of people, who might never have listened to the marvellous sweetness of his unusual voice, hear him and are happier for having heard him." Again his very conduct on the variety stage and the demands he made from the managers to satisfy his religious scruples were an ideal medium for teaching the non-Jewish masses of America something of the tenets of the Jewish faith while acquainting them with Jewish music. The announcements on the billboards that Josef Rosenblatt would not be heard on Friday evening or Saturday matinee, because he was observing his Sabbath, constituted a real *Kiddush Hashem,* a glorification of the Jewish religion. They evoked the profoundest respect and reverence in everybody.

From the explanation that the theatrical magazine Zit's found it necessary to give to its readers as to why Josef Rosenblatt always sang "Keili, Keili" instead of "Eili, Eili" and why he substituted "Adoshem" for "Adonoi," they learned that to use the authentic form of the divine appellative for non-religious purposes was to take God's name in vain. The Kiwanians of Forest Park, Chicago, discovered the Jewish dietary laws when for the first time in the history of their exclusive country club a *kosher* dinner was served on their premises, because the guest entertainer Josef Rosenblatt wouldn't touch food that wasn't prepared strictly in accordance with the requirements of his faith. Finally what other vaudevillian would ever have caused *Inside Facts* to expound on the differences, according to the Jewish code, between travel by ship or train on the Sabbath?

Of course not every vaudeville performer, as the Kansas City Journal Post noted, can tell "the owner or manager what day of the week he will work." A great many have tried to do it and failed. "Cantor Josef Rosenblatt" was "the exception." And the reason why he succeeded was because it apparently paid more to engage him at his own terms than to do without him.

His connection with vaudeville brought my father into close contact with a great many interesting people of the entertainment world whom he would otherwise never have met. When he sang on March 22 at the Chicago Theatre, Tito Schipa, foremost representative of the Italian bel canto school of musical art, came to hear him. After the performance the two of them did an impromptu duet of Irving Berlin's "When you and I were seventeen," in the alley behind the playhouse, which "would," according to the Chicago American, "have brought all the music lovers of the city," if it had been advertised. At the dinner of the Jewish Theatrical Guild in New York it was reported that "Cantor Yossele' sang an Irish ditty while Will Rogers talked Yiddish. During his stay in Los Angeles he was invited to that city's famous night club, Coffee Dan's, to share honors with the comedienne Sophie Tucker, who, starring simultaneously with him but in a different theatre, had drawn a much smaller audience than he. "It was the first time," ran the report of Inside Facts, "that Rosenblatt had attended a resort of this type." Yet despite the fact that the world into which he was now being introduced was so utterly different from that in which he had lived hitherto, he was able, thanks to his good-natured tolerance "to join in the festivities in such a manner" as to "endear himself to the hearts of all those present."

A similar impression of him was carried away by the reporter of the Forest Parker, the organ of the Chicago Kiwanians for whom he had sung on May 19. He describes him as "sitting there and smiling indulgently at the antics of the overgrown boys as they sang their Kiwanis songs . . . not as the great Cantor Rosenblatt, but just as one of the crowd taking a silent part in the romp.

"Nor did he assert his claim to the privileges that are habitually accorded a 'guest artist,' such as complete seclusion until his appearance or a dozen and one little attentions to his personal comfort. These things he ignored.

"In the matter of religion," he continues, "Josef Rosenblatt is Spartan . . . Not a pose, but a part of him as necessary as breath. Perhaps that's why he can harvest such a full enjoyment of life. And he seemed to be having a good time Tuesday night, in a quiet, unobtrusive way."

Yes, singing in vaudeville to packed houses, seeing the crowds turn out day after day to hear him and receive their plaudits, stopping the show for eighteen whole minutes, in San Francisco's Warfield Theatre, so that the next act couldn't go on, being called by the Milwaukee German-language papers "the greatest tenor alive"—all this must have been most cheering to my father—a real morale-booster aside from the material emoluments. But there was also another side to the picture. First of all there were the inroads on his time, separating him for months from his family, so that he could pay even less attention than before to his children and was thus deprived of the usual pleasures of parents. He was three thousand miles away from New York when I, his eldest son, was ordained for the rabbinate, an event that he had looked forward to with such eager anticipation. He was unable to participate for a similar reason at my installation in my first position and was absent when his first grandchild was born.

He was desperately anxious to continue his work for charity and always returned to officiate in his own synagogue on the Sabbath for which he was scheduled as well as on the great festivals. When the first ship flying a Jewish flag and bearing Jewish passengers who were going to the Holy Land to attend the opening of the Hebrew University was leaving New York, he felt impelled to be on hand to bid the pilgrims Godspeed with his familiar *"Velirusholayim Ircho."* And when the day of the university opening came around and he was in Chicago, he could not disappoint his coreligionists of that city who were waiting for him in Orchestra Hall until midnight to join them in their celebration of the event.

Sometimes, however, complications arose that made it impossible to satisfy his philanthropic impulses altogether or only at great personal sacrifice. When he entered the contract for his first week's run at the Fox Theatre of Philadelphia, it apparently slipped his mind that he had pledged himself to sing on the second night of that same week for the benefit of some charitable cause at the McKinley Theatre in the Bronx. He was most reluctant to go back on a promise made to a philanthropic institution, especially when the success of an undertaking depended on his fulfillment of that promise. But what was he to do? How could he sing in Philadelphia and New York on one and the same evening? So he went to the managers of the Fox Theatre, explained his predicament and asked them to release him for the night, which they refused to do. It would have meant too great a loss for them. Besides it would have set a bad precedent. As an alternative he besought them to at least advance the hour of his last appearance. To this they consented. But that still would not have solved his problem. How was he to get to New York, which was more than 92 miles distant from Philadelphia, in time to catch the tail end of the program at the McKinley Theatre —that is at least by 11:00 P.M.? Since commercial aviation was not yet developed as it is today, the only way was to hire from the Pennsylvania Railroad a train of three coaches by paying the company the price of 125 individual fares amounting to $405. This train, which was marked by the sign over the gate as "The Cantor Josef Rosenblatt Special," left Philadelphia at exactly 9:35 P.M. and arrived in New York 90 minutes later. It set a record at the time not only in the speed of railroad travel but also in the lengths to which a man would go and the expense he was willing to shoulder in order to make good his plighted word.

My father was very scrupulous about maintaining his dignity on the variety stage and not being dragged down by it. He wanted the public to think of him as a concert artist and would permit no stage setting or anything that smacked of theatrical affectation while he was performing. His conduct was always impeccable. Once my two youngest brothers, who were with him back-stage, passed the dressing-room of the chorus girls while the latter were changing costumes. Being boys, they peeped through the half-open door. My father, noticing what they were doing, angrily pulled them away. "Fie!" he reprimanded them. "It isn't becoming for respectable young men to look at girls in a state of undress."

However, one cannot live for months in the atmosphere of the music hall without its leaving its mark. In their eagerness to attract the public my father's managers, whose chief interest in engaging his services was box-office receipts, would resort to such advertisements as "The man with the $500,000 beard." In the course of time my father, too, unconsciously, adopted the lingo of the stage. "One day," recorded a reporter of Variety, "when Bert Wheeler asked Josef Rosenblatt his routine, the tenor startled him by saying: 'I stop the show and then I sing "Eili, Eili" for an encore and pan 'em.'" This was in a way a profanation of the holy, and caused him to be criticized in certain quarters. To be sure while there were those who found fault with him for singing in places in which acts were performed that were so incongruous with the functions of a cantor, there were many others, more numerous than his censors, who spoke up in his defense. The Chicago Chronicle, for example, accepting his explanation of the reasons that forced him to enter vaudeville, saw "nothing undignified or unworthy in his presentation." "A man of his poise and serene dignity," it added, "could sing even in a cabaret if need be (though heaven forbid) and still make his performance consistent with the highest standards. He raises his audience to his own level, instead of dropping to theirs." "Let the grumblers have done," so the editorial concludes. "And may Yossele Rosenblatt soon regain the money he has lost, with a generous sum besides."

33

An Unusual Vaudevillian

My father himself, in his heart of hearts and as he later on confided to some of his interviewers, agreed with his critics rather than his defenders. He was far from happy in his new role in spite of his successes. "It was not out of prosperity or well-being," he said to A. Alpert of the Day, "that I exchanged the pulpit for the stage, but from sheer compulsion." He realized that the place in which ballet-dancers performed was not the appropriate locale for one whose calling it was to chant sacred prayers of the synagogue. However he could not help himself. It was the only means he had of paying back his creditors. It wasn't for the vaudeville stage that he was singing, but for the "Light of Israel."

In order to ease my father's burdens and relieve him of some of the tensions brought on by the strain of his new routine, my mother now began to accompany him on his journeys to distant parts. Her presence at his side was a great source of comfort to him as well as a sort of shock-absorber. Yet this, too, through no fault of hers, of course, at times led to unfavorable consequences. Since she was always becomingly dressed, and at the age of forty-four still very attractive, some of those, who had from the very start looked askance at my father's venture into vaudeville, began to whisper that Yossele Rosenblatt was seen in the company of an actress. The error was rectified for one of these gossips, at least, when at a reception given in my father's honor in Pittsburgh, the lady in question was introduced as "Mrs. Rosenblatt." I would not have wanted to be in the tattler's place at that moment for anything. Yet I wonder how many persons went on believing that the charge was true. After all, as my father himself once remarked, we live in an age in which such goings on are by no means a rarity. Whereas formerly Jews who went on the road used to take only their wives along with them, because religious appurtenances like prayer-shawl and phylacteries were obtainable everywhere, nowadays it is the prayer-shawl and phylacteries that are carried by the scrupulous.

As the year wore on my father went through his round of vaudeville engagements, achieving triumph after triumph. After he had appeared in the East from the middle of January to the beginning of March, the route mapped out for him took him to the Middle West. In April he was back in New York for the celebration of the Passover holiday, which gave him a chance to participate in such functions as the thirty-fifth jubilee of Dr. Klein as rabbi of Ohab Zedek. In May he returned to the Middle West. From there he proceeded to the West Coast and then, via Omaha, Nebraska, he journeyed home again, with just two weeks left to spend with his family in Long Branch, celebrate his silver wedding anniversary and announce the engagement of his two oldest children.

During all this time Ned Jaakobs was his manager and he acquitted himself well of his duties. He made the necessary contacts with theater owners, took excellent care of the publicity, arranged for interviews and parties. But in addition, he served also as a buffer between my father and countless parasites who, knowing of his goodness of heart, hovered around him like moths to obtain favors. However he was not always successful in saving his client from himself. Once in Chicago a man who claimed to be a distant relative came to him with a pathetic tale about his wife who was in need of an expensive surgical operation for which he had no funds. Wouldn't Reb Yossele help him? To protect my father against exactly such requests and conserve his earnings for household expenses and the repayment of debts, he was left with very little cash to carry around. But Yossele Rosenblatt couldn't let a kinsman in so sad a plight go from him empty-handed. So he fumbled in his coat pocket and, finding there my mother's wrist watch that he was supposed to have had fixed, he gave it to the husband of the sick woman. "But what will your wife say," Ned Jaakobs interposed in an effort to stop him, "when she learns that her watch is gone?" "Don't worry about that," my father replied. "She can get another one." In St. Louis the officers of a local congregation were anxious to engage him to officiate at a Sabbath service in their synagogue. However they were unable to pay the fee of $1,000 that my father's agreement with his managers called for. The best they could do was $250. My father weakened. It was hard to refuse such a request, especially since his vaudeville engagements were providing him with a good income. But Ned Jaakobs wouldn't hear of it. It was either $1,000 or no service. After all his commission, too, was involved. So, in order to get around this obstacle, my father advised the congregation to pay his manager the full $1,000 while he gave them a return check of his own for $750.

The year 1925, which had started out so gloomily for my father, marking as it did the lowest ebb in his worldly fortunes, turned out in the end to have been a very profitable one financially, and satisfying in other respects also. He had earned enough, thanks to his vaudeville engagements, after deducting commissions and travel expenses, to pay back his creditors a sum of approximately $23,000. He was feted, wined and dined wherever he went. No less distinguished a leader of the movie-industry than Louis B. Mayer, once reputed to be the highest-salaried man in America, came to hear him officiate at the synagogue on the Day of Atonement. The managers of District Attorney Thomas C. O'Brien in the campaign for the mayoralty of Boston used him as an attraction to get out the Jewish vote of the city and were successful. Whether it was at a hospital dedication in Jersey City, a forum sponsored by the Jewish Tribune in New York, a music festival at the Brooklyn Jewish Center or a cantors' association concert, people were content to wait until midnight, when his vaudeville engagements were over, to hear him.

The publicity that the vaudeville notices in the press had brought him was priceless. He even became the subject of humorists and cartoonists like Harry Hershfield of the New York Evening Journal, one of the most widely read of America's dailies. After he had heard him at the Palace Theatre, New York, in December of 1925, these are the words that the columnist put into the mouth of his famous character, Abie the Agent:

"Listen Minsk, about the beautiful voices of angels, we got to take Conan-Doyle's word—but about Cantor Rosenblatt's voice, you can take MY word!

"And not only mine—I'll get you affidavits and testimonials from thousands of people who are afraid to sign their names to anything . . . Hearing Mr. Rosenblatt, at the Palace Theatre this week, is a privilege!

"Not a 'Samson' in stature, but certainly a 'Lion' in power of voice—but with the honeyed mellowness of the cello. He is neither the accepted picture of the tenor—but you see him not, once that golden voice is released—you see the story that he sings!

"Cantor Rosenblatt has the soul of the true artist, but it is not always for sale, for his actions continually prove it. My 'yarmilke' off to him as we say!"

After the completion of a year in vaudeville my father was established as a leader in that field of entertainment and one of the biggest box-office attractions. His name was mentioned along with such celebrities of the variety stage as Paul Whiteman, Gilda Gray, Houdini and the Fuller Dancers, during whose week of performance the Hippodrome, the largest playhouse in New York, grossed more than $40,000. Encouraged by his phenomenal success other cantors began in the early months of 1926 to emulate his example so that the New York Telegraph expressed fear of "an influx of cantors in vaudeville that would give the Charleston dancer a rival for public popularity."

Although he was inwardly and in his personal life still as far removed as ever from all that is associated with the entertainment world, its philosophy and beliefs, he was nevertheless accepted as an outstanding member of the confraternity. His patriarchal figure was included by O. O. McIntyre in his syndicated column, "New York Day by Day," among "the incessant blur of faces" to be seen in vaudeville. He was spoken of as "playing" the Keith Theatres, and he never failed to attend the social functions or to support the charitable institutions of the Theatrical Guild.

What attracted him to persons endowed with dramatic ability was the fact that, notwithstanding his deep aversion for any form of affectation, he was himself a bit of a showman. Oft sharing the spotlight with such stars of the theater as Belle Baker, Fannie Brice, Molly Picon and Sophie Tucker among women, and Eddie Cantor, Al Jolson, Lou Holtz, George Jessel and the Marx Brothers among men, he came to respect them for their gifts and to overlook the things that separated him from them. Max Gabel of the Yiddish stage in his memoirs recalls the warmth of the recognition accorded him by Yossele Rosenblatt at a concert in a fashionable summer resort. As soon as the cantor espied him in the audience, he informed his listeners of the actor's presence. "Dear friends," he said, "I am happy to inform you that we have a distinguished guest in our midst. While singing is not his field, I regard him as an outstanding performer. I give you Max Gabel." And the crowd cheered as much for Mr. Gabel as for the cantor's sportsmanship.

In the meantime, thanks to his year of apprenticeship under Ned Jaakobs and the lessons he had learned, Leo thought he knew enough about show business to take over the exclusive management of his father's professional engagements himself and thus save him the 5 percent commission charged by agents. What he was still lacking in experience he made up for amply by his youthful zeal; and he was able, for some time, to advance not only his father's fortunes but his own as well. His run-ins with the managers of the Keith-Albee outfit, with whom he had arrangements for touring many theatres in their circuit, were gradually ironed out. Once E. F. Albee, the owner of the Hippodrome in New York, threatened to cancel all my father's future engagements in the vaudeville houses of his organization because Leo had tentatively accepted an offer of $3,000 a week from the Eastman Theatre of Rochester, New York, prior to his client's appearance at Keith's Temple in the same city. It took some time to appease Mr. Albee. When the Keith-Albee outfit seemed about to break up, Leo was farsighted enough to establish connections with the Pantages interests at even more favorable terms than the $2,000 a week maximum, which was all that Keith's was willing to pay.

But even this and the additional revenue from officiating on Sabbaths, when he was free from vaudeville engagements, did not yield enough revenue to clear up the still considerable burden of debt that remained from the "Light of Israel" mess. Since his contemplated tie-up with the Philadelphia managers, which had been rescinded, his congregation Ohab Zedek had been paying him $10,000 a year for officiating on the holidays and one Sabbath a month. It could not be expected to go any higher. The only possibility of augmenting his earnings from such a source was to go out on his own, that is to engage a large auditorium in some city with a good-sized Jewish population for High Holiday services and charge admission fees high enough to assure a good income. He had threatened to do that in 1922 when his contract with the Ohab Zedek had expired. But at that time it was more or less a matter of expediency. His heart wasn't in it and he was rather glad of the opportunity that presented itself to cancel the agreement and return to his synagogue. This time the situation was different. Circumstances had changed. Harlem wasn't what it used to be. The more substantial members had moved away. The old guard, the real lovers of *Chazanuth,* who had been responsible for bringing him to America, had been replaced by younger men "who knew not Joseph." In the month of March his spiritual advisor, Dr. Philip Klein, for whom he entertained so much veneration and the prestige of whose personality had contributed so much to his remaining at his post, passed away at a ripe old age. There were no strong bonds left to keep him tied to Ohab Zedek. In addition there was the pressure of his obligations from which he wanted to free himself as soon as possible.

As early, then, as the month of January he began to cast about in search for the proper place. He did not want it to be New York, because it would have looked as though he were going into competition with the congregation that he had served for fourteen years. Besides, New York Jews had heard him often enough. His choice, therefore, fell upon Chicago, the second largest city in America with a Jewish community next in size to that of New York. The negotiations, which were initiated at a dinner given in his honor at the elite Covenant Club, were completed in February. The auditorium selected as the place of worship was the former Brilliant Palace, renamed "the Wigwam," which had a seating capacity of 3,000. He was to receive for officiating on the three days of the High Holiday festivals and for chanting the midnight *Selichos* services inaugurating the solemn season a total of $25,000. This included the cost of a choir of 35 voices, under the direction of Meyer Machtenberg, amounting to $10,000. In order to lend the enterprise an air of respectability and take it out of the category of commercialism my father selected, as the official sponsors of the service, the Beth Hamidrash Hagodol Congregation in whose synagogue he had often officiated. The beneficiary of whatever would be left over from the receipts after the payment of all incidental expenses as well as the fees of cantor and choir was to be the Beth Rachel Leah Hebrew School.

34

A Cantor without a Pulpit

After all these details had been arranged, my father resigned as cantor of the Ohab Zedek Congregation, and this time it was for good, because he himself would not and could not back out anymore. The news, which was quickly verified, naturally caused a lot of excitement, even more than it had on the two previous occasions when a similar step had been taken by him. Rumors began flying thick and fast to the effect that my father had at last been prevailed upon to give up the synagogue for the stage. "The Stage Hath Charms" read the headline of one of New York's dailies. "Noted Cantor Leaves Post for Vaudeville" reported the Boston Herald. Zit's was certain that the desire to spend more time on the variety stage had prompted my father's resignation from the synagogue. Again the press had misinterpreted my father's move and misread his intentions. Nothing was further from his mind than to cease being a *chazan*. He was, therefore, compelled to affirm once more that it was only on account of his financial troubles that he had gone into vaudeville. His singing there was only a temporary measure. The stage did not lure him. It was with a religious congregation that he had made the agreement to officiate in Chicago in a hall on the coming high holidays. "To state, therefore," he concluded, "that I have deserted the synagogue for the stage is not true."

My father's resignation from his post at the Ohab Zedek became effective officially in August, when his term of office was at an end. He still participated in the cornerstone laying of the congregation's new house of worship on 95th Street, the erection of which was necessitated by the trend in population. The farewell service to be conducted by him in the Harlem synagogue, where he had officiated during all the eventful years since his arrival in America, was held on Saturday, July 24. It was *Shabbos Nachamu,* "the Sabbath of consolation." Only a few days previous his voice had been heard chanting, over the first all-Jewish radio station to be established, the ancient laments over the destruction of Jerusalem. Now it was to resound for the last time in this miniature sanctuary with which he had become so closely identified and in which he had so often poured out his heart and presented the pleas of his congregation before their Father in heaven. The sobs could not be suppressed by the worshippers who felt as though the glory that had been Ohab Zedek's for nearly a decade and a half were about to depart from it.

As for my father, his emotions on this his last Sabbath at the Ohab Zedek were mingled. The future he was facing in leaving his synagogue was still a question mark. The prospects filled him with anxiety. On the other hand he was that day celebrating two joyous events in the life of his family which made him very happy. One was the Bar-Mitzvah of his youngest son, Ralph. The other was my return from Palestine crowned with the traditional *Semicha* in addition to my ordination from the seminary.

That summer was not spent by our family in Long Branch. We were compelled to give up our annual vacation partly in the interests of economy and partly because my father was busy—although not with rehearsing for his performance on the High Holidays in Chicago—for that he needed but little preparation. What occupied him almost up to the night of the first *Selichos* services were his vaudeville engagements, the last of which ended on August 28.

Upon his arrival in Chicago on August 19 a reception was accorded him that is usually reserved for royalty. Hundreds of people awaited him at LaSalle Street Station and Mayor Dever detailed a special police guard to escort him to his hotel. Automobiles decorated with the American colors and the blue and white flag of Israel accompanied him through the streets of the Jewish neighborhoods, and wherever he appeared he was greeted with ovations.

It was the first time that the Jews of Chicago had succeeded in luring an artist of the calibre of a Yossele Rosenblatt to their city for the High Holiday festive season, and they outdid themselves in showing him honor.

The Wigwam, in which my father conducted the High Holiday services for 3,000 Chicago Jews that year, clearly lacked the atmosphere of an Ohab Zedek. Yet, if we accept the statement of Glenn Dillard Gunn of the Chicago Herald Examiner, he "turned the bare and unlovely Wigwam Auditorium . . . into a temple" by his performance. "There is power in prayer to move the heart . . . It can even be felt by the observer who is excluded from its meaning by the barrier of language."

The High Holiday services in Chicago, the city in which he had leaped into national fame eight years previously, represented the high-water mark in my father's career as a cantor. No singer of the synagogue had ever received such generous remuneration for chanting the prayers on but four days. The $15,000 stipulated in the contract for his own share was paid in full. Manager J. Hyman was pleased, and so were the congregation, the Hebrew School and the worshippers. When my father left Chicago to go to Detroit, where he was to officiate on the first two days of the Feast of Tabernacles, a host of admirers, many of whom had become warm personal friends, came to the station to see him off and bid him an affectionate farewell.

Detroit was regarded as the proper place in which to officiate on the next important festival after the High Holidays. First because it was not far from Chicago, and secondly it had a large Jewish community that had never heard him perform on a major holiday. Thirdly he could count on the cooperation of such friends as Rabbi Tumim in whose home he had often been a guest. In order to show that he meant what he said when he stated that he had not "deserted the synagogue" and perhaps also to satisfy his own conscience for having conducted the High Holiday services in a hall, he made provision to officiate on the Feast of Tabernacles in houses of worship built for the purpose. In drawing up the agreement with his Detroit agent he insisted on inserting a clause to the effect that the places in which he would perform would be "synagogues in which men and women sit separately," according to the orthodox tradition. One time he had failed to take this precaution and there was considerable embarrassment due to his refusal to go up to the pulpit until the separation of the sexes had been effected.

The week following upon the heels of the concluding days of the festival was a very exciting one for Yossele Rosenblatt. It was during that brief interval of time that his three oldest children were married. Again a record had been broken by the Rosenblatts. Not since 1908, according to the statistics of the marriage bureau, had it happened even in a city like New York that three members of the same family should have been wedded within less than one week. Yet we had no intention of being different and attracting the publicity that the triple event received in the press. The sole reason for the unusual arrangement was the necessity of accommodating a very busy artist whose crowded schedule allowed him only six days for his children's nuptials. Sunday afternoon, Wednesday evening and Saturday night were the dates set aside for the three wedding ceremonies each of which was attended by several thousands of invitees. Immediately thereafter our father started on another one of his tours of the West. Since the details of this tour are so vividly described in Leo's memoirs, we shall quote from them almost verbatim.

"On the day after Nettie's wedding," they begin, "we entrained for the Coast, Dad, Mother, my bride and myself. Our trip across the country was very enjoyable. In Chicago and Omaha friends met and greeted us during the brief stopovers. Dad was in excellent spirits—and very careful of his bag of music, recalling his troubles of the year before. We had adjoining compartments, and every morning he would open our door a crack and call us by the pet names Doris and I had for each other. We had a half-hour stopover in Salt Lake City. Samples of the famous Utah celery were given out. Never before or since have I tasted such fresh, cooling, crunchy, tasty and immense stalks of celery. Boarding the train again we all said, 'We'll be back for more.' As the train was pulling out some serious-looking girls passed by the window of Dad's compartment. Seeing his patriarchal countenance, one of them made the sign of the cross. That incident was characteristic of the high respect with which the great Mormon city later received Dad.

"We arrived in San Francisco," the memoirs continue, "on Thursday morning (October 14) and went to the St. Francis Hotel. I reported to young Rodney Pantages, who was manager of the still new Pantages Theatre in the Golden Gate city, to arrange for the rehearsal with the orchestra. The bills at the theatre in those days changed on Saturdays. But since it was so stipulated in his contracts, Dad did not sing until just after nightfall on Saturday, October 16.

"San Francisco liked him as much as it did the previous

year, when the applause he had received was compared to
'the growing thunder of surf.' He sang 'Yahrzeit' in Yiddish
and Hebrew, 'La Campana' in Italian and 'I Hear You Calling Me' in English. He stopped the show and had to give several encores. 'Mother Machree' was his choice. The Examiner
said that the audience 'thrilled to the sweetness and power
of his notes.' On the bill with him was the twelve-year-old
Dodo Reid, child-memory marvel, and the picture was
'Broken Hearts in Hollywood' featuring Louise Dresser,
Patsy Ruth Miller and Douglas Fairbanks, Jr.

"During the week we managed to visit the Twin Peaks and
the bay and had the thrilling experience of being awakened
in the middle of one night by distant rumbles and a nearby
rocking that recalled Caruso's experiences during the great
earthquake of 1907.

"With Dad's $2,500—less the 5 percent office commission
—in my pocket I had no compunction or pangs of regret
about having left Keith-Albee, altho Mother still hadn't for-
given me for my 'daring' in leaving them."

While in San Francisco my father was very happy, as was
his custom everywhere, to lend his services to the local campaign committee of the Jewish National Welfare Fund in its
annual drive.

"We got to Los Angeles," Leo further notes, "Sunday afternoon, October 24, after a pleasant trip by daylight along the
famous California shore, and met Alexander Pantages for
the first time. Monday afternoon was the first show at the
Pantages Theatre in Los Angeles. The Examiner reported
that 'three encores and a half a dozen curtain calls are needed
before Joseph Rosenblatt is permitted to make a final bow at
the Pantages this week.' The Illustrated News said: 'There
is one thing as certain as death and taxes—a vaudeville audience knows what it likes to see. This was never more fittingly
demonstrated than yesterday at the Pantages Theatre, where
every seat was taken at the afternoon performances and oth-

ers were content to stand in bunches at the back of the house and witness the show . . . *As was expected Cantor Rosenblatt proved a tremendous sensation.'*

"With another triumph behind him, Dad displayed, according to the Express, 'an unlooked-for sense of humor in his announcement of another show in three hours when the applause continued after the added selection.' The Times questioned the wisdom of his choice of 'Mother Machree' as his encore, but added: 'However the audience seemed to like it.'

"He received many invitations to all sorts of social affairs during the week, but he accepted only that of the famous Breakfast Club. He was not pleased, however, with the 'ham and eggs' that those seated around him ate. There was also a slight drizzle—more of the 'unusual L.A. weather,' as the natives there always put it.

"Monday, November 1, Dad opened at the Pantages in San Diego—the sleepy, restful seaport town close by the Mexican border. Our hotel, the U. S. Grant, was a quaint, low-roofed building with a balcony running all around the first floor, the type you expect in a town at or near the tropics.

"San Diego found that 'perhaps the most distinctive thing about his [Dad's] voice is the range, which travels from a tone comparable to a boyish soprano to the mighty notes of an operatic basso' (San Diego Union). His program was different now—'Kaddish' in Yiddish, 'Last Rose of Summer' in English, 'La Campana' in Italian, and as an encore 'Granadinas' in Spanish—four languages in as many songs. One reviewer thought that 'the presentation of an act like Rosenblatt's on the vaudeville stage is an experiment fraught with danger for the manager, but happily in this instance his great art surmounts the difficulties of a variety theatre and he scored an emphatic success, this in spite of a somewhat restless crowd at the matinee' (San Diego Independent).

"Well, if they were restless, my wife and I were equally

restless watching a listless football game on the Saturday afternoon of that week between branches of the United States Military and Naval Services, while Dad was taking a well-earned Sabbath siesta.

"Wednesday, November 10," the memoirs continue, "found us in Salt Lake City. In addition to performing the entire week—excepting the Sabbath—Dad found time to sing at a meeting of the local Elks Lodge, visit the Capitol, sit in the governor's chair, and try out the acoustics of the famous Mormon Tabernacle. My wife and I managed once again to steal away for a few hours to watch the University of Utah trim Brigham Young by a decidedly lop-sided score, in a setting of snow-covered peaks on the outskirts of the city.

"The Salt Lake Telegraph commented on Dad's performance: 'Mr. Rosenblatt at times changes his tone in such a way as to give the impression that he has been gifted with two distinct voices.' It had reference no doubt to his change from the full voice to that unusual and finely developed falsetto which he used so effectively. At any rate he 'enthralled the audience.' (Deseret News)

"As in every city we visited on our tour, we had made special arrangements for kosher meals at the home of some orthodox Jews who had been recommended to us. In the family that thus catered to our needs in Salt Lake City there was a little girl of school age. Returning home from class one day she informed her mother that at school the teacher—a non-Jewess—had pointed out to the children that they ought to visit the Pantages Theatre to hear Cantor Rosenblatt, who appears there several times a day and whom God gives sufficient strength to carry on this arduous work, because he is a man who 'sticks to his principles' and will not work during the period of his Sabbath. He must indeed have 'enthralled his audience' to have had such an effect on Mormon school teachers."

With such recognition and praise heaped upon his father,

it was no wonder that Leo wrote: "We were loath to leave this city that took its name from the Great Salt Lake. We used to sit at our hotel windows, looking west at twilight for hours at a time, watching a sunset more golden, more lasting than anywhere else in the country, sinking into the salt lake as it were, seeking rest on the other side of the Rockies.

"Portland, Oregon," he continued, "was next on our itinerary. Dad began his week at the Portland Pantages Theatre on Monday, November 22. The story of his reception here was the same as everywhere else—the greatest possible acclaim from audience and press, continued praise for his magnificent voice, his masterly way of handling it, the wise choice of a varied program, and the pleasure all this gave to his audiences. Himself always given to variety—his essentially restless musical spirit always to the fore—he changed his program for Portland and gave 'The Last Rose of Summer' in English, 'Eili, Eili' in Yiddish and Hebrew, 'Volga Boatmen' in Russian and 'La Campana' in Italian."

There now followed three weeks of rest. But that was only so far as vaudeville engagements were concerned, not the use of his voice as such. For that he was given plenty of opportunity on the two Sabbaths on which he officiated at Shaarei Torah Synagogue, of Portland. During the intervening weekdays, he was able to make trips to the surrounding country in the company of my mother and Leo and Doris.

On the eve of the second of the two Sabbaths spent in Portland the sad news was relayed to my father that his nephew, Melech Kaufman, whom he had brought to America and who had served his congregation in Philadelphia with distinction, had passed away at the age of twenty-eight as a result of a ruptured appendix. The report came as a shock to us all. Only several weeks before Melech had sung at my installation. A strapping six-footer, he was the very picture of health. He had just succeeded, after numerous difficulties and a great deal of red tape, in bringing his fiancée over from Poland to the United States via Canada. They had been married but a short time when death overtook him, and it was not even granted to him to have his uncle present at his funeral.

"Three Bad Men and Cantor Rosenblatt" was the reading of the marquee over the entrance to the Seattle, Washington, Pantages Theatre during the week of December 13. Of course "Three Bad Men" was the title of the screen attraction. "But," as Leo observed, "when joined with the name of Dad, it gave the local quips a chance for some fun. The picture was acclaimed, but of Dad one of the newspapers (the Seattle Star) said that 'his singing the "Song of the Volga Boatmen" alone was worth the price of admission. A word should be said about his manner of presentation. His singing, in addition to its wonderful depth, astounding range, rich fullness and sweet tones, is characterized by the absence of all gestures and the utter lack of ostentation. The hearty applause which the Cantor wins is acknowledged by a simple and sedate bow and that is all.' "

Seattle, Washington, has always been noted for its fine Jewish community. By one of those unaccountable accidents of fate a number of learned Russian Jews, coming from Siberia, settled there, establishing a tradition of culture coupled with religious observance. Bikur Cholum was the leading Jewish congregation of Seattle, and my father accepted with alacrity the invitation to sing at its annual banquet which was held just prior to his week's engagement at the Pantages Theatre. In order not to appear discriminatory he agreed nine days later, after his appearance in Tacoma, to participate in the musical program of another Seattle synagogue whose spiritual leader had been his host.

Like the Seattle periodicals so, too, did the Tacoma newspapers outdo themselves in their encomiums on my father's singing. Their sole regret was that he was able to stay only one day.

Minneapolis, whose Jewish community to this day is able to pride itself on its fine Hebrew schools, was my father's first stop on his way back east. Upon his arrival just before the Christmas holidays, the following telegram from Mayor Leach awaited him:

MINNEAPOLIS IS VERY HAPPY TO HAVE YOU HERE THIS HOLIDAY TIME. YOUR OWN PEOPLE MUST BE VERY PROUD OF YOU AND YOUR WONDERFUL VOICE, AND AS MAYOR I AM ESPECIALLY GLAD TO HAVE YOU IN THIS CITY.

(signed) *Mayor Leach*

35

$70,000 Gross

When my father's earnings for the year 1926 were computed for income tax payment, it was found that he had grossed more than $70,000. Out of this sum only $11,000 was paid back to the creditors of the "Light of Israel." Business expenses, embracing payments for advertisements, Leo's salary as manager and the cost of travel and hotel accommodations accounted for another $22,000. The three weddings had cost comparatively little, but there was still a large household to be maintained. Furthermore loans had been extended by him to certain needy musicians from whom he had no hope of collecting. The long and short of it is that in spite of the $15,000 he had earned by officiating on the High Holidays in Chicago and the salary of $2,500 a week from Pantages and the royalties from the Victor Company, the cash balance my father had left in the bank amounted to but little more than $1,000. Though he was working harder than ever, he was making but little headway in clearing the debts incurred in behalf of the "Light of Israel." Nevertheless, he remained cheerful. So long as he enjoyed popular favor and the public was willing to pay to hear him sing, there was hope of reha- bilitation. "Gott wet helfen" (God will help) was his reply to every question regarding his material well-being.

With another fiscal year beginning it became necessary to make provision for the High Holidays in the fall. This time Philadelphia, which had the third largest Jewish community in America, was settled on. It had, in addition to others, the advantage of proximity to New York, which meant that the expense of travel for himself as well as the choir would be considerably reduced. The remuneration he was to get was to be the same as in Chicago and the auditorium to be used was the Academy of Music, which could accommodate more than 3,000 worshippers. Max Romm, his old standby, was se- lected as manager and Joseph Gross, a prominent Philadel- phia politician was the attorney in whose office the agreement was drawn on February 2. The proceeds, after the deduc- tion of fees and other incidentals, were to be devoted to the founding of an Orthodox congregation that would attract the youth.

This matter having been disposed of my father was able to resume his vaudeville work. However the peak had already been passed. The trips undertaken by him during the early part of 1927 did not seem to follow any definite plan or itinerary. He accepted engagements wherever he could and of whatever duration or nature they were. A week of vaude- ville in Indianapolis and Columbus, Ohio, a three-day run at Moss's Franklin in the Bronx, a night at the Regent in De- troit, and a Sabbath service in Chicago filled out his time from the middle of January until the end of February. In March he chanted the Sabbath prayers in Milwaukee, cele- brated *Purim* in Chicago, returned to New York to partici- pate in the farewell to the Rabbi of Drohobycz, officiated in my synagogue in Trenton, New Jersey, took part in a concert of the Anti-Horthy League at Carnegie Hall, New York and appeared for three days in B. F. Keith's Riviera in Brooklyn. Passover found him back again in Chicago, whither all the giants of *Chazanuth* had gravitated at that time, so that New York, the largest Jewish community in the world was, in the words of the Jewish Morning Journal, "emptied out of top-rank cantors."

During the first week of May my father sang at the Earle Theatre in Washington, D. C. Here he met for the first time in his life a president of the United States of America. The reception at the White House was conducted in the typical Coolidge manner. It was courteous but brief. The President greeted the Jewish cantor affably enough but with his usual reserve and his well-known economy of speech. The cantor responded to the greeting by pronouncing upon his host the blessing prescribed by Jewish precept for a head of state. A snapshot of the two of them shaking hands was featured in the press and may have been instrumental in moving many a Jewish resident of the Capital to contribute to the United Palestine Appeal which was then in progress. In my father's audience at the theater that week, there were among others a rear admiral of the United States Navy and his wife. The lady, in particular, was deeply impressed with the cantor's singing as well as his dignified appearance and wished that the immortal "Patti could have heard him."

Vaudeville engagements were definitely not as lucrative in 1927 as they had been the year previous, although Josef Rosenblatt's reputation was greater than ever. His name reached down to the American grass-roots. The volume of his fan-mail increased. He had become a favorite of school-children for whom he sang at assemblies. He was used as the standard by which to measure the virtuosity of other cantors. They were described as either "comparable to" or "greater than Josef Rosenblatt" or their importance was indicated, as in the case of P. S. Pinchik, by the fact that Josef Rosenblatt

headed the committee that welcomed them upon their arrival in America. Epithets like "the incomparable Cantor Rosenblatt," "the golden voiced tenor," "the sweetest singer
of the songs of all nations" had become so commonplace that
they did not excite him anymore. After his first performance
at the local Pantages Theatre the Commercial Appeal of
Memphis, Tennessee devoted an entire column to the man
whom the Kansas City Journal Post a week later dubbed "An
Unusual Vaudevillian." "Monday afternoon vaudeville audiences," it began, "are known in some respects as the most
critical of the week. Composed largely of those who seek sur-
cease after a 'tough' Saturday or weekend, the lighter forms
of entertainment generally get the best reception. There is
always present the danger of real art not being recognized, to
say the least, if not being accorded the 'guffaw.' But at yesterday afternoon's matinee at Pantages a big crowd was con-
quered by the sheer virtuosity of a singer."

36
Pioneering the Talkies

All this recognition and acclaim could not prevent the grad-
ual decline of that new source of income that had been the
cause of the temporary upturn of my father's fortunes. By
the irony of fate he himself unwittingly had a part, minor
though it was, in helping reduce the importance of vaudeville as the most popular form of amusement, next to the
cinema, of the American masses. The Warner Brothers, who
had lost a fortune in the silent movies, and were virtually
bankrupt, were just then toying with a new idea. They were
going to produce pictures which, in addition to doing panto-

mime, would have the actors speak and sing. For their first presentation they chose "The Jazz Singer," an assured Broadway success in which George Jessel had starred with great credit. Based on the life of the black-faced idol of musical comedy, Al Jolson, it is the story of the son of a cantor who became a singer of popular dance music. My father had once been asked for his opinion on the authenticity and effectiveness of the play and had given it his enthusiastic endorsement. It now occurred to the Warners that if Josef Rosenblatt could be induced to take the role of the cantor in this first "talkie," or "Vitaphone picture" as they called it, it would be a sure hit. Who wouldn't go to see it? Everybody, Jew and gentile, would be attracted by the name and voice of the principal star, and they, the producers, would be on their feet again. The only question in their minds was: "Will Josef Rosenblatt accept?" They knew of his religious scruples, of his having turned down on previous occasions the most flattering offers to enter the opera because it would have involved a little bit of acting. But perhaps this time, on account of his financial troubles, which had made him amenable to entering into vaudeville, he might be induced to stretch a point and sing for Vitaphone.

So one day in the spring of 1927 they sent three of their agents to speak to my father in person at his home and sound him out in regard to their plans for him.

"Mr. Rosenblatt," they said, introducing themselves, "we are a committee representing Warner Brothers."

"The moving picture producers?"

"Yes."

"And to what do I owe the honor of your visit?"

"You are no doubt familiar with the play 'The Jazz Singer.' "

"The one George Jessel starred in?"

"That's right. What do you think of it?"

"An excellent play."

"Well, our company is thinking of producing it on the screen with sound effects. The actors would not only be seen, but heard as well, and we were wondering whether we couldn't induce you to take the part of the father and sing some of your own liturgical compositions. We are willing to compensate you well for your efforts. There would be hardly any acting involved for you. All you would have to do is stand before the pulpit or sit at your table, as you are accustomed, and sing."

"I feel highly complimented and flattered by your offer, gentlemen. But you know what my position in these matters has always been and remains. The answer is 'No.'"

"Mr. Rosenblatt, we have been authorized to go as high as $100,000 if you could see your way clear. Think of what it would mean for raising the prestige of the Jew and his faith if a man like you were to be held up as its representative to the non-Jewish public."

"There is no use talking, my friends. I appreciate your good intentions as well as your generosity. But there isn't enough money in the world to make me profane my sacred calling by putting on an act anywhere, whether it be on the screen or the stage. Besides in order that my face might photograph well, I would have to use some make-up, and that is definitely out."

Seeing him so unalterably opposed to any active role and eager to find some tie-up for my father with the proposed talkie so that their plan might not fall through altogether, the Warner Brothers' emissaries made another proposal. "We see that we can't make even a little bit of an actor out of you, Mr. Rosenblatt. But how about just letting us have the use of your voice, without your being seen, in selections like let us say, *'Kol Nidrei'* and *'Umipnei Chatoeinu'*? That might be of some help to us in our plans."

"Did you say *'Kol Nidrei,'* that hallowed prayer that is chanted by the cantor at the inauguration of the holiest day of the year? Under no circumstances would I permit that to pass my mouth anywhere except in a house of God."

"Is there then nothing that you could do for us?" pleaded the negotiators.

"I am afraid there isn't, gentlemen," said my father firmly, and it seemed for the last time.

The Warner agents left crestfallen, disappointed, their mission unfulfilled. Later, as a result of negotiations back and forth, something was worked out. My father agreed, provided he was not photographed, to sing *Rachem* and several other such non-liturgical Jewish melodies for the Vitaphone production. But even that necessitated his presence in Hollywood in order to make certain that there would be no snag in the synchronization. The Warner Brothers could not afford to leave anything to chance in their first talkie. And so for eight weeks during this summer and in return for $10,-000 plus expenses, my father came, accompanied by my mother, Leo and Doris, to Los Angeles as the guest of the Warner Brothers.

To be in the capital of moviedom and not to get a close glimpse of its heroes would have been like visiting Rome and not seeing the pope. Always interested in and anxious to meet people, my father made it his business to come in contact with the celebrities of Hollywood. Most of all, however, did he wish to make the acquaintance of the solemn-faced comedian Charlie Chaplin. He had often laughed at his antics and been amused by his clowning, and he was curious to learn what sort of a personality there lurked behind that clumsy, uncouth hobo exterior. So he had Leo call Mr. Chaplin's home to find out whether the funny man of the movies would be able to receive him. Not only did he get an answer in the affirmative, but he was told that Mr. Chaplin was sending his own chauffeur with a car to fetch the cantor and his party.

As the automobile was approaching the Chaplin mansion in Beverly Hills, my father wondered at the reception he would be given and how he would find the real Charlie Chaplin, without the disguises. When he entered the gateway, there ran out to meet him instead of a sad-faced, woebegone, melancholy looking tramp with the Hitler mustache, a dapper, smiling, smooth-shaven gentleman, who, in a cultured voice and a beautiful Oxford English accent and with hands outstretched, greeted him: "Welcome to my abode, Cantor Rosenblatt. I am delighted to see you. I have heard so much about you and I was wondering whether I would ever have the opportunity to meet you in person."

My father returned the compliment. He, too, had seen and heard about the great actor and had wanted to make his personal acquaintance. Mr. Chaplin ushered him into the lawn, and tea was served. The actor was a charming host and a most interesting conversationalist and gave the impression of being a person of very high intelligence, everything that he was not supposed to be on the screen. He and my father had photographs taken together on the grounds. And then came the surprise of the afternoon. The host had a phonograph brought out and put on a record. "Mr. Rosenblatt," he asked his guest, "do you recognize the voice?" My father laughed. It was *his "Omar Rabbi Elozor"* that was being played.

"I have all the records you have ever produced," said his host. "I cherish them as among my most treasured possessions. Whenever I feel a little blue, I take them out and play them. They do something to me. They unite me—oh so closely—with my Jewish ancestors. Now you know why I am so happy to have the original, the master of the voice recorded on these disks, in my homestead."

My father never forgot that meeting.

There were also other celebrities whose acquaintance he made during his sojourn in California this year. One of them was the famous Russian basso of the Chicago Opera Company, Feodor Chaliapin. The tall Russian, whose singing of the "Volga Boatmen" had made that Russian folksong, which my father oft included in his vaudeville repertoire, so popular, paid him a special visit. As they conversed with each other, a crowd surrounded them. My father, because of his diminutive size, was hardly visible, while the Russian giant towered above everybody else.

When the guest was gone, my father remarked to his accompanist: "Do you know what we looked like, Chaliapin and I? Like a *Lulav* and an *Esrog*,"—the equivalent of "Mutt and Jeff" of the comics.

Of course, there were also other things my father did during his two-months' stay in Los Angeles besides recording for "The Jazz Singer" and visiting movie-stars. There wasn't a Jewish institution in that fast-growing community that left him alone nor a cause of merit toward which he did not lend his talents—with the consent, to be sure, of the Warner Brothers.

When the eight weeks were over there was barely enough time left to prepare for the High Holiday services in Philadelphia. The methods of publicizing his performance in the city on the solemn festive season adopted by his Philadelphia managers were somewhat different from those used in Chicago. Instead of receiving him with the fanfare and flourish that had heralded his arrival in the Windy City, they had him visit, in the company of Mayor Kendrick, the latter's pet project, the Shriners' Hospital for Crippled Children. His tour of the hospital and his entertainment of the youthful patients was given the widest spread in the press—an excellent bit of public relations work which must have helped in some measure to assure the attendance by close to 4,000 worshippers of the High Holiday services at the Academy of Music.

37

Back to the Synagogue

Though he could have no cause for complaint so far as the reception given his efforts by the audience was concerned, my father was inwardly not satisfied. He might at one time have thought that he would be rendering the public a real service if, instead of confining himself to just a single congregation, he could officiate for communities throughout the country. Now that he had tried it, he found it disappointing. He was tired of the gypsy life of an itinerant cantor, even though outside of the High Holidays all his chanting of religious services was done in synagogues. He longed for a pulpit of his own. He wanted to become again, what he had been before, the *Sheliach Tzibbur*, the regular representative of an established congregation. It was worth making substantial sacrifices in order to achieve once more that sense of belonging that he had had for twenty-six years prior to his first venture outside the synagogue in Chicago. And so when the Anshei Sfard Congregation of Borough Park, in which his good friend Max Jonas was prominent, offered him a ten-year contract at an annual salary of $12,000—another new high in cantorial remuneration—he took it.

His acceptance of the Borough Park position necessitated my father's transfer of his household from Harlem to the neighborhood in Brooklyn in which his new synagogue was located. It was more difficult to find an apartment large enough to suit his needs in Borough Park, however, than to dispose of the house on 120th Street, which had been given up on account of the mortgages placed on it. My mother finally solved the problem of adequate living quarters by combining two small apartments on the fifth floor of a modern building on 15th Avenue and 47th Street, Brooklyn. That yielded a total of ten spacious rooms, for which a rental of $310 a month was paid.

With my father's arrival in Borough Park, that section of New York, as the Jewish press noted, became the musical Mecca of American Jewry. Mordecai Hershman and Zawel Kwartin were already established there. Precentors of repute like Malavsky, Morgenstern and Hillman officiated in the immediate vicinity. All in all it was figured out that the Jewish community of Borough Park spent during that year no less than $100,000 to hear Jewish liturgical music sung—a large sum of money at any time.

The Anshei Sfard synagogue of Borough Park was not nearly as beautiful or elegant as the Ohab Zedek in Harlem, nor were its members as aristocratic as the constituents of the First Hungarian Congregation. I had a let-down feeling when on my first visit to my father's new theater of operations I noted the plain, unprepossessing interior. "If my father had to accept a permanent pulpit," I thought to myself, "could it not have been with a congregation that had a house of worship befitting a cantor of his calibre?" However the Anshei Sfard made up amply with the respect and affection with which they treated their new cantor for what their synagogue lacked in external beauty. Their regard for him was indicated by the flowers that were sent to his home when he moved into the neighborhood, and the party arranged in his honor by the Jonases in their *Succah* on the Feast of Tabernacles, when his tenure of office as precentor of the Anshei Sfard began.

It seems, however, that this genuine expression of love did not agree so well with their new cantor's physical health. The Feast of Tabernacles had often been fraught with hazards for my father. Although not a mechanic, he loved to busy himself personally with the construction of the foliage-covered hut prescribed by biblical ritual. "It was a *Mitzvah*," he said, "to engage in such work." One time the chemicals in the paint he put on the wooden boards two days before the feast caused a congestion in his chest so that it was only thanks to his falsetto that he was able to function on that holiday altogether. After that experience he acquired for himself a collapsible *Succah* made of canvas that enabled him to dispense with painting. This year his exposure to the elements in the insubstantial contraption in Mr. Jonas' home—no *Succah* really provides shelter against inclement weather—caused him to contract a severe bronchial cold. It later turned into pneumonia which confined him to bed for several weeks. As a consequence he was unable to fulfill his duties as a cantor toward his new congregation on the first Sabbath after the holiday period.

For a while not only his immediate family but nearly everybody else, his many patrons and admirers throughout the country, were worried. His illness was very much in the news. Flowers and messages of hope for a speedy recovery were sent by thousands of people from all over so that his sickroom, as one visitor described it, "resembled a miniature conservatory." The press carried daily bulletins on the progress of his convalescence in Lakewood from a malady that was estimated to have meant a loss to him of $10,000 worth of engagements. I had a further reason for concern. Commencing with my ordination my father had by circumstances been prevented from personal participation in the celebration of any one of the milestones in my rabbinical career. I had just been elected to the position which I still hold today in Baltimore. The date of my installation was set for December 11. Would my father be able to attend at least this one time and grace the occasion by his presence? I was hoping and praying, and my prayers were heard. By the beginning of December the patient had completely recovered from his indisposition.

There was not a trace of his illness detectable in his singing when he performed at the festivities connected with my formal induction as rabbi of Beth Tfiloh. It was a memorable day, one of the most outstanding in the annals of the congregation, which was everything Yossele Rosenblatt wanted for his son. My father's coloratura and falsetto functioned perfectly as he rendered *Omar Rabbi Elozor* to a spellbound audience that filled every seat in the large auditorium and overflowed into the aisles.

Such a start was priceless for the aspirant leader of a new flock, and I always thrill when I think of the glamor that my father's voice lent to that occasion. All the more's the pity that the man who contributed so much to the joy and happiness of others seemed so utterly powerless in furthering his own personal interests. The number of his vaudeville engagements, which had already dropped in 1927, fell off still further in 1928. During the first quarter of the latter year he appeared for one continuous week in only three variety theatres, the Marboro in Brooklyn, the Rivoli of Toledo and the Hippodrome in New York. In others, nearly all of which were located in and around his home city, he sang for periods of three days at the utmost. On top of that his Philadelphia managers had defaulted in paying his due for the High Holidays to the tune of $2,500, and he didn't have the heart to sue them. To increase his income he was forced to solicit opportunities to perform Sabbath services or sing at benefit concerts—an expedient to which he had never had to resort previously.

The reason for this state of affairs could not have been that he had lost his grip on the public. When he sang in Temple Adath Jeshurun of Syracuse in February it was not only the members of the congregation, but the sororities and fraternities of Syracuse University who attended en masse. The Anshei Sfard Congregation was compelled to charge an admission to limit the size of the crowd that was anxious to hear

him officiate in its synagogue on the Passover festival. And
the Zionist Organization was elated to be able to announce
that Cantor Josef Rosenblatt would participate in several of
its important functions. The cause of the slump could, therefore, have been only that he had been caught in the meshes
of one of the revolutions in the field of entertainment
brought on by the rapid development of technology in the
most progressive and fast-stepping country in the world. The
talkies, in which he had himself to some extent pioneered,
were beginning to displace vaudeville just as the phonograph
was being discarded in favor of radio. Why should owners of
movie theaters pay high prices to artists to perform on the
stage and run the risk of illness and other accidents, when
they could have the voices of the best singers perfectly recorded on films that could be shown in many playhouses
throughout the country at the same time? And why spend
large sums of money on collections of recorded music, when
one could hear an outstanding vocalist or a favorite symphony or opera by turning the dial of a radio receiver
bought only once in many years?

38

Europe Revisited

There was but one prospect of at least temporary relief for
my father from a recession that seemed inevitable in America. That was to try his luck again in the Old World where
singing movies had not yet usurped the place of regular concerts and the radio had not pushed out the phonograph. By
this time the European countries had stabilized their currency sufficiently to render musical recitals remunerative.

The plan of another European tour had been conceived by Leo as early as the spring of 1927. It was then that he had started negotiations with impresarios abroad. His efforts began to bear fruit in February of the year 1928. The first definite instructions were dictated by Leo from his sick-bed at the Mt. Morris Hospital, which he had entered on February 6 for an appendectomy. On Wednesday, May 2, my father was able to sail on the Mauretania, accompanied by his pianist Abraham Elstein, Mother and Leo.

The ship's passengers included a considerable number of musical celebrities. Of these cellist Hans Kindler and pianist Eugene Goossens took part together with my father in the concert given on the liner in the course of its passage. However his most distinguished shipmate, with whom he became quite friendly, was the conductor of the Boston Symphony Orchestra, Sergei Koussevitzky.

Born of Jewish parents in Russia, the great maestro had been baptized in early childhood and reared in the Greek Orthodox faith. When he saw my father with his dignified patriarchal appearance, and especially after he had heard him sing the traditional chants of his people, there were awakened in his mind long-forgotten memories of his youth. It was during the long ride from Cherbourg to Paris, when they were thrown together in the same compartment, that he said to my father: "Mr. Rosenblatt, I hesitate to impose upon you because I would not want you to exert yourself before your concert. But you see, though music is my field, I know very little about the traditional chants of the synagogue. I wonder whether it would be too much to ask you to give me a little sample?"

"Gladly," said my father. "It would be an honor to perform for a man of your distinction." And then he proceeded to give him a private audition in an undertone of his *Acheinu Kol Beis Yisroel;* and as he sang the words the meaning

of which is "Our brethren, the entire house of Israel, that
find themselves in trouble and captivity," tears rolled from
the eyes of the conductor, so deeply was he moved. This was
the beginning of Koussevitzky's return to Judaism. From that
time on he rendered great services to the Jewish Theological Seminary of America, and at the end of his long and fruit-
ful career, when he was already ailing from a fatal illness, he
organized the department of music of the first non-sectarian
university under Jewish auspices in America, Brandeis University.

The first lap of my father's second European tour covered
countries in Western and Central Europe. Starting out with a
concert in Paris on May 9, the route followed by him was Antwerp, Amsterdam, Antwerp, Brussels, Paris, Zurich, Frankfurt, Hamburg, Leipsic, Berlin, Munich, Vienna. The cities
in which he sang were for the most part such as had sizable
populations of Jews of East-European origin. While these
turned out in large numbers, fulfilling the expectations of
manager Rappaport of Antwerp, there was also a considerable attendance of the more assimilated Western Jews as well
as of non-Jewish music lovers. In Paris, Antwerp and Berlin
the police were hardly able to maintain order among the
crowds that tried to gain admittance into the synagogues or
concert halls in which he performed. On the whole the reception accorded him was favorable. However, the American
cantor and concert artist discovered very quickly that the music critics of Europe, with its traditions of culture and art,
were much more exacting in their demands of the singer
of operatic or classical music than reviewers in America. Or
was it that on account of pressure of time and many cares
that weighed on him he had failed to prepare himself ade-
quately or had not kept in trim as an artist of the highest
order must and should? At all events many of them found
fault with his manner of singing the Schubert songs while

some criticized the incongruity of his programs. On the other hand, there was virtual unanimity on his virtuosity as a cantor and on the unusual nature of his vocal equipment.

The Amsterdam Telegraaf waxed almost lyrical in its description of the "dignified presentation by the cantor in all his glory" of "the song treasure of Israel." And if the Zueriche Post was cold and aloof, its lack of enthusiasm was fully made up for by the warmth of the Koelner Tageblatt, which acclaimed him as "the unrivalled and unexcelled master of his art," and by that of the Jewish weekly of Cologne, which stated that the "artistic experience of Cologne Jewry that summer could be called 'Josef Rosenblatt.'" From that point on, his journey resembled a triumphal march. Orthodox Frankfurt hailed him as the loyal Jew even as it admired in him the gifted singer. Hamburg showed its pride in the accomplishments of its erstwhile cantor. The Jews of Leipsic would give him no rest until they had extracted from him the promise to come back a second time and conduct services in the auditorium of their Zoological Garden. In Berlin a hall with a seating capacity of 4,000 was completely filled although hardly any more publicity had been given to the concert than word-of-mouth news passed among the 50,000 to 80,000 East-European residents of the city. Zionist leaders were amazed at all the new faces they saw. There must be, so they thought, some secret power in *Chazanuth,* for even Weizmann or Jabotinsky had never been able to attract such crowds. The reporter of the Muenchener Post remarked, after my father's Munich appearance, that "even he who did not understand the words of the Yiddish and Hebrew songs" in the program, "could not help being touched by the sombre individuality of their melody" as rendered by Josef Rosenblatt. The hundreds of cantors who came to hear him and fete him in Vienna may have been somewhat smitten with envy when they thought of all the dollars he must have earned by his singing. But they could not help glorying vicariously in the musical success, as A. Tenenblat of the Riga Frimorgen put it, "of a distinguished colleague, whose talent might compete with the nightingale."

All this adulation on the part of connoisseurs and the masses alike put the visitor into excellent humor. Herman Swet of the Warsaw Moment gives us the following picture of my father on the day after his Berlin concert.

"We sit with Rosenblatt over a glass of tea in the apartment of the young Berlin cantor Manfred Lewandowski. Around Rosenblatt stand the elite of the Berlin cantorate . . .

"Yossele, in very good spirits, tells amusing stories about cantors and artists. He mimics an American cantor, a real ignoramus so far as the text of the prayers is concerned, trying to show off his virtuosity as an improviser as he recites the *Kiddush* on Friday evening. He holds the cup of wine in his hand, but instead of concluding the blessing with the words *Bore P'ri Hagofen* (that createst the fruit of the vine), he bursts out *Bore P'ri Hashabbos* (that createst the fruit of the Sabbath), confusing the end of this benediction with that of the one following.

"After that Yossele does some singing himself, and here in the company of intimates and professionals he performs real miracles. He rolls off coloratura passages, performs acrobatics with cadences, recites selections in accordance with the traditional motifs, improvises, sings in Italian and French, plays stunts with his marvellous falsetto in which, I believe, he has no rival, sings viva voce and sotto voce without a stop."

But however deep the impression my father may have made on his audiences in the West of Europe, it was as nothing compared to the stir he created among the millions of Jews of Poland and other countries of Eastern Europe, the majority of which were still relatively untouched by Western influences. To these people, most of whom followed the traditions of their fathers, for whom *Chazanuth* and music were virtually interchangeable terms, Yossele Rosenblatt was the supreme artist, the foremost interpreter in the medium of sound of their sentiments, emotions and feelings. They needed no explanation of the meaning of the prayers he sang or the contents of the text of his sacred melodies, because these were all familiar to them from daily usage. When a liturgical selection was announced as an item on the program they thrilled to it in anticipation because they already knew its movements from the recordings. All they waited for was the added pleasure of the execution by the original creator of this music in person. And so they hung on every word of the man before them, and they were fascinated not only by the voice but also by the personality from which it emanated. For Yossele Rosenblatt with his full black beard and his unsophisticated Jewish demeanor represented to them the true *Sheliach Tzibbur,* the pleader worthy of bringing Israel's petitions to its father in heaven. Even in patriarchal Poland, for all its piety, it was then already a rare occurrence that a cantor, who made his living by chanting the prayers of the synagogue, should also pray when he was not being paid for it, that an individual endowed with such talent should not arrogate to himself the privileges of genius and expect his admirers to overlook his deviations from the norm. From the first moment that Yossele Rosenblatt appeared on a public platform before his coreligionists in Eastern Europe, as more than one observer noted, there was felt a rapport between the artist and his audience that was rare. The public simply could not get enough of him. After having bought up all the seats in the Philharmonie, for example, Jews of all classes in Warsaw filled the huge Zirk three times in succession, and when he was taking his Sabbath stroll in the Saxon Garden, crowds of them followed their idol around in it like puppies.

Fist fights broke out and arrests were made in this second largest Jewish community in the world merely because there was not enough room in its concert halls to accommodate the hosts of Rosenblatt followers. In Kowno, the new capital of Lithuania, windows were shattered and roofs were smashed when he came to sing there. In Vilna, the birthplace of the famous Gaon Rabbi Elijah, bogus tickets were printed and people had themselves hoisted down into the synagogue through the skyloft in order to hear and catch a glimpse of the famous Reb Yossele.

My father had not been scheduled to conduct a Sabbath service in Riga, Latvia, even though he stayed in that city of music and culture over Saturday. However the enterprising Jewish citizens would not let him go completely scot-free. So one of them, who was the head of a little congregation that met regularly for divine services in the vicinity of the hotel in which my father was stopping, bethought himself of the following scheme. Knowing of my father's eagerness to worship in company on the Sabbath day he came on Friday afternoon to invite him to his prayer-chapel; and, in order to make sure of my father's appearance, asked my father to allow him to bring his prayer-shawl to the place of worship before the commencement of the holy day on which carrying was forbidden by Jewish precept. My father acquiesced, even though he might have worn the *Tallith* underneath his topcoat, in deference to his host's argument that such a procedure would not be dignified. Once he had arrived in the prayer-chapel he could not resist the petulant and expectant glances of the unprecedentedly large crowd that had assembled in the place, as soon as word had gotten around that Yossele Rosenblatt would be there. He had to chant at least the prayer for the new moon. But when the worshippers urged him to continue with the *Mussaph* service, he drew the line. "That far and no further!" he said. He was not going to be taken advantage of.

All these manifestations of hysteria were due to the intense hunger of the Jewish masses of Eastern Europe for a little bit of authentic *Chazanuth*. Here is how Graf Kali of the Tageblatt of Lodz described what happened in that important textile center and second largest city of Poland when Yossele Rosenblatt's first appearance was announced:

> "A hubbub, an uproar, the mass is unruly.
> Men run about frantic. They fret not unduly,
> For tickets are gone. Not one is left, truly.
> In vain do you now the box-office assail.
> Your pushing is useless and of no avail.
> For everyone's eager and has been for long
> To hear Yossele Rosenblatt, monarch of song.
> Cantors and singers we get without quota.
> We've already heard both Kwartin and Sirota.
> But this must admitted be ev'n by his *Son'im*
> That Yossele king is of all the *Chazonim*.
> When Yossele sings you're aware of God's *Sh'chineh*.
> His throat is a fiddle that's called 'Paganine'.
> The foremost musicians of each gentile nation
> Enthused and inspired are by his recitation.
>
> But be not dismay'd, ye who are now left
> Of cards of admittance completely bereft.
> We'll simply do this. Our dear guest we'll implore
> To come here and give us a concert once more."

It is no exaggeration to say that my father's presence in Poland almost caused a revolution in ultra-orthodox Jewish circles. On account of him, the pious cantor, who never appeared bareheaded in public or in private and who would not eat in restaurants that were not certified as *Kosher* by the rabbinate, many a Jew, who had never seen the interior of a theater, had been inveigled into entering such centers of frivolity.

It has been reported that in one of the prayer-chapels in

Lodz of the adherents of the *Chassidic* Rabbi of Ger, when
the young precentor went up to the pulpit to recite the
prayer of the new moon, he was pulled away from his place
by several of the worshippers with cries of "Poshe Yisroel!"
And the reason was that he had been in the Philharmonie, a
place in which men and women sit side by side and in which
ballets and other types of forbidden entertainments by female performers are given. True, the singer he had gone to
hear was Yossele Rosenblatt, a *chazan* with a long beard,
who had the reputation of leading an orthodox Jewish life,
and was known to be far more scrupulous in his observances
than the average Polish cantor. True also that the songs he
sang were for the most part the sacred prayers of the synagogue. But what right had a *Chassid* to attend a concert, even
if it was given by a Yossele Rosenblatt? And above all, how
did he dare to enter a locale like the Philharmonie whatever
the occasion?

What saved the young culprit from being torn to pieces by
his would-be-conscience-keepers and being sentenced to eternal damnation in this world and the next was the fact that
the *Gabbai* or president of the chapel was himself guilty of
the same crime as the *Baal Tefillah,* and what was good
enough for the head could not logically be held against the
lesser lights. So the youthful sinner got off scot-free this time.
But the issue as to whether it was lawful for a Gerer *Chassid*
to be present at a concert of whatever nature, be it sacred or
profane, by whomever it might be given, in the Philharmonie still remained to be settled.

And not only did Yossele Rosenblatt's visit disturb the
even course of the river of *Chassidic* life. It also disrupted
homes, especially those in which the husbands, because of
their upbringing in the old-fashioned *Chadarim,* were
steeped in tradition whereas the wives, who, for want of Jewish schools for girls, had attended the Polish *shkolas,* and
were more secular in their tastes. Here is how the head of

one Jewish household describes what he had to endure on account of Yossele Rosenblatt's *Omar Rabbi Elozor*.

"When it comes to masquerade balls," he said to his wife on his return from the first concert, "it is you who attend them. Concerts, entertainments, dances—you. If that's the case, I have a right to go to hear a cantor. That's my masquerade-ball, my theater, my concert, my pleasure in this world."

"But twenty zlotys for one ticket," screams the wife. "Murderer! Bandit! How dare you indulge in such pleasures? That's squandering your money, throwing it to the dogs. What happened to you? Did your grandmother suddenly grow rich and leave you a fortune? Is business so wonderful?"

But friend husband paid no attention to his wife's scolding. "When I came home from the first concert," says he, "I sensed an unusual sweetness inside of me. I was walking on air. Who worried about business, notes to be met, wife or mother-in-law? *Omar Rabbi Elozor* kept buzzing in my mind. It sang by itself. And the entire street, nay heaven and earth themselves, appeared to be humming along.

"I stand in front of the door and knock, knock, knock. No answer. Apparently somebody wants to get even with the spendthrift by letting him stand outside for a while. But what do I care? I am fully entertained by the second part of the song *Talmidei Chachomim Marbim Sholom Boolom*. Then suddenly the door opens a crack and I am greeted with the expected welcome:

" 'Too bad you came home already. You might just as well have gone your way gambling away your money or what have you, my beloved husband.'

"Whereunto I answer in the sweetest tone: *Omar Rabbi Elozor . . .*

" 'And you think I'll let things go on this way? I'm going to make your life miserable, you spendthrift, you gam-

bler!' and she calls her mother and her children. 'Look
at my dear husband . . . In his old age he decided to take
to gambling, to squandering money on concerts. He doesn't
care what happens to his wife or children. But wait! I'll teach
him.' "

The wife's dissatisfaction finally reaches the point where
she throws a hard object at her husband, which strikes him
on the head, and as he continues humming to himself,
his mother-in-law fears that his mind might be affected.
From then on, therefore, he is left in peace and permitted to
attend not only the second but even the third concert.

"What a pleasure! What a joy!" says he to himself. "And
for this I have to thank *Omar Rabbi Elozor, Omar Rabbi
Chanino.*"

There were also incidents of another nature that resulted
from the eagerness to hear the American cantor sing, some
of which proved to be a bit embarrassing to the visitor. His
first concert in the Zirk, for instance, had been scheduled to
take place on Saturday night and through some carelessness
of the managers—or was it that they did not care?—the advertisement had been so worded that it seemed as though
tickets of admission would be sold on the Sabbath. In the
United States such a profanation of the Jewish day of rest
might not have caused even a ripple. In Poland the mere suggestion of desecration called forth an immediate reaction.
My father was hauled over the carpet by the rabbinical tri-
bunal of Warsaw, and was forced—never had he thought that
it could come to that—to apologize for the slip-up and to
promise that he would make certain, by issuing strict orders
to his managers, that there would be no *Chillul Shabbos* on
account of his concert.

It must not be thought, however, that, enthusiastic as they
were to hear him and thirstily as they drank in every note
that issued from his mouth, the Jews of Poland and other
parts of Eastern Europe lapped up every dish he offered

them without discrimination or choice. In spite of its conservatism Poland was not a wilderness. There were among
Polish Jews many connoisseurs of not only Jewish but also
secular music. There was a critic like M. Kipnis, the member of a musical family and a person of discriminating tastes.
He liked Yossele Rosenblatt as a *chazan*. "As such," he
stated, "he knows how to grip the Jewish soul." "He warms
the heart by his manner of presentation and interpretation.
His *Rom V'nisso* . . . with its interlocking phraseology . . .
his *Omar Rabbi Elozor, Rachem No* and the other prayers
that he chanted . . . roused the audiences to ecstasy." But
"for such a cantor to sing gay Italian melodies, which in Italy
are sung only by serenaders to the accompaniment of a gui-
tar, that is entirely incongruous, out of role, shocking."

As my father gave concert after concert in rapid succession
in the largest Jewish communities of Poland, Latvia and
Lithuania signs of fatigue made themselves felt. At his first
concert in Riga, the home of the composer of Jewish liturgical music Baruch Rozovksy and one of the first communities within the Russian empire to feel the impact of the Jewish Reform movement in Germany, he was not at all in
form, so that the wiseacres in the audience remarked: "The
impresarios must have put one over on us. They got hold of
a Jew with a beard and said he was Yossele . . . Well, we
heard Yossele on the phonograph and he didn't sound at all
like this man." In Vilna, a great deal of disturbance was
caused by the influx of an unexpected crowd provided with
counterfeit tickets of admission. But the choir director Dur-
mashkin felt that even aside from this interference my father
could not have been at his best. "A cantor like Yossele," he
stated in a letter to the Vilner Tog, "should never have had
25 concerts arranged within the brief period of six weeks."
Eight appearances would have been more than ample. That
would have given him a chance to rest between appearances
and to satisfy the public that was so eager to hear him.

By the time he reached Bialestok, the third largest city of Poland and an important industrial center, my father was so worn out that he wasn't at all able to do justice to either himself or his listeners, who had welcomed him with open arms and had shown him great honor. They had expected more from him than they received and what he offered them did not correspond to their anticipation. There was, therefore, a lot of grumbling throughout the services conducted by him in the community's large and beautiful synagogue. When the devotions, which had been attended by several thousands of worshippers, were over, a brash youngster shouted directly into my father's face as he was coming out of the synagogue, in the presence of all who were there: "American bluffer!" Leo, who accompanied my father, was so incensed at this bit of unheard-of impudence that he threw himself upon the youth and let him have it. Naturally an uproar arose, as there were in the crowd persons who sympathized with the young man who had gotten the beating. The commotion first subsided when police came to learn what had caused it.

Particularly distasteful was the type of publicity given the incident in Warsaw's Unser Express. "Young Man Is Beaten up for *Chillul Hatate* [Desecration of Father—a parody of *Chillul Hashem*, Desecration of God's Name] when he calls Chazan Reb Yossele Rosenblatt 'American Bluffer!' " was the heading of a brief report from Bialestok that appeared in the said periodical. The article of apology by Pessach Kaplan who attempted to solve "the Enigma—Yossele Rosenblatt" only partially mitigated the poignancy of the blow.

The person hardest to pacify was my mother. "You have a synagogue," she said to Mr. Kaplan when he came to visit my father, "that is one in the world. But the people, brrr! . . . Imagine! All they paid was two zlotys. It would positively be a shame to tell about it in America. Eighteen cents to hear Yossele officiate! And they are not satisfied. He didn't give them their money's worth. Yes, give them a sack full for eighteen cents. And suppose they were not completely pleased! Is that a justification for shouting: 'Bluffers!' Hasn't Yossele done enough for Poland? When the relief drives were being conducted in America, Reb Yossele gave scores of concerts gratis and thousands of dollars that were thus contributed through him were sent over here. And now all they can think of is that Yossele cheated them out of eighteen cents."

As for my father, he took the whole matter more calmly. He knew that no instrument, whether mechanical or organic, could be counted on to give perfect performance on all occasions. He recalled that when he officiated in Vienna on the Sabbath after the Ninth of *Ab* (July 28) in the synagogue of the Leopoldgasse, the worshippers were at first not at all pleased. He had run through the Friday evening and the Saturday morning services like an ordinary *Baal Tefillah* and not in the style of a *chazan* who is supposed to be an artist of the *Amud*. There was grumbling that Yossele Rosenblatt had taken advantage of his Viennese admirers, that he had let them down. By the time the reading of the Torah was over the fidgeting became so loud that even *he* could not help being aware of it.

So when he had ascended the *Bema* for the second half of the morning's assignment, he turned around to his audience and said to them, with a good-humored smile: "It has come to my attention, friends, that you have been disappointed with my performance thus far. I have not given you what you expected from me. Let me tell you, then, that I am fully conscious of this failure on my part. But you must realize that a cantor is not a machine. He is no more than a human being, and a human being is not always in a mood to do his best. I assure you, however, that what you will hear now will make up for last night and this morning."

Therewith he began to recite the *Mussaph* service, *Mis-*

heberach, Av Horachamim, Kedushoh and *Tikanto Shabbos* and his listeners were so enthralled that they forgave him his previous omissions and expressed their appreciation in the most extravagant terms of praise.

The last city on the European continent in which he appeared was the free port of Danzig on the Baltic, the most important transit center at the time for Jewish emigrants from the newly created Polish republic. His critic there was the cantor of the local reform temple. He conceded to Josef Rosenblatt mastery in his special domain, the field of *Chazanuth,* but thought that his rendering of the secular portion of his program "revealed lack of training, that the use of his voice was poor and the employment of falsetto, much as it may have delighted the audience, was musically unorthodox."

This view was not at all shared by A. Romanovsky of the *Jewish Times* of London, England, in which my father brought his tour to a close. "While the talents of such renowned cantors as Sirota and Steinberg," he wrote in a lengthy article entitled "Olympus and Sinai," "were restricted entirely to the field of Jewish liturgical music, Yossele Rosenblatt stands as firmly planted on Olympus as he does on Sinai . . . He brings something of the Sinaitic into Olympus, and something of the Olympic into Sinai . . ."

On Thursday, August 23 father, mother, Leo and Abie Elstein embarked on the Olympic bound for New York. It had been a long and exhausting journey. In the space of fifteen weeks my father had given thirty-one performances in twenty-two cities located in ten countries. The experience had, except for a few minor mishaps and discordant notes, been most gratifying. He had had an opportunity to discover at first hand the extent of his popularity in the Old World. He had received the approbation of his colleagues. The foremost composer of Jewish liturgical music of the time, Cantor A. Bernstein of Vilna, had presented him, as a token of esteem, with a volume of his compositions, inscribed "to Josef Rosenblatt, the gaon of cantors." Pessach Kaplan had stated in his essay "The Enigma—Josef Rosenblatt" that he was "the teacher of the entire present generation of *chazanim,* all of whom mimic every note of his recordings and score success therewith." Financially, too, judged by European standards, the tour had been lucrative. However when an accounting was made of what the trip had actually cost, when the travelling expenses for four persons, the commissions paid to managers and advertisers and gifts to relatives, were figured up and placed against the receipts, it was found that he was coming home with empty pockets.

On his return to America my father had the pleasure of meeting for the first time his second grandson, Leo's Richard. The child was born on the day his father and grandparents landed in France. No less delighted than the members of his immediate family to welcome the much-travelled cantor-concertist back to America for the High Holiday season were his friends and admirers at the Anshei Sfard, above all the devoted Max Jonas. Overhearing a casual remark by my father about a niece in Europe whose match was about to go on the rocks for want of a dowry, he wrote out a check which he enclosed in a letter. "You know," the note read, "there is a little saying in Hebrew that if you love your wife, you must love her family too. This maxim may be applied to you. I love you and I love your family. It gives me great pleasure to send you this check for your niece. Give her my best wishes and tell her I wish her all the luck in the world."

When the fall holiday season was behind him, my father's mind was free again to turn to vaudeville and concerts. The Vitaphone production of "The Jazz Singer" had by this time been completed. It had had many successful showings all over the United States and opened up in London as recently as September 27. In order to make the most of the favorable publicity this event provided, Leo thought it might be an excellent idea to bring my father back to England where he enjoyed great favor. So he cabled several London managers for bookings, but without results. The feelers sent to Johannesburg, Berlin and Jerusalem proved equally fruitless. Meantime at home the vaudeville market, undercut by the talkies, was slumping badly. The best that could be obtained were a few scattered three or four-day runs in such theatres as Syracuse's B. F. Keith's, Pittsburgh's Harris, the Ambassador in Brooklyn, East Liberty's Sheridan Square, the McKinley Square and the New Royal in the Bronx, the Fabian in Paterson, and the Franklin Theatre in New York. During the end of the year 1928 these engagements still brought $1,000 each. At the beginning of 1929 the compensation dropped to a maximum of $800, and then vaudeville concerts stopped altogether. With creditors, who knew how seriously he took his obligations, still on his neck, he was compelled to accept invitations to perform in synagogues and Hebrew Schools at whatever terms were offered, entering even into percentage arrangements, which often netted him very little.

In April 1929 his luck seems to have taken a little bit of a turn for the better. He was engaged for two concerts in Boston, for which he received an honorarium of $1,000.

However one month of prosperity does not make up for seven lean months to follow. And since the prospect of father's earning what he had been accustomed to and was very much in need of in the United States seemed very slim at the time, Leo looked for opportunities elsewhere. A summer tour of South America, where it would be winter at the time, looked promising. Argentina and Brazil both had sizable Jewish communities. Consisting as they did for the most part of recent immigrants from Eastern Europe, they would appreciate my father's art and could be counted upon to make a visit there financially worthwhile.

So, Leo put the wheels into motion. Through Sol Bloom, a prominent member of father's former congregation Ohab Zedek and an outstanding U. S. Congressman, he secured from the Secretary of State introductory letters to the American diplomatic and consular officials in the South American countries. Impresarios in Latin America had been contacted previously. Everything was thus gotten ready for father's sailing for Buenos Aires on the steamer Eastern Prince, accompanied by Leo.

39

South America

The departure was a hectic one. It was complicated by the fact that the ship was scheduled to leave on Saturday (June 22), which posed to my father the problem of how to get his luggage on board. A further difficulty was that Leo was suffering from a nasty bronchial cold which he tried to conceal from his father out of fear that the trip might be cancelled. Only when they were a safe distance away from New York harbor did Leo make known his affliction, and then, of course, it was too late to change the plans.

The three-week voyage afforded my father ample opportunity for relaxation. Outside of participating in one courtesy concert, as was the custom, he had nothing to do during that long stretch of time. Now nothing was more difficult for him than to spend a protracted period in complete idleness. Though he was already approaching middle age he was still the bundle of energy he had always been, and energetic people must have an outlet for their activity. Being confined, then, to the narrow limits of the same ship for three seem-

ingly endless weeks, he sat up devising schemes for whiling
his leisure hours away, and Leo, who had not yet recovered
from his indisposition, had his hands full with him. For example, as the Eastern Prince was about to cross the Equa-
tor, my father suddenly vanished. After a long and frantic
search Leo found him on the captain's deck. "Papa, where
have you been? I have been looking for you all over the
ship, and my head was already full of the weirdest of imaginings."

"Don't you know," answered Leo's father. "They say that
when the pranksters find out that you are crossing the Equa-
tor for the first time in your life, they play tricks on you,
and I wanted to make certain that no such thing would happen to me. So I took refuge with the captain. In his cabin I
feel safe. Nobody would dare try a practical joke in *his*
presence."

My father was never too fastidious about food. He could
content himself with the simplest fare if edibles prepared
according to the Jewish dietary requirements were unob-
tainable. However, to subsist for more than two weeks on
raw fruits and canned vegetables was hard even for a person
of his ascetic habits. So when the Eastern Prince, skirting the
coast of Brazil, was approaching Rio de Janeiro, he decided
to resort to an expedient that he had often employed successfully in the United States when, far away from home, he
wanted to eat a cooked meal. He picked up a telephone and
called the number of the rabbi (in this case the Chief Rabbi
of Brazil).

He had never before in his life met the man or even corresponded with him. Yet such was the bond that the dietary
laws established among observant Jews that they had no hesitancy about applying to coreligionists who were perfect
strangers to them in an emergency such as this. My father
was able in addition to take advantage of the special privileges that his celebrity gave him, and the method never

failed. The mere mention of his name worked like a charm.
It certainly did so in this instance. Although it was already
late in the evening when the ship docked in the harbor and
my father apologized profusely to the rabbi for disturbing
him at such an hour, the Reverend Dr. Raffalovich, far
from being put out, seemed overjoyed, delighted and beside
himself with excitement. "Yossele Rosenblatt, the famous
Yossele Rosenblatt, who is known all over the world and
whose name has become a byword among Jews for the
best in Jewish music, coupled with philanthropy and piety,
is passing through Rio." He could hardly believe his ears.
"Be at ease, Mr. Rosenblatt. Your needs will be attended to
immediately, and I shall be up to see you together with our
committee as soon as the food can be prepared and a taxi
can bring us to the pier. After all not every day do we Jews of
Brazil have the good fortune of entertaining a guest like you."

It did not take very long before a delegation of leading
Jewish residents of Rio de Janeiro headed by their spiritual
mentor made their way, with a complete dinner under
their arms, up the gangplank leading to my father's suite.
There were warm handclasps and cordial greetings as
among friends that had known each other for years. "Reb Yossele," as Dr. Raffalovich recalled many years later, "entertained his hosts with some of his choicest liturgical
compositions interspersed with amusing anecdotes, which he
related in his own inimitable and witty manner." Ere anyone
noticed it the hours of night had sped by and day began to
break. It was time to bid the guest farewell because the
ship was about to depart for regions further south. Before
taking leave Dr. Raffalovich requested of my father that,
on his way back to the States, he give the Jews of Rio de
Janeiro and perhaps also those of Sao Paulo an opportunity
to hear him sing. He himself would take charge of all the
necessary arrangements, so as to make sure that the venture
would be a success. Father joyfully accepted the invitation

and promised to do his utmost to gratify the wishes of his Brazilian brethren.

In the summer of 1929 the Argentine republic, the second largest and certainly the richest and most progressive of all the countries of South America, was still a democracy. Its beautiful capital, Buenos Aires, a combination of Paris and New York, was the paradise of musicians, especially of opera singers. Whenever Caruso, Titta Ruffo or Galli-Curci appeared at that city's Teatro Colón, which was modelled after the Opéra of Paris, they were showered with attentions by the Latins who were willing to pay any price to listen to artists of ability.

The Jewish community of Buenos Aires had at that time already exceeded the 100,000 mark. It boasted a well-established, prosperous Yiddish press with several daily newspapers serving its large East-European contingent. It had in its *Chevra Kadisha* a mighty force for communal unity. Even if its school system was not as well developed as it should have been, it could nevertheless point to such elegant and spacious houses of worship as the synagogue on Paso Street near the Avenida Corrientes, Buenos Aires' counterpart of Broadway.

It was in the harbor of this metropolis of Argentina that my father's ship anchored on Saturday evening, July 13. A telegram from Rosa Raisa and her husband, who were in the country at the time, welcomed him upon his arrival. On Monday afternoon at 5:30 o'clock he made his first appearance at the aristocratic Odeon Theatre. His debut was handicapped from the start by faulty management. The audience, owing chiefly to poor publicity, was rather small. Also more of an effort had been made to attract non-Jewish music-lovers or curiosity seekers than to reach a strictly Jewish clientele. The hour chosen conflicted with the time during which the shops of Jewish retail merchants were still open. Finally the price of admission—six pesos—was too high for the pocket of the average Jewish patron of music.

A further mistake made was that of programming. My father had not realized that though they might not have been as developed industrially or as advanced technologically as their neighbors up North, South Americans of Argentina in particular were musically sophisticated. Their standards in this respect were very high. They knew when a song was well sung and when it did not meet the requirements, and they were as meticulous and exacting in their demands of an artist as were the audiences and critics in Europe. The result was that while most reviewers non-Jewish as well as Jewish commented favorably on my father's rendition of the Jewish selections on the program, and some paid tribute to the power and range of his voice while others praised the clearness of his diction and found his falsetto charming, they were not so laudatory in their criticism of the secular numbers. Most devastating in its appraisal of his performance was Argentina's largest and most influential Spanish-language daily La Prensa. Because its critic did not approve of the manner in which my father had sung the Andalusian song "Clavelitos" and the Italian "La Campana," he jumped to the conclusion that the "cause of Josef Rosenblatt's success in New York was neither art nor music but simply the affection for him of his coreligionists who were sensitive to the very particular style of chanting certain songs of the synagogue."

Moshe Rubin of the Argentiner Tog (July 20) consoled my father for this shabby treatment by telling the story of a Jew with a handsome beard whose striking appearance had made so deep an impression on the not overly chaste Russian empress Catherine the Great that she invited him to her palace. Overwhelmed by the honor that was about to be accorded to him, the Jew thought that if her imperial majesty could be so smitten with him as she had seen him— beard and all, how much more would she be pleased if he

were to remove his hirsute adornment. But when he presented himself to the empress, with a clean-shaven face, the
latter burst out laughing. "Foolish Jew," she said. "It was
your beard that attracted me to you. Beardless male friends
I have aplenty."

"So it is with Yossele Rosenblatt," concluded the writer.
"He stands very high in our estimation when he wears the
crown of *Chazanuth*. When he sang *Rom V'nisso* he stood
exalted before us. With his *Elokay Neshomo* he brought
inspiration into every Jewish soul. When he chanted *Omar
Rabbi Elozor*, every Jew had a good word to say about it.
But when he betook himself unto the polyglot ballads,
Jews were not inspired and non-Jewish music-lovers felt
they had greater artists than he.

"In short," said Mr. Rubin, "Yossele Rosenblatt is a cantor
by the grace of God, who occupies among us Jews a higher
position than even a Patti, a Sembrich, a Caruso or a Chaliapin. For while these were only interpretive artists distinguished for their voices and performance, he is, in addition to possessing these virtues, creative in his field as a
composer and improviser."

Most of the errors committed in connection with the concert at the Odeon were rectified by my father's second recital
in Buenos Aires which was given a week later. The place
chosen was the Excelsior, a playhouse on the Avenida Corrientes under Jewish management and in the heart of the
Jewish settlement. The hour was one that was convenient
for Jewish shopkeepers and the prices of admission reasonable. Columnist P. Niemoy predicted on the basis of these
facts that "Yossele Rosenblatt would get a royal reception at
the Excelsior, as befitted 'the king of cantors,' " and his prognosis was fully realized. "The audience that greeted him,"
the Yiddishe Zeitung noted, "was large, warm and Jewish."
Its appreciation was demonstrated by unrestrained and vociferous applause and the clamor for encores. However since

my father, in order to vary the menu and give himself an opportunity to rest his voice, still insisted on inserting non-Jewish songs between the Jewish portions of his program, some of the listeners by their calls of "Yiddish" (Jewish songs only) and "Tefillos" (Hebrew liturgical music), created a situation that was as embarrassing as it was annoying to the singer. The reporters of the Yiddish press reprimanded them for this rudeness and lack of breeding. On the other hand they were pained by the attempt on the part of a "Chazan of the reputation and stature of a Yossele Rosenblatt to assume the role of a warmblooded Italian in singing Italian serenades the text of which he does not understand, or to compete with a big-breathed Russian in singing the Volga Boat Song."

Between his first appearance at the Excelsior and his second, which took place on the week following, my father had an opportunity to visit several of the philanthropic institutions on which the Jews of Buenos Aires prided themselves so much, and his comments were given full coverage in the Jewish press. He was also accorded the honor of chanting the memorial prayer for the departed at the funeral of L. Mas, the editor and founder of the largest Jewish daily of Argentina, the Yiddishe Zeitung, who died during that week. It was reported as having been the largest public demonstration of sorrow in the annals of Argentine Jewry and the thousands who attended were deeply moved by the chant.

My father's second concert at the Excelsior was reportedly as successful as the first, although it did not pass without an incident similar to that which had occurred on the previous occasion. However it was when he officiated for the first time at a Sabbath service in the Paso Street synagogue, that he was considered at his best. After that Saturday service Moshe Rubin came out with a most enthusiastic article entitled "Yossele Rosenblatt Has Found Himself." "Not at the Odeon," it began, "nor even at the Excelsior, but in the synagogue on Paso Street did Yossele Rosenblatt find himself. So long as the soul of a cantor has not found its predestined place, it is naked, bare, like those disembodied souls that hover about in the world and are without their true garment until they find the place of repose that has been marked out for them . . .

"Yossele Rosenblatt's religious music, which was heard at the Odeon and the Excelsior, was inspiring, to be sure, but not to the point of ecstasy. That ecstasy was first aroused in the synagogue on Paso Street. The same voice, it would seem, the identical effort to display the art to the listeners, and yet what a difference!

"Let the cantors realize this, therefore, and the gifted Rosenblatt among them, so that they do not cheapen the talent with which they were endowed and thereby cause themselves more harm than good . . . And let them not feel themselves insulted when they are told the truth."

The three weeks between this his first performance at the Paso Street Synagogue and his last appearance there, prior to his departure from the Argentine, were utilized by my father in touring the provinces. He sang in several of the then already prosperous Jewish colonies founded with the money of Baron Maurice de Hirsch, and must have made a deep impression on the colonists. When I visited Argentina nineteen years later, I met a number of these colonists who, speaking most affectionately of the "unforgettable Yossele Rosenblatt," proudly brandished his autograph which they guarded like a cherished treasure. In fact it was through a family picture that my father had presented to one of them that I was recognized when I arrived at the Buenos Aires airport.

The farewell banquet tendered him by musicians, colleagues and admirers, including representatives of the Paso Street congregation, in the synagogue of which he had officiated several times, was warm and dignified. Jewish Buenos

Aires seemed to have gathered there its learning and its piety. Instead of speeches the program consisted mainly of music and prayers, sung by the cantors present as well as by
the guest of honor. After that, near midnight on Saturday August 24, the participants escorted the visitor to the
steamer Alcantara on which he left for Brazil.

On the very day on which my father boarded the Alcantara, bloody riots broke out in far-off Palestine resulting in
the massacre of several hundreds of Jews. The young Jewish settlement of Brazil, with its strong ties with the Old
World, was deeply upset by the news, and in no mood for
amusement. Yet when it was announced that Yossele Rosenblatt was going to conduct an evening service to be followed
by a concert of secular music at the Teatro Lyrico of Rio de
Janeiro on Sunday, September 1, the theater was filled to
overflowing. People came because, as the Yiddishe Volks-
zeitung remarked, "no one wanted to miss the opportunity
to hear the cantor whom the Jewish colony of New York held
in such high veneration and esteem." And this was one time
that they were not disappointed by a guest-artist. They had
so often been deceived by visiting performers who had been
over-advertised, that they breathed a sigh of satisfaction
when they found that for once the reality measured up to
their expectations.

Between this concert and the second at Rio, which was
dedicated to the victims of the Palestinian riots, my father
visited Sao Paulo and had the thrill of seeing an advertisement of "The Jazz Singer" that was being shown at one of
the local moving picture theaters. It was worded:

JOSEF ROSENBLATT
the famous Jewish cantor, who is now appearing in
S. Paulo at the Teatro Municipal, is one of the
celebrated singers, who, together with Al Jolson,
are taking part in the great singing and sound
film of Warner Brothers

THE JAZZ SINGER
(Still playing this month at the Republic)

Such being his celebrity in the far-away communities of South America, it was not at all surprising that Yossele Rosenblatt's name should have become a byword in his own home country among all sections of the population. I happened to be spending that summer with my wife's parents in Arverne, Long Island. Our David, who had just turned two, was getting his first haircut. Like most children under similar circumstances he emitted a howl when the barber's scissors touched his hair. Hearing him carry on, the barber, in an effort to quiet him, quite casually snapped back at him: "Why all this commotion, young man? Who do you think you are—Yossele Rosenblatt's grandson?" And when David's mother, who was standing by, remarked: "Well, he is," the hairdresser gave her one of those quizzical looks that meant: "Lady, you are telling a story."

My father's journey home passed without incident except that, as his ship was nearing New York, it ran out of its supply of fresh milk, which had been a very important item of my father's diet since there was little else outside of canned fish and fresh fruits for him to eat. But even this discomfort did not impair his sense of humor. After the announcement of the milk shortage was made to the wry-faced occupants of the dining-salon, my father called over the dining-room steward and, pointing to the pale-white anemic-looking mixture of powdered milk and water in his glass, said to him: "Do you mind putting a little more milk into this water?"

40

Lean Years

The interval between the New Year's Day and the Day of Atonement is, according to Jewish tradition, a period of judgment, when man's fate for the year is decreed. This time it was a favorable verdict that was awarded to Yossele Rosenblatt. Just a few days after the beginning of the Jewish calendar year 5690 he was informed by Judge Julian W. Mack, justice of the United States Circuit Court of New York City, that his discharge from bankruptcy had been granted. In a letter dated Tuesday, October 8, the distinguished jurist, who had always held my father in the highest esteem, stated to Rabbi Isaiah Levy, the successor to Dr. Philip Klein as spiritual leader of Ohab Zedek, that he was satisfied that "Mr. Rosenblatt has proven payments to the creditors of the 'Light of Israel' totalling over $50,-000." At long last his name was officially cleared. In the eyes of the law he had no further obligations to the men and women who had been hounding him for the settlement of debts incurred through the manipulations of persons who had exploited him on behalf of a supposedly idealistic venture.

However his absolution from any implications of fraud at this time did him but little real good. Only a few weeks later, on Tuesday, October 29, the stock-market crashed in Wall Street, and the disaster that pulled down millions of American citizens, and together with them countless people elsewhere in the world, could not help affecting *him* who was so ill-prepared to weather the storm.

At the beginning of 1930 he was still at the height of his artistic power. On January 20 after his concert at the Pittsburgh Y.M.&W.H.A., for instance, the Pittsburgh Sun-Telegram paid him the compliment of telling its readers: "Cantor Rosenblatt is a most unique entertainer . . . He gives us the rare opportunity to hear liturgical music of the synagogue, with its wealth of improvisation, a feature that in less clever singers pulled such music down to very low levels."

However engagements became fewer and emoluments declined sharply. "He is worth not less that $1,000," wrote Leo to a correspondent who wished to engage Cantor Rosenblatt for a Tuesday night concert in Uniontown, Pennsylvania. He compromised for $300 and would have been glad to accept $250. For an appearance of a similar nature in Philadelphia the fee was only $200.

A decade earlier my father's recordings had brought him a revenue of as much as $10,000 in a single year. The statement of his account presented to him by the Victor Company for the year ending March 31, 1930 showed instead of a surplus an unearned amount, due the company on account of advance payments made to him, of nearly $4,000.

If the Laurel-in-the-Pines of Lakewood, New Jersey, paid him the sum of $2,750 for conducting services on Passover, it is to be remembered that included in that price was the cost of the choir, which absorbed a good slice of the total.

One of the youngest members of that choir, by the way, was the now celebrated tenor of the Metropolitan Opera Company, Jan Peerce. He was then a lad possessing a remarkable soprano voice, and generally referred to by the nickname of "Pinky." When choir director Meyer Machtenberg asked my father whether he should take Pinky along to Lakewood, my father replied quite matter-of-factly, "By all means, take him along. By all means. Why do you even ask?" "Well, you know, cantor," said Machtenberg cautiously, "the boy

has a voice and makes a big hit with the public." Thereunto
my father, patting the choir leader's shoulder, replied:
"True, the little fellow does know how to sing, but for that,
my dear man, I know how to *daven*."

When July 1 came around my father was so broke that he
had to borrow $6,190 from Leo, whose entire income was
derived from commissions that he earned as his father's busi-
ness-manager.

It may seem odd that the cantor of the Anshei Sfard Congregation of Borough Park should have conducted services
on an important holiday like Passover at a hotel rather than
his own synagogue. However the never-too-affluent Anshei
Sfard was no longer in a position, despite its best intentions,
to pay him his salary; that was why it released him from his
duties on the festival this year as well as the preceding year.
Since, in addition to this situation, the acoustics of the
rickety old building of the Anshei Sfard synagogue had never
been satisfactory anyhow, it did not require too much persuasion to induce my father to resume his ties with the Ohab
Zedek. True, his relations with the congregation had not
always been happy. There had been occasional friction between him and the members of the board, tensions caused
by his absence from the synagogue just when they wanted
him. At the time when these things happened, he was annoyed and angered by them, angered by the narrowness and
lack of consideration of men who could not realize that an
artist, who was so much in demand as he was, ought not to
be chained down to hidebound rules. How was it possible
for him, in the midst of a tour far out West, for example,
suddenly to pick up and come back home because some
prominent member of the congregation was celebrating the
Bar-Mitzvah of his son? Now that time and circumstances
had mellowed him, he was beginning to view things from
their side and forgive them for their hardness of heart. They
were, after all, among orthodox Jewish congregations of

America the most established and best. They had refinement and prestige. Where else was there one like it? And
what other congregation was able now, after the Wall-
Street crash, to offer him a contract of $9,000 a year for seven
years? If it was necessary to officiate twice a month for them
at the new synagogue on 95th Street, he would do it faith-
fully and gladly. Anyhow there were no more vaudeville
engagements to detain him and concerts had become rarer.
So my father accepted the offer and moved his household
back to Manhattan, renting a large apartment on 94th Street
and Broadway, within walking distance of the synagogue
and accessible to schools and offices and theatres and to wherever one had to go.

In a way it felt good to be reunited with the congregation
that had brought him over from Europe and whom he had
served for fourteen years. It was like returning to one's
first love. The acoustical walls of the new synagogue building were so easy on the voice that it was a pleasure to officiate in it. When he ascended the platform on these High
Holidays to again lead in prayer the congregation whose
precentor he had been before, it seemed to the worshippers
that time had wrought but little change in him. Physically
and vocally he was the same. His voice was as strong as ever,
although perhaps a little more mature and mellow than
theretofore.

For a little while my father's hopes rose again as a result
of his second union with Ohab Zedek. Unfortunately when
a person is gravely ill, no matter what side you may turn
him on, his condition will not improve. Even with a guaranteed salary of $9,000 and side income from professional en-
gagements and occasional windfalls, he was not earning
enough to maintain a still large and elaborate household
and, above all, to satisfy the demands of his poorer creditors. For, as conditions in general grew worse, their need
for cash became more desperate and so they intensified

their pressure on him, knowing that, in spite of his having been freed of legal obligations towards them, he still considered himself morally bound. Under the circumstances, for relatives or friends to help him out with a couple of thousand dollars—as I and others actually did—was like pouring sand into a sack full of holes. We knew in advance that he would derive but little benefit therefrom, that the relief it would afford him was only temporary. It was, therefore, more out of a sense of filial love, in order to ease our consciences, that we did what we did, rather than from the belief that we were thereby making a constructive contribution to his economic rehabilitation.

By the end of October 1930 my father's financial situation was so critical that my mother was compelled to draw out all that remained of the cash value of her husband's life insurance policy with the Equitable Life Assurance Society of the U.S. The result was that the policy, which might one day have yielded $100,000, had the premiums been paid regularly, lapsed. When he sang that December 21 at the entertainment arranged by the Jewish Daily Forward for the benefit of the unemployed, the army of whom was steadily increasing, many of the would-be-beneficiaries of his act of humankindness must have regarded him with envy. For was he not one of the fortunate few among America's professionals who still had a good position and was drawing a respectable salary from a stable congregation? Little did they know that he was in some respects worse off than they. They were at least in a position, if they could obtain employment, to start all over again, to begin afresh. He, however, was doomed to carry a weight that continually dragged him down.

In a valiant effort to help his father in his plight Leo, who was still his personal representative, operating from my father's home instead of an office in order to cut expenses, tried sundry ways of picking up additional income. He negotiated with a widely read New York tabloid for the publi-

cation in serial form of a story of Father's life. He sought
out managers to secure engagements in theatres, in moving
pictures and radio. He corresponded with impresarios and
agencies abroad. The biography that was published three
months after the date stipulated was poorly done, and the
periodical in which it appeared never paid what it had promised, so that the publishers had to be sued in court for the
amount owed. As for the business managers that had been
hired, the first proved to be thoroughly incompetent, while
the second, who was productive, looked for every legal loop-
hole to avoid paying on time or found excuses not to pay
my father altogether what he had earned. Then, in the spring
of 1932 the Ohab Zedek Congregation broke its contract with
him.

The full story of how it came about was given in one of
New York's Yiddish dailies. The narrator tells of a visit he
paid to Yossele Rosenblatt and how he was received by him
with his usual friendly and cheerful smile. "It is natural for
cantors to smile," he says, "for as one of them once remarked
to me: 'We cantors make a living by singing,' whereunto another added: 'Yes, we sing even at funerals.'

"However of all the smiling cantors Yossele is one who is
the most so. He always made me think that the sun was
perpetually shining and that there was no cloud in the sky.
Happy man, he! so I thought.

"Now it turns out that he isn't so happy after all, although
apparently he has little to complain about, since he is today
one of the very few cantors whose earnings are still quite
respectable, notwithstanding the depression which has hit
synagogues so very hard. People still come to hear Yossele
and the public is ready to pay for the privilege even now.

"Nevertheless Yossele, too, has not been spared by the crisis. What he related to me throws some light on what goes on
in the synagogues today."

The cause of my father's unhappiness at the time was the

manner in which the congregation, that had reengaged him as its cantor two years previously, had proceeded in terminating its connections with him. According to his last contract with the Ohab Zedek he was supposed to officiate in its synagogue twice a month. He had fulfilled this stipulation quite conscientiously except for a few occasions when, on account of circumstances, it proved to be impossible. In former years, when the congregation was prosperous, such minor deviations from the strict letter of the law were never regarded as sufficient reason for a break. Cantor and congregation would get together and work out some way of making up for the omission and all would be well. But times had changed. Things had gone badly even for once well-to-do Ohab Zedek, to such a point that they were no longer able to pay their expensive cantor the high salary for which they had obligated themselves. But they were too proud to admit it. So they began picking flaws in him, charging him with breach of contract which automatically absolved them of all further obligations and served as an excuse for defaulting in the payment of his wages. That's what he resented. "I wouldn't have minded it so much if they had come to me with the truth," he declared, "and said: 'Cantor, much as we would like to have you, we can't pay you any longer because we have no money.' Things like that happen every day. One can't hold it against a person if he fails to meet his obligations for lack of means. But why make it appear as though I were the culprit and had committed so terrible a sin which justified them in their action?"

41

Unemployed

Whatever the causes were my father was now without a position. But that was not the worst that could have befallen him. Conditions being what they were, it did not, as he himself asserted, pay him at the time "to be tied to a congregation." Even in a period of depression a cantor of his renown was still sufficiently in demand to receive bids for holiday services, and he was able to make arrangements to officiate again on Passover of that year at the Laurel-in-the-Pines for a fairly good price. It was the trouble he had with his manager that well-nigh undid him. According to the understanding he had with the Renowned Artists, Inc. he was supposed to turn over to them all his earnings, except for the salary he received from his congregation and commitments previously made, while they in turn were to pay him, as their employee, a fixed sum for the services he rendered. Now the managerial firm owed him, for concerts he had given, an accumulation of $1,000. It was due on April 1. On account of the technicality that that day was Sunday the sum remained unpaid. That was, of course, as the managers saw it, perfectly legitimate, proper and fair. But when *he* failed to turn over to them in full the $1,500 that the Laurel-in-the-Pines had agreed to pay him for conducting the Passover services, the reason for it being that out of that sum $500 had already been assigned for the cost of the choir and $300 for a commission to the man who had obtained the engagement, he was charged with violation of contract and threatened, on the eve of the holiday, with an injunction to restrain him from performing for anyone but the managers for a period of twenty years.

Such was my father's situation as he was nearing his fiftieth birthday, rounding out half a century of a life crowded with success and failure, with extraordinary accomplishments and great artistic triumphs, with honor and glory on the one hand, but also extreme disappointments and depths of depression on the other. Outwardly he appeared at fifty, to most of those who observed him, as vigorous and spry as he had been as a young man of thirty. "His short quicksilver-like figure," remarked the Day, "moves about with such speed that when you walk with him in the street you always have to run after him to catch up with him." As for his voice, the reviewer of the New York Times, who heard him on January 31, thought that it had "both richness and strength." The Ledger-Dispatch of Norfolk, Virginia, where he sang the next evening, found him less tired than he had been when he appeared nine or ten years before. The Morning News of Savannah, Georgia, commenting on his performance in that city on February 23, stated that there was "no sign of strain or lessening of vocal skill" in his execution of a program of sixteen numbers. "Such a display of tone, of volume, and of subtle and varied effects, would be impossible to anyone not trained in his style of singing." So, too, did the Commercial Appeal of Memphis, Tennessee, testify on March 1 to the robustness and virility of his voice. Personally when I saw and heard him in Baltimore, where he gave a recital on April 6, on his return from another tour south and midwest, he seemed to me worn-out and tired. Although the newspaper reports the next day were quite favorable, he did not impress me as having been at his best. I was very much concerned and fearful about what would happen to him if, as is inevitable with age, his voice were to go back on him and he would be compelled to yield the place of preeminence as an artist that he had enjoyed all his life to another man. It was a thought that sometimes frightened me.

The fee my father received for this his last appearance in the city, in which I have my home and in which he had many devoted friends and ardent admirers, was $350. This was apparently the standard for the rest of his engagements and would, had he been permitted to retain it all, have made him quite comfortable. But that was, alas, not to be. When he became fifty years old in May of the year 1932, Yossele Rosenblatt, who according to the Day, "was the first member of his profession in America to lift the office of cantor to a high level," and who was "himself an institution in the domain of *Chazanuth*," was a *chazan* without a pulpit. The concert tour that had been planned in celebration of his golden jubilee did not materialize. A contemplated popular demonstration of tribute in the form of a Cantor Josef Rosenblatt Testimonial and Music Festival at the Madison Square Garden on May 1 never came off. The committee of notables, that had consented to lend their names to the project and who in their totality resembled a veritable Who's Who of New York, remained a committee on paper only. Nor did anything ever become of the Far Eastern concert tour concerning which he had received an inquiry. Whether it was the high figure set by Leo as the absolute minimum—twenty appearances at $900 per engagement plus all expenses—that was responsible for the petering out of the venture or whether there were other reasons I do not know.

If my father was busy during the last half of 1932 and the beginning of 1933, it was not with activities or functions that were income-producing. His time was taken up almost completely with soliciting help from one friend to retain another, with "borrowing from Peter to pay Paul" in the literal meaning of the phrase.

Not until years after his death was the full extent of his

suffering and anguish during this most critical period of his life revealed to me. I learned about it from close friends on the East Side, whose home he would frequent whenever he happened to be in the neighborhood and felt the need of ears willing to listen to the story of his troubles and hearts ready to give the measure of comfort that is so necessary for a person whose spirits are at a low ebb. Often he was so harassed by worry and so dazed from futile running around in desperate efforts to solve his unending financial problems that he forgot to eat. He would drop into his colleague's apartment worn out and fatigued. The latter's wife, noting how famished he was, would have to remind him that he had duties to himself and prevail upon him to take a bite with them. One day, so I was told, he appeared particularly despondent. He had gotten himself entangled with a $1,000 note which had been so drawn that, unless he redeemed it on the date on which it was due, he faced possible arrest. He had been promised a loan with which to pay off this debt by the president of a home for the aged in return for a free concert for the benefit of the institution. Up to the moment, however, the promise had not been fulfilled. His friend's wife had overheard him pleading with the said officer not to leave him in his desperate situation. Her ears had also caught the brush-off the man had given him, the brusque reply: "Cantor Rosenblatt, I have no money, and if I did, you would be one of the last persons in the world to whom I would give it. You owe enough already to many people, and there is no point in risking any more on you."

What was he to do now? Whither could he turn? He felt as if there were a knife on his throat. Ashamed and humiliated, he broke down and wept like a child.

His friends, who had never before seen the usually cheerful Reb Yossele in such a state, tried at first to becalm him. "Don't take it so much to heart, Cantor Rosenblatt. After all the world is not yet going under and you still have your voice." But when they saw that he remained disconsolate, they decided, in order to extricate him from his straits, to offer more than words. "True, we have no money of our own, Reb Yossele," they said. "But there is some of our daughter's which is deposited in our name. We will get it from the bank and relieve you in your plight."

Then my father first wept in earnest, but the tears he shed this time were tears of joy. "You, Reb Moshe and Rose, are going to help me? How truly fortunate I am! Why, you will be literally saving my life. But how will I pay you back?"

"We are not at all worried about that now. We know you'll return the money. Your credit is still good for a thousand dollars, and our daughter won't miss it. By the time she will find out, it will be back on her account and we will have performed a good deed by getting you out of trouble."

The money was thereupon secured by his friends and handed to my father in return for a note signed by him and my mother. Reb Moshe and his wife felt certain that they would have no trouble on account of the favor they were doing their beloved Yossele. Unfortunately the matter turned out differently. When the time arrived for the payment of this note, my father was in no position to meet it. Three times he was compelled to ask for postponement. When he finally did manage to lay his hands on half the amount that was due, he advised his benefactors, whose friendship towards him he was anxious to requite in some small measure, to remit a portion of it as advance commission to a certain cantorial agent who he thought would secure a position for their son as cantor. The position never materialized and, even though suit had been instituted against the agent, the money paid him could not be recovered.

My father had until this time been an inveterate optimist. No matter how bad conditions were and however gloomy the immediate prospects of improvement, he had not given way to despondency. "We must never despair of God's help," so he used to console himself and his family at critical junctures. Now, however, he seemed no longer able to bear up under his burdens. "Things are bad," he would complain to his friends. He was not earning anything and had no means of making a livelihood. More than once was it noticed that he put his hand on his heart, as if something were paining him there. "Don't take it so hard Cantor Rosenblatt," his friends would say in an effort to cheer him. "Everything will be all right." But he would not be comforted. "How can things be all right again when every day they are getting worse?" His creditors were hounding him more and more all the time and the pressure became unbearable.

Unable to pay the help any longer, my mother dismissed the cook and the maid. After enjoying for years the luxury of just being the mistress of her household and giving the orders, she went back to the kitchen and for the chores of house-cleaning took in an occasional day-worker.

My father had apparently no inkling of the fate that was in store for him when, on the High Holidays of the year 1932, the last of these Jewish solemn seasons that he was to witness on earth, he chanted the *Unesaneh Tokef* and asked the question: "Who shall live and who shall die?" Despite all the anguish that filled his heart and the weight that rested on him he went on serving his Creator and fellow-man as theretofore. The Sabbath rest was observed in his home as completely as in the years of his ascendancy and glory. When *Chanukah,* the Feast of Lights, came around, whether he was compensated for his services or not, he still participated in concerts arranged for the benefit of charitable institutions or the celebrations of this festival of the Maccabees by Zionist groups or the students of rabbinical seminaries. His contributions to Jewish cultural programs were deeply appreciated and regarded as a source of encouragement particularly to the youth. As late as January 19, 1933, the Chattanooga Times stated, after a recital he had given in a local synagogue, that he had sung "his way into the hearts of a large Jewish and Gentile audience." My brother Henry, of whose musical accomplishments he was very proud and whom he tried very much to bring before the public, was not with him on that occasion. But my father expressed the hope that he might in the not too distant future return to Chattanooga with his son, "who is probably better than I am," and sing together with him in a concert. This hope was never realized.

There was, however, another dream of his that was to be partially, at least, fulfilled. That was the wish that he had uttered as long ago as 1918 in Milwaukee, and which he had reiterated at the conclusion of his memoirs published in the Day on the occasion of his golden jubilee. It was that his last pulpit might be in the Land of Israel. South Africa did not lure him in spite of the offer made to him as recently as February 1932 by the community of Johannesburg which had been unaffected by the Wall Street crash. If he was to exchange his home in America for any other place in the world, it could be only for the Land of Israel. The zest with which he took part in the musical program of the annual conference of synagogues and organizations on behalf of the American Palestine Campaign on February 28 was a sort of precursor to the pilgrimage to the land of his dreams that he was to enter upon less than four weeks later.

He had thought about a trip to the Holy Land and possible settlement there more seriously than ever before at the beginning of 1933 when his financial situation had passed beyond the critical stage and become acute. "I am tired of the hustle and bustle of America and of American Jewry," he confided to his friend Danzis of the Day. "I have no complaints against America, mind you, or against American Jews. They have lavished upon me riches and honor. Nevertheless America robbed me of something inside of me that I will never be able to find again." He was referring to that peace of mind of which he had been deprived for the preceding ten years. He was very envious of his colleague Kwartin for having left the United States and settled in the Land of Israel. "He is a smart man, this fellow Kwartin," he used to say. "And I am a fool. But no matter, I'll go to the Land of Israel also. You will see."

An opportunity to realize his life-long ambition of seeing with his own eyes the country that he had sung about so often, presented itself when Joseph Fox, the scholarly young general manager of the Palestine American Film Company, Kol-Or, invited him to take the principal part in a talking and singing picture to be produced in the Holy Land. His role was to chant, in the ancient biblical settings, some of his own famous liturgical compositions.

The proposal was accepted most eagerly despite the fact that there was no guarantee that the venture would be financially profitable. All that the promoters of the project had to offer was their ability to photograph. Even the equipment, that is the camera and films, had to be supplied by my father. As for his travelling expenses—which they were willing to lay out—they were to be covered out of his earnings from concerts in Palestine. The only indemnification held out to him for his efforts was that the picture, when completed, would bring him a fortune. When my father asked the advice of the editors of the Forward about the prospects of the undertaking, the latter counselled caution. "After all you have nothing to go by, Mr. Rosenblatt, but the word of the promoters." Whereunto my father replied with his customary naïveté: "But who is going to be dishonest in a matter as holy as *Eretz Israel?*"

Despite all these uncertainties, I urged my father to go to Palestine. I feared for his health if he were to remain in America as long as the depression lasted. Furthermore 1933 was for Palestine, thanks to the influx into the country, since the rise of Hitler, of wealthy German Jews, a boom year. On

Friday, March 24, the Italian liner Vulcania was sailing directly for Haifa. That would bring him, my mother and my brother Henry to the Holy Land just in time for Passover. Contact was, therefore, immediately established by Leo with Herbert Glover of the Columbia Broadcasting System for a special broadcast by my father from the Wailing Wall in Jerusalem on the first day of the intermediate days of Passover, (April 13), in a portrayal of "the wandering Jew." Thus the stage was set for him to go.

Just before his departure, so I was later told, my father had planned a concert in collaboration with the choir director of the Yiddish stage, Joseph Rumshinsky. The arrangements were virtually completed and a large theater had been engaged for the affair. The deal did not go through. Rumshinsky had put the chorines of the theater on the program and my father refused, prior to his leaving for the Holy Land, to participate in a concert of liturgical music featuring female singers. "The concert," he told Rumshinsky, "must be run on strictly traditional Jewish lines. And what have women cantors to do with Jewish music?"

But, even if all preparations had not been made for my father to sail on the Vulcania when he did, something happened now that rendered it imperative that he get away at once. Some of his creditors, when they learned that he was planning to go abroad, threatened a court injunction to stop him. One of them was the daughter of his colleague Reb Moshe, whom he still owed $500. Another was a city magistrate who had been particularly irritating. My father had just barely succeeded in pacifying the former by promising her the first pay check he would receive for his appearance in whatever part of the world it might be. He had similar understandings with other creditors, whom he was thereby able to restrain from taking action that would impede his voyage. The judge, however, was not to be moved. My father was, therefore, in mortal dread of him, so much so that one

day—it was about a week before his departure—when he
spied his persecutor walking in the street, he tore himself
loose from the grasp of Henry, who was holding him by the
arm, to run to the other side. In his excitement he neglected
to make sure that the road was clear, with the result that he
was knocked down by a passing taxicab. The sight of
his father stretched out on the pavement made Henry faint.
Father, however, though he must have felt some pain, picked
himself up as though nothing had happened, and, with his
habitual smile, exclaimed: "Thank God, it's nothing. I feel
all right. Praised be the Lord for not holding up my journey to *Eretz Israel*." As a matter of fact it wasn't the trifle
that he and the physician, who examined him, thought it was
at the time. Who knows whether the brain concussion that
he suffered may not in some way have been connected with
his premature death?

But this was not the only hurdle that had to be overcome
before my parents were free to leave. There were others. For
example, the rent for the apartment on 94th Street, long
overdue, had not been paid, and there was no means of paying it. There were grocer's and other bills that were left and
had to be met. Finally there was that seamstress, a lonely
soul whom my mother had befriended, taken into the house,
provided with free board and vacations during the summer
besides paying her much more than the regular price for the
dresses she made for her. From this woman my parents had,
in their distress, when all other sources had failed, borrowed
$250. When she found out that my mother was leaving for
Palestine, she came at seven o'clock of the morning of my
parents' departure into my mother's bedroom and staged
such a scene that it was enough to drive one to distraction.
She whined and squealed, insisting that my mother pay her
the money owed her, and threatening all kinds of things to
keep her from proceeding on her journey. My mother tried
to calm her, imploring her, on bended knees, to stop. "Dear

friend," she said, "don't be so upset. I swear to you that the first $250 Mr. Rosenblatt will earn will be cabled to you. May I not live to see my children again, if this is not taken care of."

Only then did that ungrateful creature put an end to her antics. My mother kept her promise. The first $250 my father received in return for his services in Palestine were dispatched to the seamstress. But my mother vowed that the ingrate would never set foot on the threshold of her home again.

Amidst such circumstances, with only their steamship tickets, their luggage and $25 in their pockets, did my parents go aboard the Vulcania, where a radio message from David Sarnoff, president of R.C.A., greeted them. There was a terrific crowd on the ship, and my father as I beheld him then, for the last time in my life, appeared haggard and pale. "Will he be able to stand the pace?" I asked myself as I embraced him and kissed him good-bye. "Is it wise, in the condition in which he is, to let him take the long boat trip to Palestine? Will I ever see his face again?" Notwithstanding all my fears and apprehensions I was glad that I had in a small measure been responsible for his departure. Only a few weeks before, the newly elected President Franklin Delano Roosevelt had closed the banks. Money was tight in the United States. There was nothing left for my father to do here. Anything was better than to continue in the misery of the past several months.

When the Vulcania had left and the seven of us children who had remained behind returned, we immediately had all of our parents' furniture put into storage and vacated their apartment. Our unmarried brothers and sisters, who had lived with our parents, were distributed among the married ones. Thus the home was broken up and the family divided to save expenses. When the first cable sent to the old address on 94th Street by my mother, announcing the safe arrival of herself, my father and Henry in Palestine, was returned to the sender, my mother suspected what we had done. But it was the only course left to us.

42

In the Land of Israel

If it is true that every cloud has a silver lining, my father's ten-week sojourn in the Jewish national home was a serene and bright finale of a turbulent storm-tossed life. *Eretz Israel* proved to be, as I had hoped, a balm to his wounds. He had no sooner landed on its shore, than it seemed to him as though an oppressive weight had been lifted from him. He felt rejuvenated, restored, filled with new hope and zest for living. The first piano he saw was immediately put into action by him, and, after having played on it for awhile in accompaniment of a tune he was singing, he pranced around the room like a child, so that my mother felt embarrassed. "Yossel, what are you doing?" she tried to interrupt his frolicking. "You are behaving like an infant." "That's exactly how I feel. Like a newborn babe," was my father's quick retort. At times he wondered whether it was all real, whether his eyes were not deceiving him. "Henry," he was heard saying more than once during the first week after his arrival, rapping the table with his fingers, "can you believe it? It is really Tel Aviv that we are in, our own Jewish Tel Aviv, built by Jewish hands, run by a Jewish mayor, guarded by Jewish policemen, everything as it was foreseen by our prophets." He thrilled at the new Jerusalem, "Jerusalem rebuilt," with its solid architecture and its many fine institutions. "You wouldn't recognize it, Shmuli," he wrote to me. Pales-

tine was veritably a "land flowing with milk and honey,"
possessing all the virtues of the modern countries of the world
with very few of their defects. "There are no bad Jews in the
Land of Israel," he remarked to Zalman Kotler of the Jewish
Morning Journal at a casual encounter. "Even the least worthy is here full of merit as a pomegranate is full of kernels."
Like the sweet singer of medieval Spain, Jehudah Halevi,
who found Jerusalem beautiful even in its state of desolation
and ruin, so he, Josef Rosenblatt, who had so often given musical expression to Jewry's ancient prayers of longing and
yearning for Zion, could detect nothing but beauty, idealism
and nobility in the land of Jewish hopes and dreams. It may
be a matter of wonderment, to those who knew how sincerely and deeply devout my father was and the many sacrifices he had made for the sake of his religious principles, that
he should have become at the cradle of the Jewish religion,
on the sacred soil of Jerusalem, an apologete for those among
the builders of Zion who were lax in the observance of those
tenets of the Jewish faith that he had upheld with such fanat-
ical devotion and zeal. How come that he should have mus-
tered the enthusiasm he evinced for the pioneers of Israel's
new Jewish agricultural settlements, many of whom did not
measure up to the standards of piety he had set himself, and
even spurned his views? In reality the paradox of his reason-
ing was not at all difficult to resolve. While Josef Rosenblatt
was not a deep thinker, but a simple, unsophisticated person, he recognized, by means of his artistic intuition or in-
sight, that idealists could not be put into the same category
as ordinary people. They who give their all for the upbuild-
ing of a country must not be expected to comply with the
rules governing persons of average virtue and attainments.
Citing a rabbinic parable to clinch his argument he asked:
"Is it proper to find fault with the angels of heaven because
they do not fulfill the precept of, let us say, the donning of
the phylacteries at the recitation of the daily morning pray-

ers?" Even so is it wrong to speak evil of the men and women, who, at the peril of their lives, drain Palestine's marshes and transform its wilderness into gardens of the Lord, if they fail to heed all the minute regulations of the *Shulchan Aruch.* Even the most devout and pious Jew living in the Diaspora has no right to criticize, for it is easy for people who live in security and comfort to sit back and pick flaws in those who risk their health and their strength to make Israel's ageold dream come true.

This was how he loved *Eretz Israel,* every stone of it, every inhabitant, from the humblest to the most distinguished, all classes, all types—scientists and farmers, rabbis and teachers, workingmen and merchants, *Chassidim* and *Misnagdim,* those attired in the old-fashioned traditional garb and bare-headed pioneers wearing nothing but shorts. He couldn't do enough for them. He sang everywhere for every type of audience—on the first day of Passover in the Ohel Shem, the largest auditorium of Tel Aviv, and on the last day of the festival in the main hall of the *Yeshibah* of Meah Shearim, the street of the pious in Jerusalem. He appeared at a banquet of lovers of *Chazanuth,* presided over by the Hebrew poet laureate Chaim Nachman Bialik, and at the torch-dances of the mystics (*Hilula*) at the tomb of Rabbi Simon son of Jochai in Meron on *Lag B'omer.* He officiated on a Sabbath in the main house of worship of the town of Rishon Letzion, the seat of Baron Edmond de Rothschild's famous wine-cellars, and on the Feast of *Shabuot* in the great synagogue of Tel Aviv, the most capacious of its kind in the country. In between he gave a concert at the agricultural colony of Ain Charod and a recital in Tel Aviv's assembly hall Beth Haam. He also chanted prayers of the synagogue at the table of the Rabbi of Sadagora in Safed, sitting before the latter as humbly as he had in the presence of the grandfather in Sadagora more than four decades earlier.

To most of the Jewish residents of the Land of Israel the

voice of Yossele Rosenblatt was already familiar and many of them knew his recorded liturgical compositions by heart. I remember overhearing, during my year of study in Jerusalem in the winter of 1926, a youngster in the street hum his *Rachem No,* and then passing by a grocery-shop in which several eight-year-old boys were entertaining themselves by listening to the playing of my father's records, for which they paid the proprietor the price of two and a half piasters per round. But, of course, there is all the difference in the world between hearing and seeing. The effect of the actual vision of the personality producing the strains of music is far more overpowering than that of the sounds themselves.

"The first night of Passover," wrote Daniel Persky, the feuilletonist of the American Hebrew weekly Hadoar—and he was voicing the sentiments of countless others, "presented to us, the inhabitants of Tel Aviv, a precious gift, the name of which was 'Reb Yossele Rosenblatt.' " Almost all who heard him conduct the holiday services at the *Ohel Shem* were agreed that "the living Rosenblatt was not one whit inferior to the Rosenblatt who was hidden behind the disks of the phonograph. His rendition on the morning of the festival of *Umipne Chatoenu* was something out of this world. When Yossele sang 'We were exiled from our land,' we were able to envisage Israel's exile with our very eyes. Then, when he exclaimed in a robusto tone: 'Reveal the glory of Thy kingdom upon us speedily,' it was as though Israel's sovereignty had been restored in all its brilliance and splendor."

When Israel's poet laureate of the time, Chaim Nachman Bialik, heard my father sing *Shir Hamaalos,* he was roused to such a pitch of enthusiasm that he proposed that the composition be adopted as the Jewish national anthem. To this very day the Socialist *Chalutzim* claim as one of their favorite tunes the melody he had composed for the text of a hymn sung by the mystics in honor of the austere saint Rabbi Simon Bar Jochai.

The inspiration he derived from actual contact with the land, about which he had formerly only read and dreamed, the sight of the holy places about which he had so often sung without knowing what they looked like, and the enthusiastic reception he had been given—all this opened up new fountains of creativity for my father. "I have come to life again as a cantor," he confided to the aforementioned Zalman Kotler. "Never have I done so much creative work in the form of musical composition as here. Not only for the most important historic sites have I written music, but also for the new *Eretz Israel,* for the *Chalutzim,* for the Jewish colonies, for the Jewish National Fund and the Palestine Foundation Fund."

In Jerusalem where his film company had its office his headquarters was Hotel Amdursky. He felt very much at home in the atmosphere of worldly culture united with traditionalism that pervaded this hostelry, the proprietor of which was one of the old residents of the Holy City and one of the most respected members of its Ashkenazic community. Mr. Amdursky's daughter, who was an accomplished musician, would accompany him on the piano whenever he sang operatic arias or other types of classical music. What more ideal arrangement could there be than this for a vocal artist for whom music was the very breath of life?

Most treasured by him were, however, the Sabbath afternoons spent at the home of Chief Rabbi Kook, that great lover of Israel and of the Land of Israel, to whom my father was attracted as to a magnet. "He would be seated," as one of those who often met him there recalled, "at the table in the dining room, surrounded by the students of the *Yeshibah,* its directors and teachers, as well as friends and admirers. With all of them he would fraternize with the utmost cordiality, laugh heartily as he told his own or listened to other people's humorous stories and teach those present the melodies he had composed to fit the text of the poems written by the

Chief Rabbi for the outgoing of the Sabbath. Reb Yossele was lifted up to heavenly heights as he sang, and we all were uplifted together with him. Songs seemed to pour forth from his golden throat in an unending stream. 'Come let us make up, our heavenly Father (Lomir sich iberbeten *Ovinu Shebashomayim*),' he pleaded in this special hour of divine grace. It was a great and mighty plea. The entire burden of the troubled community of Israel, which was passing through the darkest night of its exile, seemed to rest on the shoulders of this little man who, crushed under its weight, was crying out for relief to the divine Redeemer."

The predilection of the admirers of his art in the Land of Israel was, of course, for his *Chazanuth*, which was in their sight the great contribution he had made to Israel's national culture. However my father was never content—and he was supported herein by my mother—to shine solely in what was his real domain. He wanted to show the world that besides being a cantor he was also able to do something of which but few cantors were capable, namely to sing music far removed from the realm of *Chazanuth*.

Once in Tel Aviv, after he had sung several selections in different languages, as had been his wont, voices from the audience were heard calling: "*Elokay Neshomoh*," while others, drowning them out with their volume, shouted: "*Rachem No*." To which my father replied: "First you will have to let me sing what I want. Then I will sing what you want." He sang a duet from the opera *La Traviata* together with Henry, and, when he had finished singing the aria, he said to the audience: "I was anxious to prove to you that I wasn't only a *chazan*, but an opera singer also." Then, after having satisfied himself, he did the audience's bidding by singing both *Rachem No* and *Elokay Neshomoh*.

My father's original intention in going to *Eretz Israel* had not been to settle there permanently, but strictly as a matter of business. He had planned to make a film, give a series of concerts and return to America. "Although I hoped eventually to make my home here," he said, "I thought that the old *Eretz Israel* was at present too old for me, for I am only fifty-one, while the young *Eretz Israel* was still too young, because I am already fifty-one." After having toured the country and having lived in it for several weeks, however, he changed his mind. The time to settle in it, he decided, was now. One could live comfortably in Israel on one fourth of what it costs in America, he wrote home. There was a movement afoot to build in Jerusalem a communal synagogue large enough to accommodate 5,000 worshippers, and there was no one else whom they would want as cantor but him. Of course, he would have liked to have his children with him, but he realized that that might be fraught with complications.

In the meantime, before taking up residence in the Land of Israel, it was necessary to earn a little money. True, he had not been doing badly with his paid engagements, considering existing conditions. But then there were travelling expenses that had been laid out and had to be reimbursed, debts to be repaid and funds to be sent home to the children for household necessities. That left no balance at all. However the European concert tour, that had been planned, looked very promising and the prospects of the film were particularly bright.

My father's last letter from Israel, addressed to Leo, was written on Friday, June 16, the day on which the Jewish labor leader, Dr. Chaim Arlosoroff, was murdered by unknown assailants. It was as cheerful and optimistic as all those that preceded it. There was not a mention in it of pain or physical discomfort even though the evening before, at the jubilee of Cantor Rivlin of Jerusalem, whose choir had often assisted him in Palestine, my father appeared, to his colleague, Zawel Kwartin, to be breathing heavily and singing with great effort. The letter expresses the usual concern for the children he had left behind in America, speaks of a visit to the Wailing Wall, where pictures had been taken of him in action and where he had had a good cry, praying for the health and well-being of his entire family. It asks Leo to get in touch immediately with an agent in South Africa where he had been told that the chances of making money were then very good. Finally he leaves Leo a forwarding address in Roumania, which was to be the first portion of the tour of Europe that had been arranged for him and that was to set him on his feet again.

On the next day, Saturday, June 17, he conducted his farewell service in the synagogue located in the courtyard, or as the Jews of Jerusalem called it the *Churvah*, of Rabbi Judah Hechassid in the old city of Jerusalem. It was the largest and most venerable of the twenty-seven Jewish houses of worship within the walls.

The farewell was, of course, meant to be only temporary, for my father had hopes of returning in the not too distant future. It was with this in view that he entrusted to Chief Rabbi Kook a little Torah scroll that was in his possession. It was to be kept for him at this synagogue and to be given back when he would come again to make his permanent home in God's Holy City.

Neither he nor anyone else who was present at this service had an idea that it was indeed a farewell service, farewell not only to the Land of Israel but to this world, and that the Land of Israel would become very soon, more quickly than he had expected, his everlasting home. They could not have known because his singing that Saturday morning seemed to them to be extraordinary. "Angels must have helped him make that music," said Chief Rabbi Kook as he looked back upon that Sabbath morning service. Yossele appeared to be floating on air. His falsetto sounded more beautiful and his voice clearer and purer than ever, and his coloratura spiralled into heavenly heights. Is it possible that an inner voice told

him that this was to be his swan-song in the synagogue, the
last time that he would lead a congregation in Israel in
prayer? Whether it was so or not, the fact remains that his
chanting was so inspired that even in so reverent a place as
the *Churvah* synagogue, in which such unbridled expressions
of enthusiasm were usually ruled out as a profanation of the
sacred, the worshippers applauded several times in the course
of the service, and, when it was over, they lifted him up on
their shoulders and carried him in triumph through the narrow lanes of the Old City.

The next morning, that sad Sunday morning on which the
funeral of the tragically murdered Chaim Arlosoroff took
place, my father left with a whole company for the Jordan
River and the Dead Sea to complete his work on the film
"The Dream of My People." He was in unusually good form
and in excellent spirits, full of joviality and banter and fun.
At the tomb of the matriarch Rachel he sang the ancient la-
ment of Jeremiah: "A voice is heard in Ramah . . . Rachel
weeping for her children"; and to those who heard him it almost seemed as though the mother of Israel had come to life
and was presenting her plea to the Almighty. His prayers at
the sepulchre of the patriarchs at the Cave of Machpelah in
Hebron were equally stirring. Then, when he stood up in a
skiff in the Jordan in the vicinity of Jericho and lifted up his
melodious voice in his own spirited, fast-moving *B'tzes Yisroel,* with its antiphonies and duets, its alto and tenor solos,
its coloratura and sudden stops, one was almost able to vis-
ualize "the sea receding and the Jordan turning back before
the invading Israelites, while the mountains skipped like
rams and the hills like young lambs." He was inordinately
happy for this opportunity to chant his favorite psalm in its
natural surroundings. His entire being felt uplifted. When
these chores were completed, the next part in the picture
called for bathing in the thick, salty waters of the Dead Sea.
It was a stiflingly hot day, and the sultry air of the lowlands

—the Dead Sea is said to be the lowest spot on earth—was almost insupportable. Also the sudden change from the rarer, purer atmosphere of Jerusalem, nearly 3,000 feet above sea level, to the torrid heat of the Dead Sea far below, was more than my father's overtaxed heart could take. He began to complain of a pressure near his stomach, and was in considerable pain when he was brought back to his hotel in Jerusalem.

Mother sent at once for the doctor. The physician examined him, gave him an injection to ease the pain, and sat at his bedside for two hours, conversing with him and indulging in pleasantries until he felt better. "How old are you, Reb Yossele?" asked the doctor, who was somewhat of a Hebrew scholar. "Don't you know?" replied the patient in his customary whimsical manner. "When we recite grace after meals, we say 'Rachem No,' and the letters of the word 'No' have the numerical value of fifty-one. That's how old I am."

43

Eternity

Outside the sickroom the doctor informed mother that her husband had had a coronary thrombosis, which often leaves those with a less robust constitution than his partially paralyzed. He prescribed absolute quiet for his patient. Mother did not have to be told twice. Her early training as a nurse and her years of experience in raising a family of eight children had taught her how important such orders were and how thoroughly they had to be carried out. Though her heart was clutched with fear over what might happen next, she did not lose herself. Tenderly she put her beloved Yossele to rest, making him as comfortable as possible. She gave him the water he had asked for to wash his hands before saying his prayers. Then she turned all lights out except for one little candle, and waited, hoping against hope that what she anticipated might not come to pass. As she watched his face, agitated and twitching, and listened to his heavy breathing, the varied events of all the thirty-three years of their life together, with their excitements, their joys and sorrows, their triumphs and heartaches, passed in review through her mind. They had been through a great deal since the time when as a raw, unworldly, somewhat difficult and yet at bottom kindly *Chassidic* youth, he had entered upon his first position in Munkacs, until he had attained world-fame and also heaped upon himself worries and burdens beyond compare in America. Artistically, professionally, in his outward demeanor and bearing he had developed, of course. Essentially he had never changed. What was in store for him now? Would he be able to sing again, and, should he recover, would there be a change in his fortunes? Would he be able to take it easier? She thought of the European tour that had been planned for him, of the repayment of his debts that the anticipated earnings would make possible, of the new era that might begin for him, when her musings were interrupted by an unearthly sound. She looked at the sick man before her and noticed his head thrown backward. For a moment she regarded him in stunned silence. She could not believe what she saw. It could not be! It could not happen, not to her Yossele! Suddenly she emitted a shriek, and ran frantically through the hotel, calling "Doctor! Doctor! Get me a doctor quickly! Something has happened to Yossele! Doctor!"

When the doctor, who happened to be in the neighborhood, came a few minutes later, it was all over. Her Yossele had gone to sleep forever. What she had feared might happen and had hoped would not come to pass when he went to the Land of Israel had alas taken place.

During the next few days Mother walked around as in a trance. She had been thoroughly unprepared for anything like this, for her Yossele was always so peppy, so full of animation and movement—the very essence of life. Now suddenly he was no longer there. He was gone from her, gone forever. She lived through the last rites and the week of mourning that followed like an automaton. Everything she did was mechanical. Her mind seemed to have stopped functioning completely. Only her body was alive, her limbs responding as if by reflex action to the prompting and prodding of those around her.

As soon as what had happened became known, the report of it spread with lightning rapidity to all the four corners of the earth. "Joseph is no more" announced one of the Palestinian Hebrew dailies, using the exclamation of the patriarch Jacob that signalized the death of his beloved son Joseph. "The master of song has become mute" was the scriptural caption of another Hebrew periodical.

The non-Jewish as well as the Jewish press throughout the world carried the news. The New York Journal had spread across its front page on Monday, June 19, the announcement, "CANTOR ROSENBLATT DIES IN PALESTINE." The New York Sun characterized him as a "Singer to the Lord." The New York World Telegram remembered that he had once been called "the Jewish John McCormack." Others mentioned the fortune he had given away for philanthropic purposes and the flattering operatic offers he had spurned on account of religious scruples. Expressions of condolence poured in from all quarters, as Jew and gentile who had heard or known him joined in bemoaning the loss.

Most moving, perhaps, in giving utterance to the grief felt by all was the elegy by the learned cantor and music critic J. L. Wasilkowsky, published in the Jewish Morning Journal under the heading of "Joseph Is No More." I have tried to render it as close to the Yiddish original as I could.

The fiddle is broken. Its strings have been severed.
The master has vanished and gone.
The singer divine from this world has departed.
None e'er sang as he has done.

The pulpit and siddur are both now deserted,
And mourners are prayer and song.
And bent down with sorrow are friend and companion,
And grief mutes the synagogue's throng.

The place of the high-priest is empty and vacant.
The melody sweet is no more.
And stopped up for aye is the fountain of music,
And hearts are left aching and sore.

Who now will make for us heavenly harmonies,
Pure as the angels on high?
Who now will cheer us with God's voice of triumph
Mingled with tear and with sigh?

The heads of the cantors are bowed deep with mourning,
Their eyes are with tears filled and dim,
As they weep and bewail the untimely departure
Of the monarch of song and of hymn.

The funeral that took place the next morning, a day after
the interment of Chaim Arlosoroff, was one of the largest
Jerusalem had ever witnessed. More than 5,000 persons attended. Eulogies were delivered by Chief Rabbi Kook and
other dignitaries, while the prayers were chanted by my father's two colleagues, the foremost contenders with him for
the crown of "King of Cantors," Zawel Kwartin and Mordecai
Hershman.

As the procession halted at the entrance of the Mount of
Olives Cemetery, the oldest in the Holy Land and the place
of repose of many saints, Rabbi Kook spoke the final words.
In the future, he stated, when posterity would visit the graves

of the righteous who sleep their eternal slumber in that sacred spot, there would be pointed out among them that of another *Tzaddik*, "Yossele Rosenblatt." Thus was Yossele Rosenblatt laid to rest. His life's dream had been, symbolically at least, fulfilled. He had had his last pulpit in the Holy City of Jerusalem for which he had yearned, ever since he had been able to think, and about which he had sung so touchingly. Now his dust was to mingle with its earth and be joined with it forever.

On the Tuesday after the week of mourning was over, the Cantors' Association of America, whom my father had served so loyally all the years of his life, arranged a memorial concert in Carnegie Hall, New York, in which a choir of more than two-hundred of my father's colleagues participated. Rabbis throughout the world discoursed about the loss that had been sustained by Jewry and articles dedicated to the memory of Yossele Rosenblatt appeared in the bulletins of countless institutions for the benefit of which he had sung at one time or another. In Palestine memorial meetings were held on the thirtieth day *(Sh'loshim)* after his demise, and regularly afterwards on every anniversary of the day of his death.

Chronologically speaking Yossele Rosenblatt died rather young, in the prime of manhood. He might have lived longer, perhaps, if he had not had the cares and worries resulting from his ill-fated business venture, brought on by his own failings. The fatal blunder he had made left its scars on his dear ones, who for a long time after his death continued to pay the price of his folly. All that is over now. The struggles and suffering are almost forgotten and what remains is a noble heritage, a wealth of inspiration, a name to conjure with and musical treasures to delight the ears not only of the present generation but of countless generations to come.

It was fortunate that Yossele Rosenblatt lived in an age in which the phonograph was already invented, so that it was possible to preserve not only the music he had composed but also to bring to the ears of posterity the sound of the living voice. In addition there are also extant a number of talking movies which reveal the figure of the man himself in action. I had never seen the film "The Dream of My People," that had technically not been completed, when it was presented during the year of mourning in the United States. But when I visited Israel in the summer following my father's death to dedicate the tombstone on his grave, I found him singing from the screen of the outdoor motion picture theater right next door to the hotel in which I stopped in Tel Aviv. He seemed so much alive, and indeed he is alive until this very day. Wherever there are Jews who heard or saw him, whether it be in America or Europe or Africa or Palestine, the memory of his personality is vivid and fresh, and many of those who had never been brought in contact with him, because they were either too young or not yet in the world when he lived, remember hearing their parents tell about him or may have among their family heirlooms some of his prized phonograph records.

What made Yossele Rosenblatt outstanding? Many answers have been given to this question. M. S. Geshuri, writing in Israel's Haaretz, thought it was a combination of factors.

"Every great cantor who achieved a reputation among Jews," he said, "distinguished himself by some unique faculty that he possessed . . . One impressed them by his fine declamation . . . or his enchanting improvisation; a second . . . by his powerful voice . . . a third by the delicacy of tone . . . Our present generation too does not have to be ashamed of its great cantors that have been richly endowed by nature. To him, however, to Yossele she has given all these gifts put together. There was something distinctive and unique about his style, a certain freshness and individuality that made his rendition of the prayers of the synagogue stand out in a class by itself.

"Even in the phonograph records there can be felt the

difference in this respect between him and other cantors. For while the latter introduced in their improvisations no new feature . . . outside of the ordinary motifs, Reb Yossele's recitation never failed to make an ineradicable impression . . . and to arouse the deepest religious feelings . . . by the variations he injected into the ancient chant.

"Thanks to this novel note struck by him in his interpretation of the Jewish liturgy [he was able to] enrich cantorial literature with compositions that raised him to the level of a creative musician.

"In all his creations," Geshuri concluded his article, "there is felt a strong Jewish ring, based on the tradition of centuries. The only trouble with them is that they are not capable of being used by every cantor. It is as though he had written them only for himself, or for cantors possessing all his attributes. That is why it is so difficult for others to execute them."

What the writer had in mind no doubt were compositions like *Meloch, Omar Rabbi Elozor, Elokay Neshomoh* and *Acheinu Kol Beis Yisroel,* which require, in order to be sung as they were intended to be, a range of three and a half octaves, a deep resonant baritone register, a robust, yet mellow tenor, a strong, well-developed falsetto and a freely moving coloratura. He may also have been alluding to selections of the class of *Nishmas* and *Lo Sachmod,* which on account of their swiftly interlocking phraseology demand perfect breath-control, or pieces of the type of *Rachem No,* written in several different keys, which only singers with a sure sense of pitch are capable of rendering properly.

B. Z. Goldberg of the Day spoke of the fascination exercised upon the Jewish masses by the personality and the voice of Yossele Rosenblatt, the love they entertained for him, on account of which they spontaneously conferred upon him the pet name of "Yossele." For Yossele Rosenblatt in their estimation, not only had the ability but also played the part of the *chazan,* the representative of the Jewish people in prayer, the instrument of its joys and sorrows, of its hopes and dreams.

"Too many of our cantors would have liked to become opera singers. They are compelled to remain cantors because the opera doesn't want them. Yossele Rosenblatt was one cantor who might, had he wished it, have become an opera singer. But he preferred to remain a cantor."

Several years ago a young cantor referred to himself in an advertisement of the services he was going to conduct as "Yossele Rosenblatt the third." "Why the *third?*" asked a person who read the announcement. "The reason is," replied the cantor, "that there never has been a second."

Glossary

Note: Unless otherwise indicated the terms or phrases explained are Hebrew.

AB, THE NINTH OF: Hebrew date of the anniversary of the destruction of the first and second temples of Jerusalem, observed by Jews as a 24 hour fast and day of mourning on which dirges are chanted in the synagogue.

ACHEINU KOL BEIS YISROEL: "Our brethren, the whole house of Israel," opening words of the last paragraph of a prayer recited by the reader in the synagogue on Monday and Thursday mornings while the scroll of the Torah is being rolled up prior to its return to the Holy Ark.

ADONOI: "My Lord," the pronunciation of the tetragrammaton in prayer.

ADOSHEM: substitute for ADONOI when not used in prayer in order not to take God's name in vain.

AKAVYOII BEN MAHALLALEL OMER: "Akavya, the son of Mahallalel, says," beginning of the third chapter of the tractate Abot of the Mishnah read on Saturday afternoons during the summer months.

AL HATZADDIKIM: "Towards the righteous," prayer for the reward of the righteous, from the silent devotion of the daily weekday services.

ALMEMAR: platform on which stands the reading desk upon which the scroll of the Torah is placed when it is read in the synagogue.

AL NAHAROS BOVEL: "By the rivers of Babylon," opening words of psalm 137.

AMUD: prayer-desk in front of which the cantor stands when he leads the congregation in prayer.

ARBA-KANFOS: four-cornered bodice with the fringes worn by Jews directly over the undershirt.

359

ATTO YOTZARTO: "Thou didst form," opening words of the variant recited in the additional service when the new-moon falls on Saturday.

AUNEG SHABBOS: "Sabbath joy."

AV HORACHAMIM: "Father of mercy," beginning of a memorial prayer in honor of Israel's martyrs recited on Sabbath mornings after the reading from the Scriptures and prior to the return of the Torah scroll to the Holy Ark.

AYE M'KOM K'VODO L'HAARITZO: "Where is the place of His glory that He might be revered," part of the KEDU-SHAH of the additional service of Saturday morning according to the Sephardic rite.

BAAL TEFILLAH: "master of prayer," reader of the divine service in the synagogue in the traditional sing-song.

BAAL TESHUVOH: penitent.

BAMEH MADLIKIN: "Wherewith may one kindle (the Sabbath lights)?" opening words of the second chapter of the tractate Shabbat of the Mishnah read just before the evening service on the eve of the Sabbath.

BAR-MITZVAH: literally "son of a commandment," a Jewish male who, having attained his thirteenth birthday, becomes charged with the responsibility of fulfilling the precepts of his faith; confirmation.

BATTE-MIDRASHIM: plural of BETH HAMIDRASH.

BEMA: synonym of ALMEMAR.

BETH HAMIDRASH: "house of study," used very commonly as a place of worship.

BORUCH EIL ELYON: "Blessed be the most-high God," opening words of hymn sung at the Sabbath morning meal.

BORUCH HU UVORUCH SH'MO: "Blessed be He and blessed be His name," response said whenever the sentence "Blessed art Thou, O Lord" is pronounced.

B'TZES YISROEL: "When Israel went forth," opening words of psalm 114.

CHADARIM: plural of CHEDER.

CHALUTZIM: pioneers of modern Israel.

CHANUKAH: the eight-day festival of dedication beginning Kislev 25 commemorating the rededication of the Temple of Jerusalem by the Maccabees in the year 165 B.C.E. It is celebrated by the kindling of lights on eight successive evenings.

CHASSID: "pious person," member of the sect of mystical pietists founded by Israel Baal Shem Tob, a Polish Jewish mystic born in the year 1700 and died in 1760.

CHASSIDIC: pertaining to the CHASSIDIM.

CHASSIDIM: plural of CHASSID.

CHASSIDISM: the mystical movement of the CHASSIDIM.

CHAZAN: cantor.

CHAZANUTH: the art of the CHAZAN, Hebrew liturgical music, the cantorate.

CHAZENDEL: diminutive of CHAZAN in the Yiddish dialects of Eastern Europe.

CHAZEREL: diminutive of CHAZIR, "pig," in the Yiddish dialects of Eastern Europe.

CHEDER: "room," the one-room private elementary school common among the Jews of Eastern Europe.

CHEVRA KADISHA: "holy brotherhood," Jewish burial society.

CHILLUL SHABBOS: desecration of the Sabbath.

CHUMISH: the pentateuch or Five Books of Moses.

CHURVAH: ruin.

DAVEN: pray (Yiddish).

DYBBUK: demon.

ECHOD: "one," end of the Jewish confession of faith beginning with the word SHEMA.

EILI, EILI: "My God, my God," beginning of psalm 22 verse 2.

EL MOLE RACHAMIM: "God full of mercy," memorial prayer for the dead.

ELOKAY AD SHELO NOTZARTI: "My God, before I was ever formed," opening words of appendage to the silent devotion of the Day of Atonement.

ELOKAY NESHOMOH: "My God, the soul. . . ," prayer at the beginning of the daily morning service, intended originally to be recited on awaking from sleep.

ERETZ ISRAEL: "the Land of Israel."

ESHKOL: "Cluster," beginning of the poetical insertion in the cantor's repetition of the additional service on the Sabbath of Shekalim.

ESROG: citron, one of the four species of plants used in the synagogue in the ritual of the Feast of Tabernacles.

GABBAI: beadle or presiding officer in the synagogue, literally "collector."

GAON: "excellency," genius, preeminent.

HABDALAH: the ritual performed at the outgoing of the Sabbath to indicate the beginning of the working week. It consists of blessings pronounced over wine, spices and light and the "distinction" between the sacred and the profane.

HABET MISHOMAYIM UR'EH: "Look down from heaven and see," from the additional supplications recited on Monday and Thursday mornings.

HAFTARAH: the reading from the Prophetical Books as the conclusion of the Scripture reading on Sabbath and holiday mornings.

HAGGADA: the ritual of the narration of the story of the exodus from Egypt on the evening of Passover.

HASHKIVEINU: "Cause us to lie down," beginning of the second paragraph following the SHEMA recited as part of the evening service.

HASKALAH: enlightenment.

KADDISH: requiem for the dead usually recited by orphans.

KASHRUTH: literally "fitness," compliance with the Jewish dietary laws, state of being kosher.

KEDUSHAH: mystical elaboration of the third paragraph in the cantor's repetition of the silent devotion.

KEDUSHOT: plural of KEDUSHAH.

KEILI, KEILI: substitute for EILI, EILI in order to avoid pronouncing God's name when not used in prayer.

KESER: "A crown," beginning of the KEDUSHAH of the additional service of Saturday according to the Sephardic rite.

KIDDUSH: "sanctification," blessing pronounced usually in conjunction with that over a cup of wine (on the evening of Sabbaths and the festivals in the synagogue) dwelling on the sanctity of the occasion.

KIDDUSH HASHEM: "sanctification of the name (of God)" by an act of heroic self-sacrifice.

KLAUS: prayer-chapel (Yiddish).

KNEIDLACH: matzoh dumplings (Yiddish), a favorite Passover dish.

KOL MEKADDEISH: "Whoever sanctifies," opening words of a Sabbath hymn sung at the meal on Sabbath eve.

KOL NIDREI: "All vows," first selection in the ritual of the eve of the Day of Atonement nullifying future self-imposed vows.

KOSHER: literally "fit," i.e., prepared in accordance with the Jewish dietary laws or complying with these regulations.

LAG B'OMER: "the thirty-third (day) of the Omer," Jewish semi-holiday serving as a break during the period between Passover and Pentecost which is a traditional period of mourning. It is very popular as a day for marriages.

LECHA DODI: "Come, my beloved," hymn sung in the synagogue at the inauguration of the Sabbath.

LO SACHMOD: "Thou shalt not covet," last commandment of the Decalogue, elaborated on and intercalated in the cantor's repetition of the silent devotion of the morning service of the second day of the Feast of Weeks.

LULAV: palm-branch, one of the four species of plants used in the synagogue in the ritual of the Feast of Tabernacles.

MAL'OCHIM HAMONEY MAALOH: "Angels, multitudes of the (heavens) on high," from the KEDUSHAH of the additional service of Saturday morning according to the Sephardic rite.

MEKIMI: "He that lifteth up," psalm 113 verse 7, which is part of the ritual of the pilgrimage festivals, new moons and Chanukah.

MELAVAH MALKAH: "accompanying the queen," meal in honor of the departure of the Sabbath for which special hymns were composed by the Jewish mystics.

MELOCH: "Reign Thou," beginning of the conclusion of the middle portion of the silent devotion of the Jewish New Year.

MENUCHOH VESIMCHOH: "rest and joy," hymn sung at the Sabbath eve meal.

MEZUMAN: quorum of three necessary for pronouncing the grace after meals jointly.

MEZUZAH: literally "doorpost," oblong box containing two portions of the SHEMA fastened to the right doorpost at the entrance of Jewish homes in compliance with Deuteronomy 6,9 and 11,20.

MINACHAL: "from a stream," conclusion of the prayer AV HORACHAMIM.

MINCHAH: afternoon service.

MISHEBERACH: "He who blessed," blessing pronounced in honor of persons called up for the reading of the Torah, also a prayer blessing the congregation recited after the Scripture reading on Saturday mornings.

MISHNAH: oldest authoritative compilation of the Jewish Oral Law edited by Rabbi Judah the Patriarch in Palestine about 200 C.E.

MITZVAH: literally "commandment," also a commendable or meritorious act.

MIZMOR SHIR LEYOM HASHABBOS: "A psalm, a song for the Sabbath day," psalm 92, sung on Friday evening at the inauguration of the Sabbath.

MIZRACH: literally "East," illustrated design usually with a picture of Jerusalem indicating the direction of the Holy City which Jews face in prayer. In countries west of Jerusalem it is hung on the east wall of the house or room.

MUSSAPH: additional service recited on Sabbath and festival mornings.

NADAN: marriage dower.

NEBICH: pitiable creature (Yiddish).

NEILAH: closing service of the Day of Atonement.

NISHMAS: "The soul of. . .," prayer concluding the recitation of the psalms in connection with morning service of the Sabbath and the festivals.

OMAR RABBI ELOZOR: "Said Rabbi Eleazar," beginning of a quotation from the end of the tractate Berakot of the Babylonian Talmud read at the Sabbath eve service as well as the additional service on Sabbath and holiday mornings.

OSHAMNU MIKKOL OM: "We are guiltier than any people," selection from the end of the penitential service of the fast-day ritual and the annual fall penitential season.

PIDYONIM: literally "ransoms," remittances or gifts to Chassidic rabbis by their devotees in return for advice and help given.

PIYUT: the poetical intercalations in the fundamental prayers of the synagogue composed by the Hebrew religious poets of the Middle Ages.

POSHE YISROEL: heretic, apostate.

P'SACH LONU SHAAR: "Open for us the gate," a sentence from the liturgy of the NEILAH service of the Day of Atonement.

PURIM: the Feast of Lots, commemorating the frustration of the plot of Haman to exterminate the Jews living in the Persian empire of the fifth century B.C.E.

RABBI ISRAEL BAAL SHEM TOB: the founder of the Chassidic movement.

RACHEM: "Have mercy."

RACHEM NO: "Have mercy, we pray Thee," opening words of the third paragraph of the Jewish grace after meals.

REBBE: literally "teacher" in the pronunciation of East European Jewry as used in Yiddish.

ROCHEL MEVAKKOH AL BONEHO. "Rachel weeping over her children," a quotation of Jeremiah 31,14.

ROM V'NISSO: "Lofty and exalted," from the prayer following the last portion of the SHEMA recited at the morning service.

ROSH HAKAHAL: lay head of the Jewish community.

SCHNORRER: beggar (Yiddish).

SEDER: order (of service), used particularly to describe the ritual at the festival meal on the first two nights of Passover.

SELICHOS: penitential prayers recited on fast-days and before dawn during the penitential season.

SEMICHA: traditional rabbinical ordination.

SHABUOT: Feast of Weeks or Pentecost observed 50 days after the beginning of Passover.

SHADCHAN: marriage broker.

SH'CHINAH: the divine Presence.

SHEBAT, FIFTEENTH OF: Jewish New Year of the trees, arbor day in the Land of Israel.

SHELIACH TZIBBUR: "emissary of the congregation," title often given to the cantor or any person who leads the congregation in prayer.

SHEMA: "Hear (O Israel, the Lord our God, the Lord is one)," Deuteronomy 6,4, which is the Jewish confession of faith and the beginning of three paragraphs from the Five Books of Moses recited every morning and evening.

SHEMA KOLEINU: "Hear our voice," beginning of a paragraph in the silent devotion of the daily weekday services, also contained in the fast-day ritual and the penitential service.

SHEMONEH ESREH: literally "eighteen (benedictions)," name usually given to the silent devotion, the prayer par excellence of every synagogue service on account of the eighteen benedictions of which the silent devotion of the three daily weekday services consisted originally.

SHIREI JOSEPH: "songs of Joseph" (Rosenblatt).

SHIR HAMAALOS: "Song of Degrees," applied in this book to psalm 126.

SHIV'OH: "seven" days of mourning immediately following the funeral of a nearest of kin.

SHIV'OH OFANEI HAKIDDUSH: "Seven (Musical) Variations (for the Recitation) of the KIDDUSH."

SHOCHET: ritual slaughterer.

SHOLOM ALEICHEM: "Peace to you," hello.

SHOMER ADOSHEM ES KOL OHAVOV: "The Lord watches all that love Him," psalm 145,20, recited among other occasions also at the beginning of the penitential ritual.

SHOMER YISROEL: "Guardian of Israel," from the daily supplicatory prayer following the cantor's repetition of the silent devotion.

SHTREIMEL: beaver hat with fox-tail rim worn by the Chassidim of Eastern Europe.

SHULCHAN ARUCH: literally "Set Table," the most authoritative code of Jewish law, compiled by Rabbi Joseph Karo in the sixteenth century and usually looked upon as the last word for the conduct of the orthodox.

SIMCHAT TORAH: Festival of "the Rejoicing over the Torah," the last day of the Jewish fall festival season, celebrating the completion of the reading of the Five Books of Moses.

SOGACHZ: declamation (Yiddish).

SON'IM: enemies.

SUCCAH: booth used as dwelling during the week of the Feast of Tabernacles.

TALLITH: literally "cloak," used most commonly as a designation of the prayer-shawl with fringes worn in the synagogue at the morning services.

TALMIDEI CHACHOMIM MARBIM SHOLOM BOOLOM: "The disciples of the wise increase peace in the world," from OMAR RABBI ELOZOR.

TALMUD: the interpretation and elaboration of the MISHNAH by the Jewish scholars of Palestine and Babylonia during the 3rd, 4th and 5th centuries C.E.

TEBUOT SHOR: "Products of the Ox."

TFILOS JOSEF: "Prayers of Josef" (Rosenblau).

TIKANTO SHABBOS: "Thou didst institute the Sabbath," opening words of the middle paragraph of the silent devotion of the additional service of Saturday morning.

TORAH: the Five Books of Moses, which constitute the basic "law" or "doctrine" of Judaism.

TZADDIK: literally "righteous man," title given to the Chassidic saints and heads of the Chassidic dynasties.

TZADDIKIM: plural of TZADDIK.

UMIPNEI CHATOENU: "And on account of our sins," from the silent devotion of the additional service of the festivals.

UMOS HO-OLOM: the nations of the world.

UNESANEH TOKEF: "So let us declare the might (y holiness of the day)," poem introducing the KEDUSHAH of the additional service of the New Year's Day and the Day of

Atonement. Its impressiveness is due to the fact that it speaks of man's fate.

UV'NUCHO YOMAR: "And when it rested, he would say," beginning of a series of scriptural verses recited as the Torah scrolls are returned to the Holy Ark.

V'CHOL MAAMINIM: "And all believe," poem in alphabetic acrostics recited immediately after the KEDUSHAH of the additional service of the New Year's Day and the Day of Atonement.

V'LIRUSHOLAIM IRCHO: "And unto Jerusalem Thy city," from the silent devotion of the daily weekday services.

YAHRZEIT: anniversary of death (Yiddish), observed by the recitation at every synagogue service on that day of the KADDISH.

YAHUDIM: literally "Jews," designation by the East European Jews of their wealthy assimilated coreligionists of the West.

YEHI ROTZON MILIF'NEI OVINU SHEBASHOMAYIM: "May it be the will of our Father who is in heaven," beginning of prayer recited as the Torah scroll is being rolled up after the Scripture reading on Monday and Thursday mornings.

YESHIBAH: Talmudical academy.

YESHIBOT: plural of YESHIBAH.

Y'HI ROTZON: "May it be the will," opening phrase of the prayer for the new moon recited on the Sabbath preceding the beginning of a Jewish month.

YISHTABACH: "Praised be," beginning of the last paragraph of the prayer concluding the recitation of the psalms in connection with the daily morning service.

YOH RIBBON: "Lord, master" (Aramaic), hymn sung at the meal on Sabbath eve.

YOMIM NOROIM: the Jewish High Holidays.

YOM KIPPUR KOTON: minor Day of Atonement, observed on the eve of Jewish new moons occurring during the week.

ZEMIROS: "melodies" sung during the Sabbath meals.

ZEMIROS JOSEF: "melodies of Josef" (Rosenblatt).

ZOREA ZEDOKOS: "Sower of righteous deeds," from the blessings preceding the SHEMA recited in connection with the daily morning service.

Discography

a list of phonograph recordings by Josef Rosenblatt in the possession of his children

ACHEINU KOL BETH ISRAEL
Victor, blue seal, 45204A&B
ADOSHEM MOLOCH GEUS
Victor, blue seal, 55152B
AHEIM, AHEIM
Victrola, red seal, 9011B
(H)AKAVYO BEN MAHALLA(L)EL
Victrola, red seal, 9304A
AL CHET
Victor, blue seal, 55274A
ATTO YOTZARTO
Victrola, red seal, 9443A&B
Columbia, green seal, E5067 (37025)
BIRCHAS KOHANIM
Columbia, green seal, E5067 (37019)
DIE NEVIOH
Columbia, green seal, E2699
EILI, EILI
Victor, blue seal, 55197
Victrola, red seal, 9792B
Columbia, orange seal, E5143 (59458)
EL MOLE RACHAMIM
Victor, black seal, 35312B
Columbia, green seal, E5126 (59435)
Columbia, 12 in., 57044F
ELEGIE
Victor, 45518B
Columbia, orange seal, E5143 (59454)
ELOKAY AD SCHELO NOZARTI
Victor, blue seal, 55164A

ELOKAY NESHOMOH
Victor, blue seal, 55125A
ES ZEMACH DOVID
Columbia, green seal, E1933 (39523)
GEISHEM
Victor, blue seal, 55199A&B
HABEN JAKIR LI
Columbia, green seal, E5148 (59475)
Columbia, 12 in., 57043F
HABET MISHOMAYIM
Victor, blue seal, 55139A&B
HAMAVDIL
Victor, 45479A&B
HA(Y)OM HARAS OLOM
Victrola, 4034A
HINENY HEONY
Victrola, red seal, 9108A
Columbia, green seal, E5172 (59532)
IIU ELOKEINU
Columbia, green seal, E1965
KEL DAR BAMOROM
Victrola, red seal, 9119A
KOL NIDRE
Victor, black seal, 35312A
Victrola, red seal, 9792A
Columbia, green seal, E5126 (59436)
Columbia, 12 in., 57044F
KOL NIDRE (DIE NEUER)
Victor, blue seal, 55197B
KVAKORAS
Victor, blue seal, 55274B
Columbia, green seal, E3750 (58853)

Columbia, 10 in., 8214F
LECHU NRANENU
Columbia, green seal, E5121 (59405)
L'KEIL ORECH DIN
Victrola, red seal, 9119B
Columbia, green seal, E3750 (58852)
Columbia, 10 in., 8214F
LOMIR SICH IBERBETEN
Victor, blue seal, 55291A
LO SACHMOD
Victrola, red seal, 4183A&B
Columbia, green seal, E2900
MEKIMI MEOFOR DOL
Columbia, green seal, E1965
MELECH RACHAMON
Columbia, green seal, E2900
MELOCH AL KOL HOOLOM
Victor, black seal, 35325A
Columbia, green seal, E5148 (59474)
Columbia, 12 in., 57043F
MI SHEBERACH
Victor, 67548A
MISRATZE B'RACHMIM
Victrola, red seal, 9120B
MY YIDDISHE MOMME
Victor, 45518A
NISHMAS
Victor, blue seal, 55293A&B
OMAR RABBI ELOSOR
Victor, black seal, 17448A
Columbia, green seal, E3034 (44066)
Columbia, 10 in., 8207F
OMAR RABBI ELOSOR
(DER NEUER)
Victor, blue seal, 55142A
OMAR RABBI ISHMUEL
Victrola, red seal, 4084A&B
OSHAMNU MIKOL OM
Columbia, green seal, E4070
Columbia, 10 in., 8211F
OVINU MALKEINU

Victor, blue seal, 55163B
Columbia, green seal, E5173 (59533)
PASTUCHEL
Victor, blue seal, 55228A
RACHEM
Columbia, green seal, E5198 (59594)
RACHEM NOO
Victor, blue seal, 55201A&B
RCA Victor, 38-1020A&B
REZEH ASIROSOM
Victrola, red seal, 9120A
Columbia, green seal, E1933 (39541)
RIBONO SHEL OLOM
Victrola, red seal, 9072A&B
ROCHEL MEVAKKOH
Columbia, green seal, E4070
Columbia, 10 in., 8211F
ROM W'NISSO
Victor, 55230A
RCA Victor, 38-1022B
SHIR HAMAALOS
Victrola, red seal, 9299A
SHIVISI
Columbia, green seal, E5198 (59595)
SHLOF IN SISSER RUH
Victor, blue seal, 45425B
SHOIFER SHEL MOSHIACH
Victor, blue seal, 45425A
Columbia, green seal, E2699
SHOMER ISRAEL
Victor, blue seal, 55125B
SOG ZE REBENJU
Victor, blue seal, 55291B
TAL
Victor, blue seal, 55195A&B
RCA Victor, 38-1021A&B
TANCHUM
Victor, blue seal, 55228B
TIKANTO SHABBOS
Victor, blue seal, 55142B
TISGADAL V'SISKADASH

Columbia, green seal, E2819
T'KA B'SHOFAR
　Victor, 45484A
　Columbia, green seal, E2700
UMIPNE CHATOENU
　Victor, blue seal, 45242A&B
　Columbia, green seal, E1932 (39524)
　(39525)
UVNUCHO YOMAR
　Victrola, red seal, 9234A&B
UVYOM SIMCHASCHEM
　Victor, 45484B
　Columbia, green seal, E2700
V'CHOL MAAMINIM
　Victor, blue seal, 55164B
　Columbia, green seal, E2819
V'KOREV P'SUREINU
　Columbia, green seal, E2800
V'LIRUSHOLAIM
　Victor, black seal, 17400A
　Columbia, green seal, E3034 (44065)
　Columbia, 10 in., 8207F
V'SEOREV
　Victor, black seal, 17450A&B
WE'AF IIU IIOYOII MISCHAVEN
　Victor, blue seal, 55163A
　Columbia, green seal, E5173
WEAL JEDE
　Victor, black seal, 35325B
WEHU RACHUM
　Victrola, red seal, 9304B

YAALE
　Victrola, red seal, 9108B
　Columbia, green seal, E5172 (59531)
YAALE V'YOVO
　Victor, 55254A
YEHI ROZON
　Victor, black seal, 17449A&B
　Columbia, green seal, E3033
　Columbia, 10 in., 8210F
　Okeh, orange seal, 14026A
YEKUM PURKON
　Victor, black seal, 17400B
YHI ROZON MILIFNE
　Victor, 55220A&B
　RCA Victor, 38-1022A
YISHTABACH
　Victor, blue seal, 55152
YISM'CHU
　Victor, 55254B
YOHRZEIT
　Victrola, red seal, 9011A
ZADDIK RABBI ELOSOR
　Columbia, green seal, E3103A&B
ZADIK ADOSHEM BECHOL
DROCHOW
　Columbia, green seal, E5121 (59404)
ZION, ZION
　Victrola, red seal, 9299B
ZOREA ZEDUKOS
　Victor, black seal, 17448B
ZUR ISRAEL
　Victor, 55230B

See next page for Addenda to the Discography

Addenda to the Discography

Under the heading, ATTO YOTZARTO, add: Odeon, 18000A&B

After the item under the heading, BIRCHAS KOHANIM, list:

B'TZES YISROEL

Okeh, 14018

After the item under the heading, HAMAVDIL, list:

THE NEW HATIKVOH

Columbia, green seal, E4437

Under the heading, HA (Y) OM HARAS OLOM, add: Okeh, 14018

Under the heading, MI SHEBERACH, add: Odeon, Am 8004

After the item under the heading, OMAR RABBI ISHMUEL, list:

ONWARD JEWISH LEGION

Columbia, green seal, E4437

After the items under the heading, OSHAMNU MIKOL OM, list:

OV HORACHMIN

Columbia, green seal, E5066 (37030)

After the item under the heading, SOG ZE REBENJU, list:

SOLDIERS OF ZION

Columbia, green seal, E4030 (84569)

After the item under the heading, TANCHUM, list:

TFILOH L'MILCHOMEH

Columbia, green seal, E4030 (84570)

Under the heading, TIKANTO SHABBOS, add: Columbia, green seal, E5066 (37030)

Under the heading, T'KA B'SHOFAR, add: Odeon, 8003A

Under the heading, UVYOM SIMCHASCHEM, add: Odeon 8003B

Under the heading, WEAL JEDE, add: Columbia, green seal, E2818

After the item under the heading, YEKUM PURKON, list:

YEVONIM

Columbia, green seal, E2818

Under the heading, ZADDIK RABBI ELOSOR, add: Odeon, 8002A&B

After the item under the heading, ZADIK ADOSHEM BECHOL DROCHOW, list:

ZAROH CHAYU

Columbia, green seal, E3278 (44871)

Odeon, 8004B

Under the heading, ZOREA ZEDUKOS, add: Columbia, green seal, E3278 (44871); Odeon, Am 8004